THE School Efficiency Series comprises about twelve volumes by as many educational experts on Elementary School and Kindergarten, High School, and Vocational Instruction, Courses of Study, Organization, Management and Supervision. The series consists of monographs based on the report of Professor Hanus and his associates on the schools of New York City, but the controlling ideas are applicable as well in one public school system as in another.

Among the authors contributing to these volumes are included Professor Paul H. Hanus, Professor of Education, Harvard University, who is also general editor of the whole series; Dr. Frank P. Bachman, General Education Board; Dr. Edward C. Elliott, Director of the School of Education, University of Wisconsin; Dr. Herman Schneider, Dean of the College of Engineering, University of Cincinnati; Dr. Frank W. Ballou, Director of Promotion and Educational Measurement, Boston Public Schools; Dr. Calvin O. Davis, Assistant Professor of Education, University of Michigan; Dr. Frank V. Thompson, Assistant Superintendent of Schools, Boston; Dr. Henry H. Goddard, Director Department of Psychological Research, New Jersey Training School for Feeble-Minded Boys and Girls; Mr. Stuart A. Courtis, Supervisor of Educational Research in the Public Schools, Detroit; Dr. Frank M. McMurry, Professor of Elementary Education, Teachers College, Columbia University; Dr. Ernest C. Moore, Professor of Education, Harvard University; Dr. Ellwood P. Cubberley, Professor of Education, Leland Stanford Junior University.

SCHOOL EFFICIENCY SERIES

Problems in Elementary School Administration

SCHOOL EFFICIENCY SERIES

Edited by PAUL H. HANUS

Problems in Elementary School Administration

A constructive study applied to New York City

By FRANK P. BACHMAN, PH. D.

AUTHOR OF "PRINCIPLES OF EDUCATION," ETC.

YONKERS-ON-HUDSON, NEW YORK

WORLD BOOK COMPANY

1915

SES: BPESA—I

EDITOR'S PREFACE

THREE important contemporary problems in the administration of elementary schools are treated in this volume by a method which is commending itself increasingly to students of Education, and has a special significance for all officers of school administration and supervision. These problems arise when the establishment of intermediate schools (or junior high schools) is under consideration; when we seek to ascertain what a satisfactory rate of promotion is, and under what conditions we may hope for a maximum rate of promotion; and when we try to secure age-grade standards that will yield us usable and valid information concerning the number of normal-age, over-age, and under-age children in the schools: and the method employed in dealing with these problems is the statistical or objective method—the method that is free from personal bias or general opinion, and seeks to arrive at valid conclusions on the basis of incontestable and well-organized data.

Dr. Bachman's brief but comprehensive introduction states these problems clearly, and also the principles of method on which his studies are based. The main body of the volume consists of three parts, each dealing with one of the problems under consideration. Parts I and II constitute Dr. Bachman's contribution to the report submitted by me to the Committee on School Inquiry of the Board of Estimate and Apportionment of the City of New York in 1912; and Part III is a report made to that Committee after my term of service had closed.

I welcomed the opportunity to publish these three important reports substantially unchanged in a volume of the School Efficiency Series, both because they contain comprehensive data of much intrinsic value, and because they illustrate in detail Dr. Bachman's objective method of reaching conclusions, a method that can be advantageously employed in the study of school administration anywhere.

PAUL H. HANUS.

HARVARD UNIVERSITY.

CONTENTS

Contents

Problems in Elementary School Administration

PROBLEMS IN ELEMENTARY SCHOOL ADMINISTRATION

INTRODUCTION

THE objective or statistical method is applied, in this volume, to the solution of certain practical problems related to the administration of the elementary schools.

In the solution of administrative problems there are three general methods of procedure in common use. The first of these may be called the method of personal judgment. A superintendent or principal studies the question of forming a class for backward children, and gives his judgment, which is essentially his personal opinion. Again, a number of persons canvass a field—for example, the causes of non-promotion—and submit a joint report. In such a report, the opinion of the individual is modified by the opinion of the group. This method may be termed the method of collective or group judgment. Finally, there is the objective or statistical method. Here the facts collected and presented, or the objective standards of measurement employed, become the prime factor in determining the conclusion reached, and there is little place left either for the opinion of the individual or of the group. Each of these methods has its use and its value. It is conceded, however, that, where applicable, the objective or statistical method is the preferable one to employ, and that in a judicious use of this method lies our hope of education becoming a science.

Few topics in the field of the elementary school are receiving to-day as much attention as the intermediate school, called also the junior high school. Part I of this volume is devoted to a consideration of a number of questions to which superintendents want satisfactory answers before they are willing to recommend the bringing together of the seventh and eighth grade pupils into a central building. For example, when children are sent from the home school to a distant intermediate school, will fewer or more of them continue beyond the sixth grade; will a larger or smaller number complete the elementary course of study; will their progress through the school be more or less rapid? What educational opportunities and advantages does the intermediate school offer over the ordinary school having all grades? What is the difference in the cost when the regular seventh and eighth grades are in a central school? These and other questions are answered in the light of the experience of New York City with the intermediate school. This experience should be helpful to those who have under consideration the segregation of the children of the upper grades.

In the management of the elementary school it is of the highest importance that children be properly classified and that they advance regularly from grade to grade. Accordingly, Part II of this volume has to do with the classification and progress of school children. Progress from grade to grade is conditioned on promotion and non-promotion. In the first section of Part II, the general problem of promotion and non-promotion, what the rate of promotion should be, and the conditions favorable to a maximum rate of promotion are treated in detail. An analysis is also made of the factors which contribute to non-promotion, such as size of class, absence, over age, inability to use the English language, and the short school day or part time. The data presented in this connection not only shed light on the causes of non-promotion, but also on the value of special classes, such as classes for children unable to speak the English language and classes for backward children.

The relation between the age of the child and the grade in which he should be enrolled, and the relation between the length of time a child has been in school and the number of units of work or the grades he has completed, have of late years been widely discussed. Indeed, we have come to appreciate that insight into these age-grade relations is fundamental, not only to the proper classification of children, but to the adaptation of the work and the life of the school to their capacities and needs. While the value of definite knowledge of the relation between the ages of the children and the grades they have completed is generally accepted, there is by no means a like unity of opinion with regard to the method to be employed to determine whether or not a child is under age, normal age, or over age. There should be a common method of determining over age, both for the sake of exactness and for the sake of comparison of one system of schools with another. The second section of Part II takes up the essential features of such a method, dealing with the age-grade standards to be used, when and how to make age-grade reports, when to take the ages of children, how to take the ages of children, and what children to include in an age-grade report.

This volume thus contains a large amount of data that may be used in determining educational policies. Useful particularly to those who would base their policies on facts and who would measure the results of their work are the examples contained herein of the application of the objective or statistical method to the solution of administrative problems.

Part I

The Intermediate School

No data have ever been collected by the Board of Education on these points.

First Objection: That More Pupils Leave the 6B Grade without Completing this Grade

Do a larger per cent. of pupils leave the 6B grade without completing it in schools having only 1A-6B grades than leave this grade in schools having all grades?

A final answer to this question would involve collecting data for a number of terms on children leaving 6B classes in schools having only 1A-6B grades, and on children leaving the same classes in schools having all grades. With the time at our disposal it was impossible to do this. We have, however, collected such data for the February-June term of 1911, not only for the 6B, but also for the 5B and 6A, grades. See Table I.[1]

Table I shows, for the February-June term of 1911, the enrollment [2] in the 5B, 6A, and 6B grades, and the number of pupils who left [3] these grades in schools having all grades (1A-8B); and also, by grades and for the same schools, the per cent. of the enrollment leaving. The same facts are also shown for neighboring schools having 1A-6B grades.

[1] The schools having all grades (1A-8B) compared in this report with intermediate schools are attended by about the same type of pupils as attend the intermediate schools; hence the cost of operation and the educational results achieved in the two kinds of schools should be about the same.

The data in all the tables of this study, unless it is otherwise stated, were taken from schools located in the same districts with intermediate schools 24, 159, and 62, or located in districts contiguous to these intermediate schools. Also, the data collected are from all the schools in the given districts of the particular kind under discussion; that is, from all the schools in the given districts having only 1A-6B grades, from all the schools in the given districts having all grades (1A-8B), and from the three intermediate schools.

[2] Enrollment, as used here and throughout this study, includes all pupils, exclusive of transfers, on the register during the term.

[3] Leaving, as used here and throughout this study, includes all pupils, exclusive of transfers, who left school during the term.

TABLE I[1]

(1) Pupils Leaving Schools Having All Grades (1A-8B)

Schools	Districts		5B Grade Boys	5B Grade Girls	5B Grade Total	6A Grade Boys	6A Grade Girls	6A Grade Total	6B Grade Boys	6B Grade Girls	6B Grade Total	Grand Total Boys	Grand Total Girls	Grand Total Total
72	17	Enrollment...	.....	144	144	.....	165	165	.....	170	170	.....	479	479
		Leaving....	.....	7	7	.....	16	16	.....	16	16	.....	39	39
83	17	Enrollment...	441	.....	441	358	.....	358	282	.....	282	1,081	.....	1,081
		Leaving....	21	.....	21	45	.....	45	30	.....	30	96	.....	96
168	17	Enrollment...	.....	202	202	.....	308	308	.....	265	265	.....	775	775
		Leaving....	.....	10	10	.....	43	43	.....	32	32	.....	85	85
171	17	Enrollment...	198	.....	198	119	.....	119	201	.....	201	518	.....	518
		Leaving....	12	.....	12	9	.....	9	15	.....	15	36	.....	36
68G	21	Enrollment...	.....	76	76	.....	63	63	.....	88	88	.....	227	227
		Leaving....	.....	7	7	.....	5	5	.....	10	10	.....	22	22
90	21	Enrollment...	.....	118	118	.....	170	170	.....	144	144	.....	432	432
		Leaving....	.....	7	7	.....	14	14	.....	16	16	.....	37	37
119	21	Enrollment...	.....	174	174	.....	170	170	.....	134	134	.....	478	478
		Leaving....	.....	19	19	.....	17	17	.....	9	9	.....	45	45
22	4	Enrollment...	137	.....	137	114	.....	114	137	.....	137	388	.....	388
		Leaving....	4	.....	4	14	.....	14	6	.....	6	24	.....	24
31	4	Enrollment...	.....	102	102	.....	89	89	.....	74	74	.....	265	265
		Leaving....	.....	1	1	.....	6	6	.....	9	9	.....	16	16
147	4	Enrollment...	138	54	192	89	50	139	80	55	135	307	159	466
		Leaving....	9	3	12	5	1	6	7	2	9	21	6	27
110	4	Enrollment...	40	140	180	24	77	101	8	86	94	72	303	375
		Leaving....	1	7	8	3	4	7	1	8	9	5	19	24
34	3	Enrollment...	123	.....	123	104	.....	104	186	.....	186	413	.....	413
		Leaving....	5	.....	5	2	.....	2	12	.....	12	19	.....	19
7	2	Enrollment...	42	37	79	81	47	128	73	37	110	196	121	317
		Leaving....	3	2	5	2	4	6	8	1	9	13	7	20
Total		Enrollment...	1,119	1,047	2,166	889	1,139	2,028	967	1,053	2,020	2,975	3,239	6,214
		Leaving....	55	63	118	80	110	190	79	103	182	214	276	490
Per cent. of enrollment leaving.			4.92	6.02	5.45	9.00	9.66	9.37	8.17	9.78	9.01	7.19	8.52	7.88

[1] Unless otherwise stated, the figures in this and all other tables in this book were taken from the reports to the Committee on School Inquiry, June, 1911.

(2) Pupils Leaving Schools Having 1A-6B Grades

Schools	Districts		5B Grade			6A Grade			6B Grade			Grand Total		
			Boys	Girls	Total	Boys	Girls	Total	Boys	Girls	Total	Boys	Girls	Total
101	17	Enrollment...	.....	104	104	.....	96	96	.....	50	50	.....	250	250
		Leaving....	.....	3	3	.....	1	1	.....	4	4	.....	8	8
57	20	Enrollment...	.....	207	207	.....	211	211	.....	165	165	.....	583	583
		Leaving....	.....	15	15	.....	17	17	.....	9	9	.....	41	41
78	20	Enrollment...	.....	151	151	.....	227	227	.....	106	106	.....	484	484
		Leaving....	.....	19	19	.....	15	15	.....	11	11	.....	45	45
103	20	Enrollment...	227	104	331	147	95	242	91	99	190	465	298	763
		Leaving....	8	9	17	16	6	22	9	6	15	33	21	54
39	21	Enrollment...	338	84	422	302	54	356	207	47	254	847	185	1,032
		Leaving....	26	10	36	37	12	49	32	3	35	95	25	120
89	21	Enrollment...	176	.....	176	167	.....	167	152	.....	152	495	.....	495
		Leaving....	21	.....	21	13	.....	13	16	.....	16	50	.....	50
100	21	Enrollment...	.....	45	45	.....	33	33	.....	32	32	.....	110	110
		Leaving....	.....	1	1	.....	4	4	.....	2	2	.....	7	7
12	4	Enrollment...	92	133	225	90	86	176	73	193	266	255	412	667
		Leaving....	14	8	22	13	3	16	10	14	24	37	25	62
88	4	Enrollment...	.....	51	51	.....	44	44	.....	39	39	.....	134	134
		Leaving....	.....	1	1	.....	.....	.....	.....	3	3	.....	4	4
98	4	Enrollment...	155	52	207	137	41	178	100	43	143	392	136	528
		Leaving....	7	4	11	14	5	19	10	4	14	31	13	44
42	3	Enrollment...	.....	153	153	.....	128	128	.....	109	109	.....	390	390
		Leaving....	.....	14	14	.....	8	8	.....	11	11	.....	33	33
62G	3	Enrollment...	.....	89	89	.....	82	82	.....	85	85	.....	256	256
		Leaving....	.....	.....	.....	.....	.....	.....	.....	.....	.....	.....	.....	.....
75	3	Enrollment...	198	.....	198	178	.....	178	188	.....	188	564	.....	564
		Leaving....	11	.....	11	7	.....	7	9	.....	9	27	.....	27
92	3	Enrollment...	.....	114	114	.....	122	122	.....	120	120	.....	356	356
		Leaving....	.....	11	11	.....	15	15	.....	9	9	.....	35	35
2B	2	Enrollment...	220	.....	220	197	.....	197	201	.....	201	618	.....	618
		Leaving....	13	.....	13	13	.....	13	20	.....	20	46	.....	46
65BG	2	Enrollment...	111	103	214	104	74	178	83	65	148	298	242	540
		Leaving....	6	8	14	14	4	18	5	5	10	25	17	42
177	2	Enrollment...	.....	138	138	.....	120	120	.....	141	141	.....	399	399
		Leaving....	.....	10	10	.....	12	12	.....	13	13	.....	35	35
Total		Enrollment...	1,517	1,528	3,045	1,322	1,413	2,735	1,095	1,294	2,389	3,934	4,235	8,169
		Leaving....	106	113	219	127	102	229	111	94	205	344	309	653
Per cent. of enrollment leaving.			6.99	7.39	7.19	9.61	7.22	8.37	10.14	7.26	8.58	8.74	7.29	7.99

It will be observed that the losses, both in schools having all grades and in schools having only 1A-6B classes, are large. These large losses in the 5B, 6A, and 6B grades are due to the fact that many children are fourteen years old or over by the time they complete the 5A grade. Twenty-five per cent. of the children in these grades of the foregoing schools on the lower East Side were found to be fourteen years old and above.[1] These over-age children, being able to obtain labor certificates, leave school, from choice or necessity, in large numbers.

The total loss in the 5B, 6A, and 6B classes of schools having all grades is 7.88 per cent. of the total enrollment; in schools having 1A-6B grades, 7.99 per cent., or a difference of .11 of 1 per cent. in favor of schools having all grades. So slight is the difference in the holding power of these two kinds of schools in the 5B, 6A, and 6B grades that, had the 8,169 pupils in these grades in schools having only 1A-6B grades been in schools having all classes, only nine fewer pupils would have left these schools during the February-June term of 1911.

It should be observed, however, that the losses in schools having only 1A-6B grades are 1 per cent. less in 6A classes, and in 6B .43 of 1 per cent. less than in the corresponding classes of schools having all grades, and that only in 5B classes are the losses in schools having all grades less than in schools having only 1A-6B grades. If more 5B pupils drop from schools having only 1A-6B grades, there are of course fewer left to drop from the 6A and the 6B grades, hence it may be that .11 of one per cent. represents the actual difference in the holding power of these two kinds of schools. Such a difference is, however, too small to serve as a basis of judgment.

There are, however, reasons why schools having only 1A-6B classes should be able to hold relatively more 6B pupils than schools having all grades. The highest class in any school is the object of special attention and considera-

[1] From reports to the Committee on School Inquiry, June, 1911.

tion. In schools having all grades this class is the 8B; in schools having only 1A-6B grades it is the 6B. Hence, more attention and consideration are given to 6B pupils in schools having only 1A-6B grades than are given such pupils in schools having all grades. The inevitable effect of this special attention and consideration is to increase the power of schools having only 1A-6B grades to hold 6B pupils who might otherwise drop out.

From the foregoing it appears that there is at least no ground in the data collected for the February-June term, 1911, for the prevailing opinion that more children leave the 6B classes in schools having only 1A-6B grades than leave the corresponding classes in schools having all grades. Indeed, the reverse seems to be true.

Second Objection: That More Pupils Promoted from the 6B Grade do not Enter the 7A Grade

Do a larger per cent. of pupils promoted from the 6B grade fail to enter the 7A grade when they must go to an intermediate school than fail to enter the 7A grade when they can advance to this grade in their home school?

Table II shows the total number of 6B promotions January 31, 1911, in schools having all grades, and the total number of 7A beginners [1] in these schools for the February-June term of 1911; also the per cent. of 6B promotions entering the 7A grade. The table also shows the same facts for contributing schools and for intermediate schools 24, 159, and 62. (See page 16.)

Few pupils in the foregoing schools, promoted from the 6B grade in January, 1911, failed to enter the 7A grade in February—only twenty-eight out of a total of 3,008. In neither kind of school does the number failing to enter the

[1] Includes all pupils along with transfers to other schools, in attendance at least one school day.

7A grade amount to 1 per cent. of the 6B promotions, whereas .03 of 1 per cent. measures the difference in the total per cent. of loss. This difference is in favor of the schools having all grades; but it is so small that, had the same rate of loss prevailed as prevailed in schools having

TABLE II[1]

(1) 6B PROMOTIONS AND 7A BEGINNERS—SCHOOLS HAVING ALL GRADES (1A-8B)

Total 6B Promotions Jan. 31, 1911	Total 7A Beginners Feb.-June Term 1911	Per Cent. of 6B Promotions Entering 7A Grade
1,524	1,510	99.08

(2) PROMOTIONS AND 7A BEGINNERS—CONTRIBUTING SCHOOLS AND INTERMEDIATE SCHOOLS 24, 159, AND 62

Total 6B Promotions from Contributing Schools Jan. 31, 1911	Total 7A Beginners P. S. 24, 159, and 62, Feb.-June Term 1911	Per Cent. of 6B Promotions Entering 7A Grade
1,484	1,470	99.05

all grades, not a single additional pupil out of 1,484 would have entered the 7A of intermediate schools. In a word, the same relative number of 6B promotions actually entered the 7A grade of these two kinds of schools during the February-June term of 1911.

Table III shows the number of 6B promotions June 30, 1911, in schools[2] having all grades, and the number of 7A beginners[3] in these schools, for the September-January term of 1911-12; also the per cent. of all 6B promotions entering the 7A grade. The table also shows the same facts for contributing schools and intermediate schools 24, 159, and 62.

[1] The figures for this table were taken from special reports made by the principals and are for the schools given in Table III.

[2] See note on page 11.

[3] From reports to the Committee on School Inquiry, June, 1911.

TABLE III[1]

6B PROMOTIONS AND 7A BEGINNERS

(1) SCHOOLS HAVING ALL GRADES[2] (1A-8B)

Schools	Districts	Promotions 6B Grade June 30, 1911			Beginners' 7A Grade Sept.-Jan. Term, 1911-12		
		Boys	Girls	Total	Boys	Girls	Total
72	17	....	143	143	....	137	137
83	17	238	....	238	224	....	224
168G	17	....	185	185	....	174	174
171	17	161	....	161	155	....	155
68G	21	....	66	66	....	63	63
90	21	....	120	120	....	118	118
119	21	....	125	125	....	112	112
22B	4	125	....	125	122	....	122
31	4	....	65	65	....	63	63
147	4	63	48	111	54	43	97
110	4	....	85	85	....	82	82
34	3	155	....	155	150	....	150
7	2	....	....	98	....	....	98
....	....	....	....	....	....	....	....
....	....	....	....	....	....	....	....
Total	....	....	....	1,677	....	....	1,595
Per cent. of 6B promotions entering 7A grade........				95.11			

(2) SCHOOLS CONTRIBUTING 6B PUPILS TO P. S. 24, 159, AND 62

Schools	Districts	Promotions 6B Grade June 30, 1911		
		Boys	Girls	Total
39	21	159	38	197
89	21	124	....	124
103	20	104	85	189
78	20	....	95	95
57	20	....	153	153
157	19	1	....	1
159P	20	....	67	67
184	19	18	18	36
2B	2	170	....	170
75	3	158	....	158
42	3	....	97	97
62GP	3	....	74	74
92	3	....	110	110
177	2	....	112	112
65G	2	2	....	2
Total	....	736	849	1,585
Per cent. of 6B promotions entering 7A grade.......		95.51	93.52	94.44

(3) INTERMEDIATE SCHOOLS (7A-8B)

Schools	Districts	Beginners' 7A Grade Sept.-Jan. Term, 1911-12		
		Boys	Girls	Total
24	21	383	....	383
159G	20	....	416	416
62	3	320	378	698
....	....	....	....	....
....	....	....	....	....
....	....	....	....	....
....	....	....	....	....
....	....	....	....	....
....	....	....	....	....
....	....	....	....	....
....	....	....	....	....
....	....	....	....	....
....	....	....	....	....
....	....	....	....	....
....	....	....	....	....
Total	....	703	794	1,497

[1]The figures for this table were taken from special reports made by the principals.
[2]Includes all pupils along with transfers to other schools, in attendance at least one school day.

The number of children leaving school is always smaller between the Fall and Spring terms when there is practically no interruption in the work of the school than between the Spring and Fall terms when there is a long vacation. It is, therefore, not surprising, as shown in Table III, that, in the schools having all grades, 4.89 per cent. of the pupils promoted from the 6B grade in June failed to enter the 7A grade in September, and that 5.56 per cent. of the 6B pupils promoted from contributing schools failed to enter the 7A grade of intermediate schools. The pupils lost in going from contributing schools to intermediate schools were, however, greater by only .67 of 1 per cent. (5.56—4.89) than the pupils lost between the 6B and 7A of schools having all grades—a difference of ten pupils.

The factors influencing the exact number of 6B promotions entering the 7A are so many and so complex that the small difference revealed by the foregoing data might have been due to the action of any one of several factors. To illustrate: In Public School Number 159 [1] forty 6B promotions from contributing schools failed to attend during the September-January term a single day:

Disappeared (moved, leaving no address)	5
Working papers	15
Parochial schools	8
At home, over age	5
Moved to the country	5
At home, illness	1
Horace Mann School	1
Total	40

Had the five children that disappeared and the five children that moved to the country asked for transfers, this simple fact alone would have erased any difference for the September-January term of 1911-12 in the number of 6B promotions entering the 7A of these two kinds of schools.

Apart from losses due to such causes as sickness, entering a private or parochial school, moving to another city, there

[1] From special report made by the principal.

is only one group of pupils, promoted from the 6B grade, that can fail to enter the 7A, viz., children who are fourteen years of age and over. There are large numbers of such children—approximately each fourth child in the schools of the city in the 6B grade has attained his fourteenth year. Any considerable difference, therefore, between the number of 6B promotions entering the 7A of schools having all grades and of intermediate schools must lie in the difference in attractiveness of these two kinds of schools for pupils fourteen years of age and over. There is no inherent reason why intermediate schools should not be even more attractive to such children than schools having all grades.

It has been shown, therefore, that the only ground for believing that more pupils promoted from the 6B enter the 7A of schools having all grades than of intermediate schools lies in the fact that for the spring term of 1911 the difference in per cent. of 6B promotions entering these two kinds of schools was .03 of 1 per cent., and for the September-January term of 1911-12 .67 of 1 per cent.—differences so small that out of 3,069 promoted pupils from contributing schools for the calendar year 1911 only ten fewer pupils failed to enter the 7A of intermediate schools than would have entered had these 6B promoted pupils been able to enter the 7A of their home school. These differences supply no adequate basis for the foregoing belief, and hence supply no grounds for the City Superintendent and the Board of Education to change their favorable attitude toward intermediate schools.

Third Objection: That More Pupils Leave the 7A-8B Grades without Completing these Grades

Do a larger per cent. of seventh and eighth year pupils leave the seventh and eighth grades without completing these grades in intermediate schools than leave these grades in schools having all grades?

TABLE IV

(1) Withdrawals—Schools Having All Grades (1A-8B)

Schools	Districts		7A Grade			7B Grade			8A Grade			8B Grade			Grand Total		
			Boys	Girls	Total	Boys	Girls	Total	Boys	Girls	Total	Boys	Girls	Total	Boys	Girls	Total
72	17	Enrollment	.....	152	152	.....	142	142	.....	135	135	.....	86	86	.....	515	515
		Leaving	.....	8	8	.....	18	18	.....	10	10	.....	2	2	.....	38	38
83	17	Enrollment	249	.....	249	220	.....	220	142	.....	142	130	.....	130	741	.....	741
		Leaving	31	.....	31	28	.....	28	9	.....	9	1	.....	1	69	.....	69
168	17	Enrollment	.....	212	212	.....	165	165	.....	147	147	.....	110	110	.....	634	634
		Leaving	.....	42	42	.....	29	29	.....	18	18	.....	11	11	.....	100	100
171	17	Enrollment	145	.....	145	121	.....	121	134	.....	134	95	.....	95	495	.....	495
		Leaving	13	.....	13	9	.....	9	8	.....	8	5	.....	5	35	.....	35
68	21	Enrollment	.....	93	93	.....	81	81	.....	67	67	.....	64	64	.....	305	305
		Leaving	.....	9	9	.....	7	7	.....	11	11	.....	5	5	.....	32	32
90	21	Enrollment	.....	110	110	.....	140	140	.....	106	106	.....	68	68	.....	424	424
		Leaving	.....	9	9	.....	22	22	.....	4	4	.....	1	1	.....	36	36
119	21	Enrollment	.....	138	138	.....	122	122	.....	127	127	.....	87	87	.....	474	474
		Leaving	.....	9	9	.....	12	12	.....	6	6	.....	3	3	.....	30	30
22	4	Enrollment	215	.....	215	227	.....	227	176	.....	176	165	.....	165	783	.....	783
		Leaving	27	.....	27	25	.....	25	15	.....	15	2	.....	2	69	.....	69
31	4	Enrollment	.....	79	79	.....	80	80	.....	87	87	.....	48	48	.....	294	294
		Leaving	.....	7	7	.....	4	4	.....	11	11	.....	.....	.....	.....	22	22
147	4	Enrollment	158	148	306	152	104	256	108	102	210	115	75	190	533	429	962
		Leaving	15	16	31	6	8	14	10	6	16	2	.....	2	33	30	63
110	4	Enrollment	3	104	107	5	103	108	6	104	110	1	97	98	15	408	423
		Leaving	.....	6	6	.....	8	8	1	12	13	.....	2	2	1	28	29
34	3	Enrollment	103	.....	103	74	.....	74	134	.....	134	99	.....	99	410	.....	410
		Leaving	9	.....	9	11	.....	11	11	.....	11	7	.....	7	38	.....	38
7	2	Enrollment	145	153	298	107	108	215	.....	.....	.....	.....	.....	.....	252	261	513
		Leaving	15	13	28	4	4	8	.....	.....	.....	.....	.....	.....	19	17	36
Total		Enrollment	1,018	1,189	2,207	906	1,045	1,951	700	875	1,575	605	635	1,240	3,229	3,744	6,973
		Leaving	110	119	229	83	112	195	54	78	132	17	24	41	264	333	597
Per cent. of enrollment leaving			10.81	10.01	10.38	9.16	10.72	9.99	7.71	8.91	8.38	2.81	3.78	3.31	8.18	8.89	8.56

(2) WITHDRAWALS—INTERMEDIATE SCHOOLS (7A-8B)

Schools	Districts		7A Grade			7B Grade			8A Grade			8B Grade			Grand Total		
			Boys	Girls	Total	Boys	Girls	Total	Boys	Girls	Total	Boys	Girls	Total	Boys	Girls	Total
24	21	Enrollment	454	.....	454	375	.....	375	310	.....	310	283	.....	283	1,422	.....	1,422
		Leaving	61	.....	61	42	.....	42	18	.....	18	13	.....	13	134	.....	134
159	20	Enrollment	.....	441	441	.....	375	375	.....	332	332	.....	272	272	.....	1,420	1,420
		Leaving	.....	43	43	.....	29	29	.....	23	23	.....	5	5	.....	100	100
62	3	Enrollment	316	350	666	291	349	640	254	368	622	314	360	674	1,175	1,427	2,602
		Leaving	28	19	47	20	21	41	15	24	39	5	5	10	68	69	137
Total		Enrollment	770	791	1,561	666	724	1,390	564	700	1,264	597	632	1,229	2,597	2,847	5,444
		Leaving	89	62	151	62	50	112	33	47	80	18	10	28	202	169	371
Per cent. of enrollment leaving			11.56	7.84	9.67	9.31	6.91	8.06	5.85	6.71	6.33	3.02	1.58	2.28	7.78	5.94	6.81

Table IV shows for the February-June term, 1911, the enrollment in schools having all grades in 7A, 7B, 8A, and 8B grades, and the number leaving each of these grades; also grade for grade and for the same schools the per cent. of the total enrollment leaving. The table also shows the same facts for intermediate schools 24, 159, and 62. (See pages 20-21.)

The per cent. of pupils leaving these two kinds of schools varies grade for grade, and is different for boys and girls. While the per cent. of loss of boys in the 7A, 7B, and 8B grades is slightly greater in intermediate schools than in schools having all grades (less than 1 per cent. in each case, amounting to a difference of six, one, and one pupils respectively), when boys and girls are taken together, .71 of 1 per cent. more 7A pupils, 1.93 per cent. more 7B pupils, 2.05 per cent. more 8A pupils, and 1.03 per cent. more 8B pupils left schools having all grades than intermediate schools. The highest per cent. of loss, it will be observed, is in the 7A in both kinds of schools. The 7A grade is apparently the most trying of the four upper grades, and particularly trying in the intermediate school. Friendships in the old school are broken off; new acquaintances need to be formed, and the pupil must adjust himself to a new school life. Despite these facts, the holding power of the 7A grade in intermediate schools is apparently greater than the holding power of the 7A grade in schools having all classes.

The total per cent. of 7A-8B pupils leaving schools having all grades is 1.75 per cent. (8.56—6.81) greater than the total losses in intermediate schools. Had the same rate of loss prevailed as prevailed in intermediate schools, 122 fewer pupils, out of the total of 6,973, would have left schools having all grades.

There is, therefore, no basis in the foregoing for the expressed opinion that more children leave the seventh and eighth year classes in intermediate schools than leave the corresponding classes in schools having all grades.

FURTHER COMPARISONS

That further comparisons might be made between schools having all grades and intermediate schools, data were collected on promotions and on terms of work lost and gained.

Relative Rate of Promotion in the 7A-8B Grades

Table V shows for the February-June term, 1911, the enrollment in schools having all grades in the 7A, 7B, 8A, and 8B grades, and the number of pupils promoted June 30, 1911, in each of these grades; also grade by grade and for the same schools the per cent. of the total enrollment promoted. The table also shows the same facts for intermediate schools 24, 159, and 62. (See pages 24-25.)

The per cent. of boys promoted in the 7A, 7B, and 8B grades, as shown by Table V, is less by 7.87 per cent., 4.97 per cent., and 4.42 per cent. respectively in intermediate schools than in schools having all grades. A larger per cent. of boys in the 8A by 4.42 per cent., and a larger per cent. of girls in all four grades by 5.78 per cent., 11.40 per cent., 5.72 per cent., and .73 per cent. respectively were, however, promoted in intermediate schools than in schools having all grades; so that while in schools having all grades 83.65 per cent. of the total enrollment was promoted, in the intermediate schools the per cent. of promotion was 85.69 per cent.—a clear difference in favor of intermediate schools of 2.04 per cent. Had the same rate of promotion prevailed in the two kinds of schools, 142 more pupils, out of a total of 6,973, would have been advanced in schools having all grades.

A high percentage of promotion does not necessarily indicate a high degree of efficiency. Yet when due regard is paid to proper standards, that school is best which succeeds in advancing the largest percentage of its children.

TABLE V

(1) Rate of Promotion—Schools Having All Grades (1A-8B)

Schools	Districts		7A Grade			7B Grade			8A Grade			8B Grade			Grand Total		
			Boys	Girls	Total	Boys	Girls	Total	Boys	Girls	Total	Boys	Girls	Total	Boys	Girls	Total
72	17	Enrollment	.....	152	152	.....	142	142	.....	135	135	.....	86	86	.....	515	515
		Promoted	.....	127	127	.....	110	110	.....	117	117	.....	84	84	.....	438	438
83	17	Enrollment	249	.....	249	220	.....	220	142	.....	142	130	.....	130	741	.....	741
		Promoted	204	.....	204	179	.....	179	128	.....	128	124	.....	124	635	.....	635
168	17	Enrollment	.....	212	212	.....	165	165	.....	147	147	.....	110	110	.....	634	634
		Promoted	.....	145	145	.....	107	107	.....	105	105	.....	94	94	.....	451	451
171	17	Enrollment	145	.....	145	121	.....	121	134	.....	134	95	.....	95	495	.....	495
		Promoted	116	.....	116	93	.....	93	113	.....	113	89	.....	89	411	.....	411
68	21	Enrollment	.....	93	93	.....	81	81	.....	67	67	.....	64	64	.....	305	305
		Promoted	.....	47	47	.....	49	49	.....	52	52	.....	55	55	.....	203	203
90	21	Enrollment	.....	110	110	.....	140	140	.....	106	106	.....	68	68	.....	424	424
		Promoted	.....	98	98	.....	117	117	.....	102	102	.....	67	67	.....	384	384
119	21	Enrollment	.....	138	138	.....	122	122	.....	127	127	.....	87	87	.....	474	474
		Promoted	.....	108	108	.....	91	91	.....	100	100	.....	76	76	.....	375	375
22	4	Enrollment	215	.....	215	227	.....	227	176	.....	176	165	.....	165	783	.....	783
		Promoted	180	.....	180	197	.....	197	149	.....	149	163	.....	163	689	.....	689
31	4	Enrollment	.....	79	79	.....	80	80	.....	87	87	.....	48	48	.....	294	294
		Promoted	.....	65	65	.....	70	70	.....	62	62	.....	48	48	.....	245	245
147	4	Enrollment	158	148	306	152	104	256	108	102	210	115	75	190	533	429	962
		Promoted	137	118	255	135	81	216	96	85	181	110	73	183	478	357	835
110	4	Enrollment	3	104	107	5	103	108	6	104	110	1	97	98	15	408	423
		Promoted	3	98	101	5	95	100	5	92	97	1	95	96	14	380	394
34	3	Enrollment	103	.....	103	74	.....	74	134	.....	134	99	.....	99	410	.....	410
		Promoted	83	.....	83	61	.....	61	85	.....	85	90	.....	90	319	.....	319
7	2	Enrollment	145	153	298	107	108	215	.....	.....	.....	.....	.....	.....	252	261	513
		Promoted	116	140	256	96	102	198	.....	.....	.....	.....	.....	.....	212	242	454
Total		Enrollment	1,018	1,189	2,207	906	1,045	1,951	700	875	1,575	605	635	1,240	3,229	3,744	6,973
		Promoted	839	946	1,785	766	822	1,588	576	715	1,291	577	592	1,169	2,758	3,075	5,833
Per cent. of enrollment promoted			82.42	79.56	80.88	84.55	78.66	81.39	82.29	81.71	81.97	95.37	93.23	94.27	85.41	82.13	83.65

(2) Rate of Promotion—Intermediate Schools (7A-8B)

Schools	Districts		7A Grade			7B Grade			8A Grade			8B Grade			Grand Total		
			Boys	Girls	Total	Boys	Girls	Total	Boys	Girls	Total	Boys	Girls	Total	Boys	Girls	Total
24	21	Enrollment......	454	.....	454	375	.....	375	310	.....	310	283	.....	283	1,422	.....	1,422
		Promoted.....	304	.....	304	279	.....	279	260	.....	260	244	.....	244	1,087	.....	1,087
159	20	Enrollment......	.....	441	441	.....	375	375	.....	332	332	.....	272	272	.....	1,420	1,420
		Promoted.....	.....	359	359	.....	328	328	.....	293	293	.....	258	258	.....	1,238	1,238
62	3	Enrollment......	316	350	666	291	349	640	254	368	622	314	360	674	1,175	1,427	2,602
		Promoted.....	270	316	586	251	324	575	225	319	544	299	336	635	1,045	1,295	2,340
Total		Enrollment......	770	791	1,561	666	724	1,390	564	700	1,264	597	632	1,229	2,597	2,847	5,444
		Promoted.....	574	675	1,249	530	652	1,182	485	612	1,097	543	594	1,137	2,132	2,533	4,665
Per cent. of enrollment promoted......			74.55	85.34	80.01	79.58	90.06	85.04	85.99	87.43	86.79	90.95	93.99	92.51	82.09	88.97	85.69

Number of Terms of Work Lost and Gained by 7A-8B Pupils

Table VI[1] shows, for certain schools having all grades, the number of graduates June 30, 1911, the terms of work lost and gained in the seventh and eighth years by these graduates, and the net terms of work lost; also the same facts for intermediate schools 24, 159, and 62. These figures were taken from special reports made by the principals of the schools represented in the table. (See page 27.)

Table VI shows that the 881 graduates from the schools having all grades together lost, during their seventh and eighth years, 186 terms of work and gained fifty-eight, a net loss of 128, or the equivalent of a loss of a term's work for each group of seven pupils; the 1,137 graduates from intermediate schools, while losing 215 terms of work, gained 203, a net loss of only twelve, the equivalent of a term's work for each group of ninety-four pupils. Hence, had the same rate of loss prevailed in the two kinds of schools, the 1,137 graduates from intermediate schools would have lost 165 terms of work ($128 \div 881 \times 1{,}137$), or thirteen times as many terms of work as were actually lost by these graduates.

This difference between the number of terms of work lost in schools having all grades and in intermediate schools suggests a wide difference in the two kinds of schools in the chances of losing or gaining a term's work. In schools having all grades, during the seventh and eighth years, three terms of work are lost to one term's work gained, whereas in intermediate schools the terms of work lost and gained are about equal.

This difference in terms of work lost and gained suggests also that schools having all grades afford small opportunity

[1] Table VI contains data from certain schools having all grades in the same districts with intermediate schools 24, 159, and 62, and in districts contiguous to these intermediate schools. It was impossible, owing to the rush of work at the close of the school year, to collect data from all such schools in these districts.

to children to complete the course of the seventh and eighth years in less than the regular time—four terms, and that

TABLE VI

ACCELERATION AND RETARDATION

(1) SCHOOLS HAVING ALL GRADES (1A-8B)

Schools	Districts	Number Graduated June 30, 1911	Terms of Work Lost during Seventh and Eighth Years	Terms of Work Gained during Seventh and Eighth Years	Net Terms of Work Lost during Seventh and Eighth Years
72	17	84	10	2	...
83	17	124	45	4	...
168	17	94	38	0	...
171	17	89	20	6	...
22B	4	163	10	1	...
31	4	48	0	11	...
110	4	96	0	26	...
147	4	183	63	8	...
Total........		881	186	58	128

(2) INTERMEDIATE SCHOOLS (7A-8B)

Schools	Districts	Number Graduated June 30, 1911	Terms of Work Lost during Seventh and Eighth Years	Terms of Work Gained during Seventh and Eighth Years	Net Terms of Work Lost during Seventh and Eighth Years
24	21	244	83	53	...
159	20	258	41	16	...
62	3	635	91	134	...
Total........		1,137	215	203	12

intermediate schools afford large opportunities to shorten the course. The difference in such opportunity is reflected in the number of terms required by the foregoing graduates to complete the course of the seventh and eighth years. In schools[1] having all grades 6.58 per cent. did the work in 3 terms; 75.82 per cent. did the work in 4 terms; 14.08 per cent. did the work in 5 terms; 3.52 per cent. did the work in 6 terms. In intermediate schools[1] .97 per cent. did the work in 2 terms; 15.92 per cent. did the work in 3 terms; 68.07 per cent. did the work in 4 terms; 11.17 per cent. did the work in 5 terms; 3.87 per cent. did the work in 6 terms.

Though terms of work lost and gained and the time required to do the last two years of the elementary school are not in themselves measures of efficiency, yet, when all things are taken into account, that school is the most efficient which does most to accelerate the progress of its pupils and which contributes the least to their retardation.

In these respects, the superiority of the intermediate school over schools having all grades is marked. Only 6.58 per cent. of the graduates from schools having all grades completed the last two years of the course ahead of time; this was accomplished by 16.89 per cent. of the graduates from intermediate schools. Further, 17.60 per cent. of the graduates from schools having all grades were retarded in the last two years of their course, while but 15.04 per cent. of the graduates from intermediate schools took more than the regulation time.

To be sure, pupils may be advanced from grade to grade without regard to their attainments. That pupils are not so advanced in intermediate schools is indicated by a study made by Mr. Coleman D. Frank.[2] Mr. Frank studied the successes and failures of pupils entering in 1910 the February class of the DeWitt Clinton High School. The schools selected were 160, 188, and 10, Manhattan, schools having all grades, and 24 and 62, intermediate schools. These five schools send, as a rule, the largest number of pupils to DeWitt Clinton High School.

[1] Based on special reports by principals of these schools.

[2] Report of the Committee on Secondary Education, New York City, 1911.

The per cent. of pupils of these schools who succeeded and who failed to do all the work of the first and second terms was:

	School	Successes	Failures
First Term:	160	80%	20%
	188	69%	31%
	10	47%	53%
	62	72%	28%
	24	67%	33%
Second Term:	School	Successes	Failures
	160	80%	20%
	188	72%	28%
	10	52%	48%
	62	72%	28%
	24	96%	4%

When the schools of the two kinds are grouped, the per cent. of successes and failures is:

First Term:	Successes	Failures
Schools Having All Grades	68%	32%
Intermediate Schools	70%	30%
Second Term:		
Schools Having All Grades	72%	28%
Intermediate Schools	82%	18%

It appears that the highest per cent. of successes was attained in the first term by pupils from a school having all grades; in the second term, by pupils from an intermediate school. When the pupils coming from the different schools of each of the two kinds are taken together, the highest per cent. of successes was achieved in both terms by intermediate school graduates—at least partial evidence of the quality of the work done in these schools.

SUMMARY OF THE FOREGOING CONSIDERATIONS

Schools having all grades and contributing and intermediate schools have now been compared with reference to five points:

1. Number of pupils leaving the 6B grade without completing this grade.
2. Number of pupils promoted from the 6B grade not entering the 7A grade.
3. Number of pupils leaving the 7A-8B grades without completing these grades.
4. Relative rate of promotions in the 7A-8B grades.
5. Number of terms of work lost and gained by 7A-8B pupils.

The difference in the efficiency of the two kinds of schools with respect to the foregoing points may be summarized as follows:

1. Number of pupils (per 1,000) leaving the 6B grade without completing the grade:
   a. In schools having all grades.......... 90
   b. In schools having only 1A-6B grades.. 86
2. Number of pupils (per 1,000) promoted from the 6B grade not entering the 7A grade:
   a. In schools having all grades......... 49
   b. In intermediate schools............. 56
3. Number of pupils (per 1,000) leaving the 7A-8B grades without completing these grades:
   a. In schools having all grades.......... 86
   b. In intermediate schools............. 68
4. Relative rate of promotion (per 1,000) in the 7A-8B grades:
   a. In schools having all grades.......... 836
   b. In intermediate schools............. 857
5. Net terms of work (per 1,000) lost by 7A-8B pupils:
   a. In schools having all grades......... 145
   b. In intermediate schools............. 11

Hence, we conclude:

(a) That fewer pupils leave the 6B classes in schools having only 1A-6B grades by .43 of 1 per cent. than leave the corresponding classes in schools having all grades.

(b) That more 6B promoted pupils by .67 of 1 per cent. fail to enter the 7A grade of intermediate schools than fail to enter the 7A when they can advance to this grade in their home school.

(c) That fewer pupils leave the seventh and eighth year classes of intermediate schools by 1.75 per cent. than leave the corresponding classes of schools having all grades.

(d) That more seventh and eighth year pupils are promoted in intermediate schools by 2.04 per cent. than are promoted in schools having all grades.

(e) That thirteen times as many terms of work are lost by seventh and eighth year pupils in schools having all grades as are lost by such pupils in intermediate schools.

In only one respect do schools having all grades show a higher efficiency than intermediate schools, and in this respect the higher efficiency is slight. In all other points the intermediate schools show a greater efficiency than schools having all grades.

The data on which the foregoing conclusions rest, with the exception of the data on pupils promoted from the 6B grade and not entering the 7A grade, cover but the February-June term of 1911. These data, however, in the case of 6B losses cover 4,409 pupils; in the case of losses between the 6B-7A grades, 6,270 pupils; in the case of losses from the 7A-8B grades, 12,417; in the case of relative rate of promotion, 12,417; in the case of terms of work lost and gained, 2,018 graduates—numbers sufficiently large and taken from schools operating under conditions sufficiently similar to the conditions surrounding intermediate schools to indicate tendencies. Final conclusions with respect to the educational efficiency of schools having all grades and intermediate schools would, of course, require the collection of data similar to the above for a number of terms.

CHAPTER II

ECONOMY OF THE INTERMEDIATE SCHOOL

EDUCATION should be conducted as economically as possible. Hence, in carrying on any given kind of school work, the expense of different ways of accomplishing the same end should be considered.

Any difference in the expense of schools having all grades and intermediate schools is due almost exclusively to differences in (1) the number of schoolrooms needed; (2) the number of teachers required; and (3) the supplies and equipment needed to instruct a given number of seventh and eighth year pupils. Comparisons with respect to these three points will, therefore, bring out the difference between the cost of instructing seventh and eighth year pupils in these two kinds of schools.

The schools having all grades selected for the purpose of these comparisons are, with few exceptions, the same as those selected for the foregoing comparisons with respect to educational efficiency. Their selection, however, does not imply the suggestion that the 7A-8B pupils in them could be brought into intermediate schools. Hence, the comparisons to be made will merely indicate what the probable saving would be where conditions are such that 7A-8B children in schools having all grades can be brought into intermediate schools.

(1) DIFFERENCE IN THE NUMBER OF SCHOOLROOMS REQUIRED

To instruct seventh and eighth year pupils, at least four different kinds of schoolrooms are needed: regular classrooms, manual training shops, cooking rooms, and gymnasiums.

Difference in Number of Regular Classrooms Required

Table VII shows for the February-June term of 1911, the enrollment in 7A-8B classes in schools having all grades, the number of regular classrooms used in instructing these classes, and the average number of 7A-8B pupils per regular classroom. The table also shows the same facts for intermediate schools 24, 159, and 62.

The average number of 7A-8B pupils per classroom varies, as shown by Table VII, in the foregoing schools from thirty-five to fifty-two. These variations are due to differences in size of classrooms and to the particular number of 7A-8B pupils to be instructed.

TABLE VII

CLASSROOMS REQUIRED

(1) SCHOOLS HAVING ALL GRADES (1A-8B)

Schools	Districts	7A-8B Enrollment, Feb.-June Term, 1911	Number of Regular Classrooms	Average Number of Pupils per Classroom
72	17	515	11	46
83	17	741	15	49
168	17	634	13	48
171	17	495	12	41
68	21	305	8	38
90	21	424	12	35
119	21	474	12	39
22	4	783	18	43
31	4	294	7	42
110	4	423	8	52
147	4	962	23	41
34	3	410	10	41
7	2	513	12	42
Total		6,973	161	43.31

(2) INTERMEDIATE SCHOOLS (7A-8B)

Schools	Districts	7A-8B Enrollment Feb.-June Term, 1911	Number of Regular Classrooms	Average Number of Pupils per Classroom
24	21	1,422	28	50
159	20	1,420	32	44
62	3	2,602	59	44
Total..................		5,444	119	45.75

It will also be observed that the average number of pupils per classroom in schools having all grades is 43.31, in intermediate schools, 45.75—an average difference in favor of the intermediate school of 2.44 pupils. Hence, had the average number of pupils per classroom been the same in the two kinds of schools, to provide for the 6,973 7A-8B pupils in schools having all grades would have required only 152.42 classrooms (6,973 ÷ 45.75) instead of 161, or 8.58 fewer than were used.

It therefore appears that when 7A-8B pupils are brought together in intermediate schools the number of regular classrooms required is 5.33 per cent. (8.58 ÷ 161) less than when seventh and eighth year pupils are taught in schools having all grades.[1]

[1] It will be observed that the average number of pupils per classroom in both schools having all grades and intermediate schools is high. Because comparisons are made under these conditions, the inference should not be drawn that we favor overcrowded classrooms. We

Difference in the Number of Manual Training Shops Required

Table VIII shows, as of April, 1911, for schools having all grades the number of single shops, the number of seventh and eighth year pupils instructed in each shop, and the average number instructed per shop. The table also shows the same facts for intermediate schools 24 and 62. Intermediate school 159 is a girls' school, and hence has no shop.

In schools having all grades the average number of seventh and eighth year pupils instructed per shop is 260; in intermediate schools, 358—an average difference in favor of intermediate schools of ninety-eight pupils. Had the same average prevailed as prevailed in intermediate schools, to provide for the 4,945 seventh and eighth year pupils in schools having all grades, only 13.81 shops (4,945÷358) instead of nineteen would have been required, or 5.19 fewer than were used. It therefore requires 27.32 per cent. (5.19 ÷ 19) fewer shops to care for a given number of seventh and eighth grade pupils in intermediate schools than to care for the same number of such pupils in schools having all grades.

Manual training is regularly taught only in the seventh and eighth years. The Board of Superintendents, however, may authorize the giving of such instruction to other than seventh and eighth year pupils. This is done particularly in case of over-age boys in the 6A and 6B grades. Manual training shops may consequently be used by other than seventh and eighth year pupils.

Table IX shows, as of April, 1911, for schools having all grades, the number of single shops, the total number of pupils instructed in each shop, and the average number in-

favor the opposite. The comparisons are made on the assumption that whatever the average number of pupils per classroom in theory, in practice the difference in the actual number of pupils per classroom in schools having all grades and in intermediate schools would be similar to the difference found for the February-June term, 1911.

TABLE VIII

(1) Shops Required—Schools Having All Grades (1A-8B)

Schools	Districts	Number of Single Shops	Number of Seventh and Eighth Year Pupils as of April, 1911, Instructed in Each	Average Number Seventh and Eighth Year Pupils Instructed per Shop
20	6	1	438	
21	1	1	161	
23	1	1	190	
25	6	1	405	
29	1	1	31	
34	3	2	408	
44	1	1	74	
64	7	1	501	
79	6	2	334	
83	17	2	728	
114	1	1	257	
147	4	2	527	
160	5	2	569	
188B	7	1	322	
Total		19	4,945	260

(2) Shops Required—Intermediate Schools (7A-8B)[1]

Schools	Districts	Number of Single Shops	Number of Seventh and Eighth Year Pupils as of April, 1911, Instructed in Each	Average Number Seventh and Eighth Year Pupils Instructed per Shop
24	21	3	1,368	
62	3	4	1,138	
Total		7	2,506	358

[1] The figures for this table were taken from the Teachers' Schedule of Assignment and from the Principals' Statement of Shop Work, on file at the office of the Board of Education.

structed per shop. The table also shows the same facts for intermediate schools 24 and 62. (See page 39.)

In schools having all grades the average number of all pupils instructed per shop was 289; in intermediate schools, 358—an average difference in favor of intermediate schools of sixty-nine pupils. Had the same average prevailed as prevailed in intermediate schools, to provide for the total of 5,501 pupils in schools having all grades, only 15.37 shops (5,501÷358) instead of nineteen would have been required, or 3.63 fewer than were used.

When, therefore, manual training is extended to other than seventh and eighth year pupils, thus increasing the total use of shops, only 19.11 per cent. (3.63÷19) fewer shops are required in intermediate schools than in schools having all grades, to provide for the same number of pupils.[1]

Hence, intermediate schools require 27.32 per cent. (see above) fewer shops than schools having all grades, only when the instruction of seventh and eighth year pupils alone is taken into account.

Difference in the Number of Cooking Rooms Required

Owing to a lack of uniformity in the method of using cooking rooms, it is impossible to compare intermediate schools and schools having all grades with respect to the number of seventh and eighth year pupils taught per cooking room. In schools such as 13, 71, 72, and 137, Manhattan, the group method of instruction is followed, i. e., instead of doing the work themselves, the pupils observe cooking done in whole or in part by the teacher. In some schools, such as 90, 159, and 188 G, due to the lack of adequate individual equipment, children are given considerable theory; this reduces by one half or one third the amount of actual cooking. In other schools, the entire time assigned

[1] See closing sentence of this section, page 44.

TABLE IX[1]

(1) Shops Required—Schools Having All Grades (1A-8B)

Schools	Districts	Number of Single Shops	Total Number of Pupils as of April, 1911, Instructed in Each Shop	Average Number Instructed per Shop
20	6	1	438	
21	1	1	180	
23	1	1	190	
25	6	1	405	
29	1	1	63	
34	3	2	641	
44	1	1	127	
64	7	1	501	
79	6	2	483	
83	17	2	728	
114	1	1	332	
147	4	2	527	
160	5	2	564	
188B	7	1	322	
Total................		19	5,501	289

(2) Shops Required—Intermediate Schools (7A-8B)

Schools	Districts	Number of Single Shops	Total Number of Pupils as of April, 1911, Instructed in Each Shop	Average Number Instructed per Shop
24	21	3	1,368	
62	3	4	1,138	
Total................		7	2,506	358

[1]The figures for this table were taken from the same sources as the figures in Table VIII.

TABLE X[1]

(1) Cooking Rooms Required—Schools Having All Grades (1A-8B)

Schools	Districts	Number of Single Cooking Rooms	Single Periods Used per Week for Seventh and Eighth Year Pupils, April, 1911	Average Number Single Periods Used per Week for Seventh and Eighth Year Pupils
1	1	1	28	
4	5	1	30	
21	1	1	12	
23	1	1	26	
31	4	1	28	
63	6	1	34	
68	21	1	26	
90	21	1	28	
91	6	1	30	
110	4	1	30	
119	21	1	30	
168	17	1	27	
188G	7	1	24	
Total................		13	353	27.15

(2) Cooking Rooms Required—Intermediate Schools (7A-8B)

Schools	Districts	Number of Single Cooking Rooms	Single Periods Used per Week for Seventh and Eighth Year Pupils, April, 1911	Average Number Single Periods Used per Week for Seventh and Eighth Year Pupils
62	3	2	63	
159	20	2	68	
Total................		4	131	32.75

[1] The figures for this table were taken from the Teachers' Schedule of Assignment and from Principals' Statement of Cooking, on file at the office of the Board of Education.

to the study is given to cooking. It is possible, however, to compare schools having all grades and intermediate schools with reference to the periods per week cooking rooms are used.

Table X shows, as of April, 1911, for schools having all grades the number of cooking rooms; the number of single periods each cooking room was used per week for the instruction of seventh and eighth year pupils; and the average number of single periods per week in use. The table also shows the same facts for intermediate schools 62 and 159. (See p. 40.)

Table X shows that in schools having all grades, cooking rooms were used in the instruction of seventh and eighth year pupils on the average 27.15 single periods per week; in intermediate schools, 32.75—an average difference in favor of intermediate schools of 5.60 periods. Had the same average prevailed as prevailed in intermediate schools, the 353 periods of instruction given in schools having all grades could have been given in 10.78 cooking rooms (353 ÷ 32.75) instead of thirteen, or in 2.22 fewer than were used.

It therefore appears that 17.10 per cent. (2.22÷13) fewer cooking rooms are required to provide for a given number of seventh and eighth year pupils in intermediate schools than to provide for the same number of such pupils in schools having all grades.

Like manual training, cooking is regularly taught only in the seventh and eighth years. The Board of Superintendents may, however, authorize the giving of cooking to other pupils. This is done particularly in case of over-age girls in the 6A and 6B grades. Cooking rooms may consequently be used by other than seventh and eighth year pupils.

Table XI shows, as of April, 1911, for schools having all grades, the number of cooking rooms, the total number of

TABLE XI [1]

(1) Cooking Rooms Required—Schools Having All Grades (1A-8B)

Schools	Districts	Number of Single Cooking Rooms	Total Number of Single Periods Used per Week for All Pupils	Average Number Single Periods Used per Week for All Pupils
1	1	1	35	
4	5	1	30	
21	1	1	30	
23	1	1	30	
31	4	1	30	
63	6	1	34	
68	21	1	28	
90	21	1	32	
91	6	1	30	
110	4	1	30	
119	21	1	30	
168	17	1	30	
188G	7	1	30	
Total		13	399	30.69

(2) Cooking Rooms Required—Intermediate Schools (7A-8B)

Schools	Districts	Number of Single Cooking Rooms	Total Number of Single Periods Used per Week for All Pupils	Average Number Single Periods Used per Week for All Pupils
62	3	2	63	
159	20	2	68	
Total		4	131	32.75

[1] The figures for this table are taken from the same sources as the figures in Table X.

single periods each cooking room was used per week, and the average number of single periods per week in use. This table also shows the same facts for intermediate schools 62 and 159.

Cooking rooms are used on the average, in schools having all grades, a total of 30.69 single periods per week; in intermediate schools, 32.75—an average difference in favor of intermediate schools of 2.06 single periods. Had the same average prevailed in the two kinds of schools, the total of 399 periods of instruction given in schools having all grades could have been given in 12.18 cooking rooms (399÷32.75) instead of thirteen, or in .82 fewer than were used.

When the total use of cooking rooms in intermediate schools is compared with the total use in schools having all grades, it appears that only 6.31 per cent. (.82÷13) fewer are required in intermediate schools than in schools having all grades to instruct the same number of pupils.

Hence, it is only when the instruction of seventh and eighth year pupils is taken into account that intermediate schools require 17.10 per cent. (see pages 41-42) fewer cooking rooms than schools having all grades.

The foregoing difference of 27.32 per cent. in the number of shops and 17.10 per cent. in the number of cooking rooms needed by intermediate schools and by schools having all grades, to instruct a given number of seventh and eighth year pupils, is due to the fact that shops and cooking rooms in the intermediate schools are kept in use practically the entire school day. In consequence, they cannot be used to instruct pupils below the 7A grade, even were it practical to send such pupils to an intermediate school merely for manual training and cooking. To provide for the pupils below the 7A grade now instructed in schools having all grades would, therefore, require shops and cooking rooms in addition to those needed in the intermediate schools.

Hence, in considering the saving in shops and cooking rooms that might be effected by bringing 7A-8B pupils into intermediate schools, the use of shops and cooking rooms to instruct other than seventh and eighth year pupils in schools having all grades should be taken into account (see the first note, page 45). Moreover, should intermediate schools be made universal and manual training and cooking be made general for over-age 6A-6B pupils, the saving in shops and cooking rooms might be less than the above estimates, even when the instruction of pupils below the 7A is taken into account, because under such conditions, to provide manual training and cooking for such over-age pupils might require relatively more shops and cooking rooms than under present conditions.

Difference in the Number of Gymnasiums Required

Table XII gives the number of gymnasiums in schools having all grades, the number of single periods per week each was used during the February-June term, 1911, for the instruction of seventh and eighth year pupils, and the average number of single periods per week in use. The table also shows the same facts for intermediate schools 24, 159, and 62. (See page 45.)

Gymnasiums, it appears, are used in schools having all grades on the average 34.17 single periods per week; in intermediate schools, 41.75—an average difference in favor of intermediate schools of 7.58 single periods.

Had the same average prevailed in the two kinds of schools, the total of 205 periods of instruction in schools having all grades could have been given in 4.91 gymnasiums (205÷41.75) instead of six, or in 18.17 per cent. fewer gymnasiums than were used.

Summary

In view of the foregoing data, it appears that to provide for a given number of 7A-8B pupils in intermediate schools requires:

5.33 per cent. fewer regular classrooms
27.32 per cent. or 19.11 per cent. fewer shops[1]
17.10 per cent. or 6.31 per cent. fewer cooking rooms[1]
and
18.17 per cent. fewer gymnasiums

than to provide for the same number of such children in schools having all grades.

The saving in money, represented by these differences in the number of rooms required in intermediate schools and in schools having all grades, is brought out, if these differences are considered in relation to caring for 20,000 7A-8B pupils.[2] On the basis of the rooms required to care for the foregoing 7A-8B pupils in schools having all grades, and

TABLE XII

(1) GYMNASIUMS REQUIRED—SCHOOLS HAVING ALL GRADES (1A-8B)

Schools	Districts	Number of Gymnasiums	Single Periods Used per Week for Seventh and Eighth Year Pupils	Average Number of Single Periods Used per Week for Seventh and Eighth Year Pupils
1	1	1	36	
4	5	1	45	
23	1	1	36	
44	1	1	16	
91	6	1	40	
114	1	1	32	
Total		6	205	34.17

[1] According as the use of shops and cooking rooms in schools having all grades to instruct other than seventh and eighth grade pupils is disregarded or taken into account.

[2] This illustration does not imply the suggestion that 20,000 7A-8B pupils out of the 100,000 now in the schools of New York could be brought into intermediate schools. With the time at the disposal of the Committee on School Inquiry, it is impossible to determine the exact number that could be advantageously segregated in intermediate schools.

(2) GYMNASIUMS REQUIRED—INTERMEDIATE SCHOOLS (7A-8B)

Schools	Districts	Number of Gymnasiums	Single Periods Used per Week for Seventh and Eighth Year Pupils	Average Number of Single Periods Used per Week for Seventh and Eighth Year Pupils
24	21	1	45	
159	20	1	22	
62	3	2	100	
Total		4	167	41.75

in intermediate schools, to provide for 20,000 such pupils, equally divided between boys and girls, there would be needed in:

	Schools Having All Grades	Intermediate Schools	Difference in Favor of Intermediate Schools
Regular classrooms.........	462	438	24
Manual training shops......	39	28	11 or 4[1]
Cooking rooms.............	35	27	8 or 4[1]
Gymnasiums..............	27	21	6
	563	514	49 or 38[1]

To care for 20,000 7A-8B pupils, there is a difference of forty-nine in the number of rooms needed in these two kinds of schools—a difference of 8.70 per cent. (49÷563) in favor of intermediate schools; when the use of shops and cooking rooms in schools having all grades to instruct other than seventh and eighth year pupils is taken into account, there is a difference of thirty-eight, or 6.75 per cent., in the rooms required. This difference, at the least of thirty-eight rooms, represents not less than $400,000 [2] in original

[1] See first note on page 45.

[2] The estimated cost of a thirty-nine-room building is $330,000; of the site $70,000. These estimates are based on the cost of new buildings as given in the Corporate Stock Requirements submitted by the Board of Education, March, 1911, and on the cost of sites, as given in the annual Financial and Statistical Report of the Board of Education for 1910.

investment, and an annual difference of 6.88 per cent. in cost of upkeep and operating expenses.

(2) DIFFERENCE IN THE NUMBER OF TEACHERS REQUIRED

In the instruction of seventh and eighth year pupils, three kinds of teachers are employed: regular class teachers, manual training teachers, and cooking teachers.

Difference in the Number of Regular Class Teachers Required

Table XIII shows, for the February-June term of 1911, the enrollment of 7A, 7B, 8A, and 8B classes in schools having all grades, the number of regular class teachers in each grade, and the average number of pupils per teacher. The table also shows the same facts for intermediate schools 24, 159, and 62. (See page 48.)

It will be observed that the number of pupils per teacher in schools having all grades ranges from thirty-two to fifty-five, and that there were at least twenty over-size classes—classes having an enrollment of more than fifty pupils.

The average number of pupils per regular class teacher in schools having all grades is 43.31; in intermediate schools, 45.75—an average difference in favor of intermediate schools of 2.44 pupils. Hence, had the average number of pupils per regular class teacher been the same as in intermediate schools, the 6,973 7A-8B pupils in schools having all grades would have been instructed by 152.42 teachers (6,973÷45.75) instead of 161, or by 8.58 fewer teachers than were engaged. Further, had these 6,973 pupils been in intermediate schools, it would have been possible, without increasing the number of teachers, to have reduced the foregoing over-size classes, whereas in schools having all grades to have done this would have required additional teachers.

TABLE XIII

(1) TEACHERS REQUIRED—SCHOOLS HAVING ALL GRADES (1A-8B)

Schools	Districts	7A Grade			7B Grade			8A Grade			8B Grade			Grand Total		
		Enroll-ment	Regular Teachers	Pupils per Teacher	Enroll-ment	Regular Teachers	Pupils per Teacher	Enroll-ment	Regular Teachers	Pupils per Teacher	Enroll-ment	Regular Teachers	Pupils per Teacher	Enroll-ment	Regular Teachers	Pupils per Teacher
72	17	152	3	50	142	3	47	135	3	45	86	2	43	515	11	46
83	17	249	5	49	220	4	55	142	3	47	130	3	43	741	15	49
168	17	212	4	53	165	4	41	147	3	49	110	2	55	634	13	48
171	17	145	4	36	121	3	40	134	3	44	95	2	47	495	12	41
68	21	93	2	46	81	2	40	67	2	33	64	2	32	305	8	38
90	21	110	3	36	140	4	35	106	3	35	68	2	34	424	12	35
119	21	138	4	34	122	3	40	127	3	42	87	2	43	474	12	39
22	4	215	5	43	227	6	37	176	4	44	165	3	55	783	18	43
31	4	79	2	39	80	2	40	87	2	43	48	1	48	294	7	42
110	4	107	2	53	108	2	54	110	2	55	98	2	49	423	8	52
147	4	306	7	43	256	6	42	210	5	42	190	5	38	962	23	41
34	3	103	2	51	74	2	37	134	4	33	99	2	49	410	10	41
7	2	298	6	49	215	6	35	....	....	....	....	....	....	513	12	42
Total.....		2,207	49	45.05	1,951	47	41.51	1,575	37	42.57	1,240	28	44.29	6,973	161	43.31

(2) TEACHERS REQUIRED—INTERMEDIATE SCHOOLS (7A-8B)

Schools	Districts	7A Grade			7B Grade			8A Grade			8B Grade			Grand Total		
		Enroll-ment	Regular Teachers	Pupils per Teacher	Enroll-ment	Regular Teachers	Pupils per Teacher	Enroll-ment	Regular Teachers	Pupils per Teacher	Enroll-ment	Regular Teachers	Pupils per Teacher	Enroll-ment	Regular Teachers	Pupils per Teacher
24	21	454	9	50	375	7	53	310	6	51	283	6	47	1,422	28	50
159	20	441	10	44	375	9	41	332	7	47	272	6	45	1,420	32	44
62	3	666	15	44	640	15	42	622	14	44	674	15	44	2,602	59	44
Total.....		1,561	34	45.91	1,390	31	44.84	1,264	27	46.81	1,229	27	45.52	5,444	119	45.75

It therefore appears that to instruct the same number of 7A-8B pupils, intermediate schools require fewer regular class teachers than schools having all grades by 5.33 per cent. (8.58÷161). Also that classes can be made more nearly uniform in size. This tends to equalize opportunity and to add to the effectiveness of the instruction.

Difference in the Number of Manual Training Teachers Required

Table XIV shows, as of April, 1911, for schools having all grades, the number of seventh and eighth year pupils instructed in manual training, the number of manual training teachers giving their whole time to the instruction of seventh and eighth year pupils, and the average number of seventh and eighth year pupils per teacher. The table also shows the same facts for intermediate schools 24 and 62.

The average number of seventh and eighth year pupils per manual training teacher in schools having all grades is 338; in intermediate schools, 368—an average difference of thirty pupils. Hence, had the same number of pupils been instructed per manual training teacher in schools having all grades as were instructed in intermediate schools, to have taught manual training to the 4,945 seventh and eighth year pupils in schools having all grades would have required 13.44 manual training teachers (4,945÷368) instead of 14.61, or 1.17 fewer than were engaged.

It therefore appears that intermediate schools need fewer manual training teachers than schools having all grades by 8.01 per cent. (1.17÷14.61) to give shopwork to the same number of seventh and eighth year pupils.[1]

[1] The extension of manual training and cooking to over-age 6A-6B pupils might, as stated above, lessen the estimated saving in manual training and cooking rooms, but such an extension would not affect the estimated saving in manual training and cooking teachers, because this extension would in no wise affect the number of teachers required to instruct a given number of 7A-8B pupils in the two kinds of schools.

TABLE XIV[1]

(1) MANUAL TRAINING TEACHERS REQUIRED — SCHOOLS HAVING ALL GRADES (1A-8B)

Schools	Districts	Seventh and Eighth Year Pupils Instructed as of April, 1911	Number of Manual Training Teachers Giving Whole Time to Seventh and Eighth Year Pupils	Average Number of Seventh and Eighth Year Pupils per Teacher
20	6	438	1.00	
21	1	161	.46	
23	1	190	.51	
25	1	405	.96	
29	1	31	.17	
34	3	408	1.38	
44	1	74	.23	
64	7	501	1.00	
79	6	334	1.40	
83	8	728	1.93	
114	1	257	.80	
147	4	527	1.94	
160	5	569	1.94	
188B	7	322	.89	
Total................		4,945	14.61	338

(2) MANUAL TRAINING TEACHERS REQUIRED—INTERMEDIATE SCHOOLS (7A-8B)

Schools	Districts	Seventh and Eighth Year Pupils Instructed as of April, 1911	Number of Manual Training Teachers Giving Whole Time to Seventh and Eighth Year Pupils	Average Number of Seventh and Eighth Year Pupils per Teacher
24	21	1,368	3.00	
62	3	1,138	3.80	
Total................		2,506	6.80	368

[1] The figures for this table were taken from the Teachers' Schedule of Assignment and from the Principals' Statement of Shop Work, on file at the office of the Board of Education.

Difference in the Number of Cooking Teachers Required

Owing to differences in cooking instruction, it is impossible to compare the number of cooking teachers needed, in schools having all grades and intermediate schools, to instruct the same number of seventh and eighth year pupils. Cooking classes are, however, organized and conducted in the same way as classes in manual training, and the same general conditions affect the size of class and the number of pupils per teacher.

It is, therefore, fair to infer that were it possible to compare the number of cooking teachers required, in schools having all grades and in intermediate schools, to teach a given number of seventh and eighth year pupils, the same difference would be found in the number of cooking teachers needed as is found in the number of manual training teachers required—that is, it is but fair to infer that intermediate schools require fewer cooking teachers than schools having all grades by 8.01 per cent. to give cooking to the same number of seventh and eighth year pupils.

Summary

In view of the foregoing data, it appears that to instruct a given number of 7A-8B pupils in intermediate schools, in comparison with instructing the same number of such pupils in schools having all grades, requires:

5.33 per cent. fewer regular class teachers
8.01 per cent. fewer manual training teachers
8.01 per cent. fewer cooking teachers

The saving in money, represented by these differences in the number of teachers required in intermediate schools and in schools having all grades, is brought out, if these differences are considered in relation to instructing 20,000

7A-8B pupils.[1] On the basis of the teachers required to instruct the foregoing 7A-8B pupils in schools having all grades, and to instruct such pupils in intermediate schools, to provide for 20,000 7A-8B pupils, equally divided between boys and girls, there would be required in:

	Schools Having All Grades	Intermediate Schools	Difference in Favor of Intermediate Schools
Regular class teachers....	462	438	24
Manual training teachers..	30	28	2
Cooking teachers.........	30	28	2
	522	494	28

In caring for 20,000 7A-8B pupils, there is a difference of twenty-eight in the number of teachers required in these two kinds of schools—a difference of 5.36 per cent. (28÷522) in favor of intermediate schools. This difference of twenty-eight teachers represents an annual difference in cost of not less than $35,000.[2]

(3) DIFFERENCE IN THE AMOUNT OF SUPPLIES AND EQUIPMENT REQUIRED

The term "supplies" is used by the Board of Education to include all material aids to instruction. A distinction, however, should be drawn between supplies which are directly consumed by pupils—for example, paper pads, pencils, ink, textbooks, etc.—and supplies which are to a greater or less extent permanent—for example, maps, globes, science apparatus, gymnasium, cooking room, and shop equipment.

It is obvious that bringing 7A-8B pupils into intermediate schools would effect no saving in supplies which are directly consumed. It is, however, equally obvious that great saving would thereby be effected in supplies which are to a

[1] See second note on page 45.

[2] Estimated on the basis of the average annual salary of 7A-8A, 8B, and of manual training and cooking teachers, as stated in the Board of Education's Estimate, 1912.

greater or less extent permanent. The saving on equipment in shops, cooking rooms, and gymnasiums would be in direct relation to the difference in the number of these required in intermediate schools and in schools having all grades to instruct a given number of 7A-8B pupils. Hence, there would be a saving of 19.11 per cent. or 27.32 per cent. on equipment for shops; of 6.31 per cent. or 17.10 per cent. on equipment for cooking rooms—according as the use of shops and cooking rooms in schools having all grades to instruct other than seventh and eighth year pupils is taken into account or disregarded—and a saving of 18.17 per cent. on equipment for gymnasiums.

It was impossible to obtain data on what is spent for seventh and eighth year pupils on such permanent equipment as maps, globes, science apparatus, etc. Hence, it is impossible to estimate what saving would be effected by bringing 7A-8B pupils into intermediate schools. This saving would, however, be no inconsiderable sum.

SUMMARY OF THE FOREGOING CONSIDERATIONS

Schools having all grades and intermediate schools have been compared with respect to economic efficiency on three points:

1. The number of schoolrooms required.
2. The number of teachers required.
3. The amount of equipment required.

It has been shown:

(a) That intermediate schools require fewer rooms by 8.70 per cent. or by 6.75 per cent.[1]

(b) That intermediate schools require fewer teachers by 5.36 per cent.

[1] According as the use of shops and cooking rooms in schools having all grades to instruct other than seventh and eighth year pupils is disregarded or taken into account.

(c) That intermediate schools require less equipment in shops by 19.11 per cent. or by 27.32 per cent.,[1] in cooking rooms by 6.31 per cent. or by 17.10 per cent.,[1] and in gymnasiums by 18.17 per cent.

In view of these differences in requirements, and hence differences in cost, could 20,000 7A-8B pupils be brought into intermediate schools[2] the immediate saving would be sufficient to provide at the very least for the erection of a school building of thirty-nine rooms, and for the annual total cost of operating such a school.[3]

[1] See note on page 53.
[2] See second note, page 45.
[3] See note on page 46 and second note on page 52.

CHAPTER III

EDUCATIONAL OPPORTUNITIES AFFORDED BY THE INTERMEDIATE SCHOOL

THE intermediate school should not be judged, however, only by what it now is, but also by what it might become.

Intermediate schools, at the present time, are conducted in most ways like schools having all grades. The two kinds of schools have the same course of study for the seventh and eighth years, the same departmental organization, and practically the same methods of classifying and promoting pupils. In a word, the intermediate school is merely an enlargement, with slight modifications, of the seventh and eighth grades of schools having all classes. But to limit the activities of the intermediate school in this way is to fail to take advantage of important educational opportunities it may be made to afford.

These educational opportunities suggest themselves when we consider the wisdom of offering to seventh and eighth year pupils more than one course of study; of a better adaptation of the instruction to the two sexes; of a more thoroughgoing classification of pupils; of a more just method of promotion; and of a better adaptation to the needs of seventh and eighth year pupils of certain general features of school organization.

OPPORTUNITY TO OFFER DIFFERENT COURSES OF STUDY

The wisdom of offering more than one course of study in the elementary schools of New York City to seventh and eighth year pupils is discussed elsewhere.[1] By reason of the large number of pupils in attendance in the same grade, the intermediate school affords peculiar opportunity for different courses of study. As is pointed out in our discussion on the course of study, these courses meet the needs of three classes of pupils: (a) those who are planning to go to an "academic" or "general" high school, and perhaps to college; (b) those who look forward to entering a vocational high school; and (c) those who intend, as soon as they are fourteen years old, to enter an elementary vocational school, or who must leave or choose to leave school as soon as they are legally exempt from further school attendance. In all these courses the separate educational needs of the two sexes, as well as their common needs, should be provided for, as is indicated in the next section.

OPPORTUNITY TO ADAPT THE INSTRUCTION TO THE TWO SEXES AND TO THE REQUIREMENTS OF HIGH SCHOOLS AND VOCATIONAL SCHOOLS

The differences between boys and girls point to the necessity of differences in the instruction they should receive. The desirability of making the instruction of boys and girls different is already recognized in providing for boys manual training, and for girls cooking and sewing; also in providing different physical training for boys and for girls. This differentiation of work, however, should be carried much further in the elementary school than it now is. The intermediate school affords particular opportunity to differentiate, according to the needs of the two sexes, both in the general scope of the different courses of study and in their details.

Good opportunity is also afforded by the intermediate school to experiment with courses of study, to the end that these may on the one hand be adapted to the capacities, desires, and intentions of different groups of children, and

[1] See Part II, pages 114-117.

may on the other hand be brought to articulate so closely with the courses in high schools and vocational schools, that pupils graduating from the intermediate school are well prepared to profit by and do the work of the particular kind of subsequent school they may enter.

Again, by reason of the number of children in intermediate schools who are approaching the time when they must choose a pursuit, and who need advice that they may choose wisely, and by reason of the number of teachers having to deal only with such children, the intermediate school affords the best possible opportunity to experiment with and to develop systematic vocational guidance.

Hence, in judging of the worth of the intermediate school, the opportunity it affords to adapt the instruction to the needs of the two sexes, and to the needs of different groups of children, and to lay the foundation for work in a subsequent school should be given serious consideration.

OPPORTUNITY TO CLASSIFY PUPILS ACCORDING TO ABILITY

In schools having all grades, it is impracticable, because of numbers, to group pupils within a particular grade, to any considerable extent, according to ability. Children of widely different capacity must, in consequence, work in the same class, with the inevitable result that one part of the class is kept comfortably busy; a second part has too much to do, and a third part too little.

But, so far as possible, every child has the right to work at all times up to his capacity. The intermediate schools can supply such conditions of work more easily than other schools; for, by reason of numbers, the pupils of a given grade may at least be grouped as slow pupils, normal pupils, and exceptionally bright pupils, and the instruction adapted to the requirements of each group.

Further, in schools having all grades, when a pupil is not promoted, he must, because of the relatively few failing in a given grade, take the work over with pupils who are in the class for the first time. The pupil consequently has no opportunity to pay special attention to the particular subjects in which he has failed. In the intermediate school, however, it is possible, by reason of numbers, to bring together into one class children who have failed in the same branches. Such a grouping affords opportunity to help pupils where there is need, and hence to strengthen them where they are weak.

OPPORTUNITY FOR PROMOTION BY STUDIES

In schools having all classes, children are promoted by grades. Hence, if a pupil is not advanced, he must go over a second time all the work of the grade instead of having to repeat only the studies in which he is deficient.

The pupil has the right, so far as possible, to be advanced as rapidly or as slowly as his several abilities permit or require. His advancement in all studies, therefore, ought not to be conditioned by his weakness in certain branches. Whether promotion by grades is necessarily inherent in schools having all grades should be made the subject of consideration. However that may be, the intermediate school can readily adopt such a system of promotion that each child may go forward whenever he is prepared to advance. That is, the intermediate school can be so organized that promotions are made by studies rather than by grades. The administrative difficulties of promotion by studies should be no greater in the intermediate school than they are in the high school; and no one would think of promoting high-school pupils otherwise than by subjects.

OPPORTUNITY TO ADAPT TO THE NEEDS OF SEVENTH AND EIGHTH YEAR PUPILS CERTAIN GENERAL FEATURES OF SCHOOL ORGANIZATION

It is well understood that at about the age of twelve or fourteen years boys and girls need a kind of care and discipline different from the care and discipline of younger children. In schools having all classes, relatively the same organization prevails throughout the school. To be sure, certain modifications are made in favor of seventh and eighth year pupils—for example, departmental teaching—but these modifications must necessarily be few. The intermediate school, however, having to do only with seventh and eighth year pupils, can adapt its organization to the particular needs of children passing from late childhood into the period of early youth.

The intermediate school may be so organized that larger place is given than it is possible to give in the average school having all grades to athletics and competitive games, to club work, and to social activities; larger opportunity can be given for pupil self-government; larger individual freedom of thought and action can also be permitted. In a word, the intermediate school can be so organized, such opportunity can be given for the expression of spontaneity, and for the exercise of initiative, judgment, and self-direction, that school life will make a stronger appeal to seventh and eighth year pupils than it now does, as a rule, in most schools. The need of this stronger appeal is revealed in the fact that 4,218 7A-8B boys and 3,948 7A-8B girls, a total of 8,166 7A-8B pupils, left the elementary schools of the City of New York during the spring term of 1911 without completing these grades.[1]

PROBABLE EFFECTS OF REALIZING THE FOREGOING POSSIBILITIES

Certain of the foregoing possibilities are now being realized, to a limited extent, in intermediate schools—notably in Public School Number 62; but should different courses of study be introduced; should a differentiation of the instruction for boys and girls be made and the courses of study be made to articulate with high schools and vocational

[1] From reports made to the Committee on School Inquiry, June, 1911.

schools; should pupils within a grade be grouped according to ability; should promotion by studies be inaugurated; should an organization be developed, that is adapted to the particular needs of seventh and eighth year pupils, and should the effects of these innovations be studied carefully for a series of terms, it would be found, it is believed, that such an intermediate school would not only be far more efficient in caring for seventh and eighth year pupils than a school having all grades, but also far more efficient than are the intermediate schools already established.

LOCATION AND ESTABLISHMENT OF AN INTERMEDIATE SCHOOL

Finally, there are two fundamental conditions that directly influence the location of an intermediate school: first, there must be adequate school provision within ready reach of the 1A-6B pupils who would live in the immediate vicinity of the intermediate school; and, second, there must be a sufficient number of 7A-8B pupils within ready walking distance to justify the establishment of such a school.

A serious difficulty to be reckoned with in the establishment of intermediate schools is the attitude of the principals and of the teachers in the schools affected. The schedule of salaries is higher for 7A-8B than for 1A-6B teachers; also, in schools having from six to seventeen rooms in which there are grades above the 6B, the head teacher or assistant principal in charge is relieved from teaching a class. There is necessarily, however, no such exemption in schools having the same number of rooms but in which the highest grade is the 6B.[1] It is, therefore, only natural, when the 7A-8B grades are removed from given schools in order to organize an intermediate school, that the principals and the teachers of these schools feel that their professional standing is unfavorably affected. Unless some way is found to allay this feeling it will continue to make difficult the active

[1] Schedule of Teachers' Salaries, 1912, pages 8 and 9.

extension of the intermediate school. In planning to increase the number of intermediate schools, there is also the question, which should be carefully considered, of the effect of removing from a school seventh and eighth year pupils. The question to be considered is whether the removal of seventh and eighth year pupils affects favorably or unfavorably the conduct, the ambition, and the work of younger children.

RECOMMENDATIONS

In view of the educational and economic efficiency of the intermediate schools now in existence, when judged on the basis of the data collected for the February-June term, 1911, and in view of the educational possibilities of such schools, we recommend:

(1) That similar data be collected for a number of terms, and should the foregoing findings be substantiated, we would further recommend:

(2) That an immediate study be made by the Board of Education of all localities where conditions seem favorable to the establishment of intermediate schools.

(3) That intermediate schools be established wherever conditions are favorable.

(4) That, when established, intermediate schools should not only serve the purpose they now serve, but should be planned and carried on so as to aim at the fuller realization of the educational opportunities they may be made to afford, as outlined in this report.

(5) That special care be taken to maintain sympathetic relations between the intermediate schools and the contributing schools on the one hand, and the closest articulation possible with high schools and

vocational schools on the other; and that the peculiar opportunity to develop systematic vocational guidance be fully utilized.

(6) That complete records of the work and cost of such schools be kept and that these records be used to improve intermediate schools and to judge of their efficiency.

Part II

Progress and Classification of School Children

CHAPTER IV

THE PROBLEM OF PROMOTION AND NON-PROMOTION

THE State, through its Compulsory Education Law, seeks to guarantee to each child of the City of New York, by the time he is fourteen years old, an education equal to graduation from the elementary school.[1] Physical and mental defects, as well as conditions in the home and in the school, which militate against children completing the elementary school course of study are, therefore, of both social and educational interest.

The factors which contribute to prevent children from graduating from the elementary schools of the City of New York by the time they are fourteen years of age, as is contemplated by the Compulsory Education Law, fall under three heads: late entrance into school, slow progress through the school, and late entrance and slow progress together.

Failure to complete the elementary school course of study by the fourteenth year, in so far as this is due to slow progress, is the direct result of the child's failure to secure regular promotion. To determine the causes which prevent children from receiving promotion, eight committees were appointed, in the fall of 1909, by the City Superintendent of Schools. These eight committees were in substantial accord in reporting the following, among others, as the chief causes of failure on the part of pupils to secure regular promotion:[2]

[1] See Section 622 of Compulsory Education Law.

[2] Twelfth Annual Report of the City Superintendent of Schools of the City of New York, pages 80 and 81.

"*Part time,* which prevents pupils from doing the work of the lower grades thoroughly."

"*Excessive size of classes,* which prevents teachers giving necessary individual instruction."

"*Irregular attendance.* Due to poor home conditions; looseness of parental control; ignorance of parents; lack of opportunities for home study; poverty of home, requiring pupils' assistance; sickness of other members of the family; lack of proper clothing; feeble health of individual pupils; poverty of surroundings."

"*Late entrance into school.* Due to two causes: the presence of immigrant children, and the fact that many children are sent to private schools before they enter the public schools."

"*Sluggish mentality.* Sometimes this feature takes the form of positive mental defect, and sometimes it characterizes pupils as slow in receptivity and response. Sometimes it takes the form of moral defects, such as dishonesty, lying, and cheating, which are intensified by improper reading, the following of bad examples, and petty defiance of law in the streets."

"*Ignorance of the English language.* Due to foreign birth and to the fact that English is not the language of the home."

From conference with members of the foregoing committees, it was learned that no comprehensive study of the causes of non-promotion was made by these committees, and that their conclusions were based on the personal impressions of the several members.

The studies made of the causes of non-promotion up to the present time may be characterized as descriptive studies, or as preliminary surveys. They are, nevertheless, very valuable. Their worth lies, however, in focusing the attention of teachers and superintendents on the problem of non-promotion, in suggesting probable causes, and in indicating where improvements should be made and the need of further investigation, rather than in having determined finally the causes of non-promotion and the extent to which non-promotion is due to each cause.

Even the data collected, and herewith reported in the following tables, supply no adequate basis for *final* conclusions. Because, although there appears to be, for example, a direct connection between the per cent. of promotion and the number of days absent, there is no way of telling from the table on absence whether part of the difference in the per cent. of promotion might not be due to causes other than absence —to the fact that pupils were in different kinds of classes (in part-time classes or whole-time classes), or in classes of different sizes, or were of different ages, or were of different nationalities. Until the retarding force of these and other probable causes is equalized or neutralized—i. e., until the pupils in the several groups, when grouped, for example, on the basis of the number of days absent, are from the same kind of class, from classes of the same size, are of the same age, of the same sex, of the same nationality—until this is done—and it was impossible to do it in this investigation—it is unscientific to draw more than *tentative* conclusions about the causes of non-promotion and the retarding force of particular causes.

Though no *final* conclusions can be properly drawn from the collected data, with regard to the causes of non-promotion or with reference to what extent non-promotion is due to each cause, *these data do supply the basis for tentative conclusions,* and for certain recommendations, and supply, also, a fund of valuable information.

The register in regular classes at the end of the February-June term, 1911, the number promoted, and the number not promoted—the basis of this report—were, for the several grades and the sexes, as follows:

TABLE XV

Grades	On Register before Promotion June 30, 1911			Promoted on June 30, 1911			Not Promoted on June 30, 1911		
	Boys	Girls	Total	Boys	Girls	Total	Boys	Girls	Total
1A	21,898	21,114	43,012	16,726	15,972	32,698	5,172	5,142	10,314
1B	25,302	24,530	49,832	22,358	21,862	44,220	2,944	2,668	5,612
2A	20,370	19,237	39,607	18,061	17,209	35,270	2,309	2,028	4,337
2B	22,488	22,120	44,608	20,336	20,071	40,407	2,152	2,049	4,201
3A	20,264	19,916	40,180	18,101	17,978	36,079	2,163	1,938	4,101
3B	21,496	21,415	42,911	19,373	19,564	38,937	2,123	1,851	3,974
4A	19,560	19,013	38,573	17,437	17,260	34,697	2,123	1,753	3,876
4B	20,174	19,735	39,909	18,110	17,878	35,988	2,064	1,857	3,921
5A	18,556	18,267	36,823	16,391	16,329	32,720	2,165	1,938	4,103
5B	17,653	18,382	36,035	15,703	16,634	32,337	1,950	1,748	3,698
6A	16,351	16,522	32,873	14,532	14,730	29,262	1,819	1,792	3,611
6B	15,632	15,502	31,134	13,898	13,949	27,847	1,734	1,553	3,287
7A	13,579	14,088	27,667	11,898	12,439	24,337	1,681	1,649	3,330
7B	12,176	12,615	24,791	10,891	11,203	22,094	1,285	1,412	2,697
8A	10,248	10,864	21,112	9,155	9,745	18,900	1,093	1,119	2,212
8B	9,587	9,958	19,545	9,002	9,458	18,460	585	500	1,085
Total	285,334	283,278	568,612	251,972	252,281	504,253	33,362	30,997	64,359

In the elementary schools of the city, the regular time for making promotions is the last day of the school term. Promotions are, however, also made during the course of the term. The total number of promotions for a term is,

TABLE XVI

Grades	Per Cent. of Promotion in Borough of					Per Cent. of Promotion in Entire City of New York
	Manhattan	Brooklyn	The Bronx	Queens	Richmond	
1A	75.37	76.49	76.13	76.97	75.75	76.02
1B	88.88	88.34	90.13	88.40	86.92	88.74
2A	88.90	88.76	90.24	89.28	89.76	89.04
2B	91.28	89.90	90.25	90.52	91.08	90.58
3A	90.08	89.54	89.46	90.66	87.12	89.79
3B	91.25	89.94	90.74	91.60	91.64	90.74
4A	90.51	89.38	89.58	90.68	88.26	89.95
4B	90.76	89.58	89.09	91.43	90.05	90.18
5A	89.52	88.21	88.45	89.93	84.91	88.86
5B	90.32	89.06	88.94	91.02	89.82	89.74
6A	89.01	89.16	88.19	89.86	87.67	89.02
6B	90.07	89.08	88.52	89.32	89.53	89.44
7A	88.31	87.08	88.82	89.31	87.21	87.96
7B	89.32	88.26	90.37	90.13	89.92	89.12
8A	89.92	88.78	89.15	91.28	90.87	89.52
8B	93.71	94.45	95.38	96.14	97.25	94.45
Total	88.96	88.22	88.71	89.47	88.30	88.68

therefore, the sum of the promotions made during the term and those made on the last day of the term.[1] *The data herein presented, it should be observed, relate only to promotions and non-promotions made at the end of the term,* and it should also be noted that these data have to do only with

[1] See Annual Report of the City Superintendent of Schools for 1910-11, Table XXXVII, pages 66 and 67.

promotions and non-promotions in regular classes[1] of the elementary school, exclusive of the kindergarten.

RATE OF PROMOTION IN EACH BOROUGH AND IN THE ENTIRE CITY OF NEW YORK

The City of New York includes the Boroughs of Manhattan, Brooklyn, The Bronx, Queens, and Richmond. Table XVI gives for each of the boroughs and for the Greater City the per cent. of promotion by grades at the end of the February-June term, 1911.

The difference between the per cent. of total promotion in the several boroughs, it will be observed, is small. The lowest per cent. of total promotion was, in Brooklyn, 88.22 per cent., and the highest, in Queens, 89.47 per cent.—a variation of but 1.25 per cent.

In each of the boroughs the lowest per cent. of promotion was in the 1A, and the highest in the 8B grade, but, within the same grade, the rate of promotion varied little among the boroughs. The per cent. of promotion ranged in the

1A from 75.37% to 76.97%—a variation of 1.60%
1B from 86.92% to 90.13%—a variation of 3.21%
2A from 88.76% to 90.24%—a variation of 1.48%
2B from 89.90% to 91.28%—a variation of 1.38%
3A from 87.12% to 90.66%—a variation of 3.54%
3B from 89.94% to 91.64%—a variation of 1.70%
4A from 88.26% to 90.68%—a variation of 2.42%
4B from 89.09% to 91.43%—a variation of 2.34%
5A from 84.91% to 89.93%—a variation of 5.02%
5B from 88.94% to 90.32%—a variation of 1.38%
6A from 87.67% to 89.86%—a variation of 2.19%
6B from 88.52% to 90.07%—a variation of 1.55%
7A from 87.08% to 89.31%—a variation of 2.23%
7B from 88.26% to 90.37%—a variation of 2.11%
8A from 88.78% to 91.28%—a variation of 2.50%
8B from 93.71% to 97.25%—a variation of 3.54%

[1] Regular classes are to be distinguished from "C" classes (for non-English-speaking pupils); from "D" classes (for over-age pupils preparing for employment certificates); from "E" classes (for over-age and retarded pupils), and from classes for defective children.

If the several grades, exclusive of the 1A and the 8B (fourteen grades), are grouped according to per cent. of promotion, the distribution in each of the boroughs is as follows:

Boroughs	Number of Grades Promoting Less Than 87%	Number of Grades Promoting from				Number of Grades Promoting 91% and Above
		87% to 88%	88% to 89%	89% to 90%	90% to 91%	
Manhattan..	0	0	3	4	5	2
Brooklyn....	0	1	5	8	0	0
The Bronx...	0	0	5	4	5	0
Queens......	0	0	1	5	4	4
Richmond...	2	3	1	4	2	2
Total Number of Grades Promoting a Given Per Cent........	2	4	15	25	16	8

In the great majority of the grades in the schools of each borough, it will be noted, the per cent. of promotion ranged between 88 per cent. and 91 per cent., while the most common per cent. of promotion was from 89 per cent. to 90 per cent.

In the Greater City, as in the several boroughs, the lowest per cent. of promotion was in the 1A, and the highest in the 8B grade. In the remaining fourteen grades the rate of promotion was from 87 per cent. to 88 per cent., in one grade; from 88 per cent. to 89 per cent., in two; from 89 to 90 per cent., in eight; and from 90 per cent. to 91 per cent., in three. With the exception of the 1A and the 8B grades, the most frequent rate of promotion, both in the Greater City and in the boroughs, was, therefore, from 89 per cent. to 90 per cent.

RATE OF PROMOTION IN THE 1A GRADE

The rate of promotion, as we have seen (Table XVI), was the lowest in the 1A grade. In the other grades, taken together, only one child in ten failed of promotion, but in the 1A almost each fourth child failed of advancement, with the result that 10,314 1A pupils were left back in June to reënter this grade in September, to overcrowd classes, and to congest the school.[1]

The requirements of the 1A grade should be relatively no higher than the requirements of other grades; hence, conditions being the same, the rate of promotion should be no lower. As a matter of fact, however, the rate of promotion for the 1A grade is, as a rule, lower than for other grades. Whether this is necessarily so is a matter of doubt, and deserves careful investigation.

From conferences with administrative officials, principals, and teachers, it was learned that they held the low rate of promotion in the 1A grade due to (a) the number of pupils unable to use the English language; (b) immaturity of pupils; (c) over-size classes; (d) part-time classes, and (e) irregular attendance and late entrance during the course of the term.

Inability to Use the English Language as a Factor

The total register of the 1A grade, June 30, 1911, was 43,012. According to the reports made to us, there were 3,648 1A pupils who were unable to use the English language on entrance to the grade,[2] leaving 39,364 1A pupils who, in the opinion of the teachers, had no unusual difficulty with our language. Of these 39,364, 30,531 were promoted, and 8,833 were not promoted. Hence, the rate of promotion for 1A pupils, when all those unable to use the English language are excluded, was 77.56 per cent., which is but

[1] See Table XV, page 68. [2] See Table XLII, page 157.

1.54 per cent. higher than the rate (76.02 per cent.) for the grade as a whole.[1]

Assuming that all other conditions affecting promotion and non-promotion were the same for the two groups of children—those able, and those unable, to use the English language—the per cent. of promotion in the 1A grade was, therefore, lower by but 1.54 per cent. than it otherwise would have been, because of the presence of 1A pupils unable to use the English language. Hence, inability of pupils to use the English language on entrance to the grade is, at best, but a minor factor in causing the low rate of promotion in the 1A grade.[2]

Immaturity as a Factor

The maturity of a child may be judged (a) in view of his physical development; (b) in view of his mental development; and (c) in view of his age. Maturity can be judged best in view of physical and mental development, but so difficult is it so to judge maturity and so crude is education as yet in its methods, that the maturity of children is judged very largely in view of age alone. Hence, in school practice, age is taken as the index of maturity. Accordingly, certain age limits have been fixed as the normal age for each grade of the school, and a child whose age falls within the normal age limits fixed for a grade is regarded as being sufficiently mature, both physically and mentally, to do the work of that grade. The age-grade standard is therefore the only basis we can use here in judging of the maturity or immaturity of the children found in a grade. To be sure, when maturity is judged by such standards, children will be found in all grades who are of the normal age for the grade, but who are manifestly immature for the grade.

[1] See Table XVI, page 69.

[2] The effect of inability to use the English language on the rate of promotion in the 1A grade should not be confused with its effect on the actual number of non-promotions in this grade. See Table XLV, page 161.

Table XVII gives, by grades, the number of children out of a thousand under normal age, of normal age, under one year over normal, between one and two years over normal, between two and three years over normal, and three years and more over normal, when the distribution is made on the basis of the per cent. of children of the corresponding age in the grade June 30, 1911:

TABLE XVII[1]

Grades	Below Normal Age	Normal Age	Under 1 Year Over Normal	Between 1 and 2 Years Over Normal	Between 2 and 3 Years Over Normal	3 Years and More Over Normal
1A	10	857	91	29	7	6
1B	10	805	127	38	12	8
2A	21	706	177	61	22	13
2B	19	703	171	67	25	15
3A	30	606	206	100	35	23
3B	21	602	204	103	42	28
4A	33	499	249	127	58	34
4B	26	517	229	133	62	33
5A	32	461	241	161	74	31
5B	28	482	236	160	67	27
6A	41	431	267	181	64	16
6B	39	466	270	163	53	9
7A	53	448	290	160	43	6
7B	47	511	274	134	29	5
8A	71	505	275	122	23	4
8B	75	551	243	106	22	3

It will be observed that a larger proportion of the children in the 1A grade are of normal age than in any other grade. Hence, the ages of the children in the 1A grade correspond more nearly to the normal age fixed for the 1A grade than is the case in any other grade of the elementary school.

[1] Table XVII is based upon Table XXXVII; see page 144. The age-grade standards employed in Table XVII are those of the City Superintendent of Schools.

When judged by the age-grade standards as determined by the City Superintendent of Schools, there is, therefore, no ground for holding that 1A pupils, in large numbers, are immature for their grade and, consequently, for assuming that immaturity is any considerable factor in causing the low rate of promotion found in the 1A grade.

Over-Size Classes as a Factor

1A classes, according to the By-laws of the Board of Education, should not contain more than fifty pupils, and fifty is regarded in most cities as too large for the most effective work. Hence, 1A classes having more than fifty pupils may be considered over-size.

There were in the 1A grade, June 30, 1911, according to the reports made to us, 15,025 pupils in classes having more than fifty pupils. The rate of promotion for 1A pupils in these over-size classes was 73.46 per cent.[1] If the 15,025 pupils in over-size classes are subtracted from the total register of 1A pupils (43,012), there remain 27,987 pupils in classes of fifty and under. The rate of promotion for these classes was 77.40 per cent.[1] Hence, the per cent. of promotion in the 1A grade, when all 1A pupils in over-size classes are excluded, was 1.38 per cent. higher than the per cent. of promotion for the grade as a whole.

Assuming that all other conditions affecting promotion and non-promotion were the same in classes of fifty and under, and in over-size classes, the per cent. of promotion in the 1A grade was, therefore, lower by 1.38 per cent. than it otherwise would have been, because of 1A pupils in over-size classes. Hence, it appears that over-size classes are a slight factor in causing the low rate of promotion in the 1A grade.

Part Time as a Factor

According to the reports made to us, the per cent. of promotion in the 1A grade, when all 1A pupils in part-time

[1] See Table XXXI, page 129.

classes are excluded, was 76.96 per cent.,[1] which is but .94 of 1 per cent. higher than the per cent. of promotion (76.02 per cent.) for the grade as a whole.

Consequently, had there been 1A whole-time classes only, the per cent. of promotion in the 1A grade as a whole would have been 76.96 per cent. Assuming that all other conditions affecting promotion and non-promotion were the same in the two kinds of classes, the per cent. of promotion in the 1A grade was, therefore, lower by but .94 of 1 per cent. because of 1A pupils in part-time classes.[2]

Absence as a Factor

In the reports made to us it is impossible to distinguish between absence due to irregular attendance and absence due to late entrance during the course of the term, the reports giving merely the days absent.

Table XVIII gives the number of 1A pupils on register at the end of the February-June term, 1911, absent ten days and less, absent eleven to twenty, etc.; it gives the per cent. of the total register of 1A pupils absent ten days and less, absent eleven to twenty days, etc., and the per cent. of the pupils absent ten days and less, absent eleven to twenty days, etc., promoted and the per cent. not promoted:

TABLE XVIII [3]

	Absent 10 Days and Less	Absent 11 to 20 Days	Absent 21 to 30 Days	Absent 31 to 40 Days	Absent 41 Days and Above
Number	17,215	8,708	5,010	3,188	8,891
Per Cent. of Total Register of 1A Pupils	40.02	20.25	11.65	7.41	20.67
Per Cent. Promoted	89.47	85.75	79.02	71.01	40.56
Per Cent. Not Promoted	10.53	14.25	20.98	28.99	59.44

[1] See Table XLVII, page 169. [2] See note 2, page 73.

[3] These data were compiled from Table XXXII, page 133, and from Table XXXIV, page 137.

11.65 per cent. of 1A pupils were absent, it will be observed, more than a month—that is, more than a fifth of the term; 7.41 per cent. were out of school a month and a half; and 20.67 per cent. were out more than forty-one days, or one 1A pupil out of each five was absent more than two-fifths of the entire time.

The rate of promotion, it will be noted, varies inversely with the increase in the days absent. For pupils absent ten days and less the rate of promotion was 89.47 per cent.; for those absent forty-one days and more, 40.56 per cent. Further, the rate of promotion for pupils absent ten days and less (89.47 per cent.) is higher than the rate for the grade as a whole (76.02 per cent.) by 13.45 per cent. Consequently, had all other conditions been the same as among pupils absent ten days and less, and had there been in the 1A grade pupils absent ten days and less only, the per cent. of promotion for the grade, as a whole, would have been 89.47 per cent. The rate of promotion in the 1A grade was, therefore, lower by 13.45 per cent. than it otherwise would have been, because of pupils who were absent more than ten days.[1]

Summary

The foregoing discussion of the assigned causes of the low rate of promotion in the 1A grade may be thus summarized: The per cent. of promotion in the 1A grade, at the end of the February-June term, 1911, was lower than it otherwise would have been by 1.54 per cent., because of the pupils who were unable to use the English language; by 1.38 per cent., because of pupils being in over-size classes, and by .94 of 1 per cent., because of pupils being in part-time classes, and by 13.45 per cent., because of absence. Immaturity was a negligible factor. It is, therefore, clear that absence (including late entrance) was the preponderating cause of the low rate of promotion in the 1A grade at the end of the February-June term, 1911.

[1] See note, page 132.

INCREASING THE RATE OF PROMOTION IN THE 1A GRADE

The problem of increasing the per cent. of promotion in the 1A grade is, therefore, not so much a question of increasing the number of special classes for pupils unable to use the English language, of reducing the number of oversize classes, and of part-time classes—all of which should be done—as it is a question of getting 1A pupils in school at the beginning of the term and of keeping them there during the term. Hence, the problem of increasing the per cent. of promotion in the 1A grade is chiefly one of how to improve attendance among 1A pupils.

It is to be expected that 1A pupils will attend school somewhat less regularly than pupils in other grades. Many parents do not feel the need of keeping such young children in school regularly; the children themselves, not having as yet formed the school-going habit, are, at times, inclined to remain at home when there is no good reason why they should. Infectious and contagious diseases are also more prevalent among 1A pupils than among pupils of the other grades. Granting all this, there is little doubt but that the amount of absence in the 1A grade can be materially reduced.

To be sure, large numbers of 1A pupils are under seven years of age, and are, therefore, not amenable to the Compulsory Education Law. Indeed, of the 83,766 pupils admitted to the 1A grade during the school year 1910-11, 65,682,[1] or 78 per cent., were under seven years of age. With these all that can be done is for the Board of Education to pass rules and regulations controlling their entrance and attendance, and for principals and teachers to use, to the utmost, their influence with parents and pupils. (See recommendations, page 79.)

There were, however, among the 1A entries during the school year 1910-11, 18,084[1] pupils, or 22 per cent. of the

[1] Annual Report of City Superintendent of Schools for 1910-11, Table XXXIII, page 61.

total 1A entries, who were seven years of age and older. Teachers and principals should not only use their influence with the parents to send these pupils to school at the beginning of the term, but every effort should be put forth to keep them regular in attendance. Further, parents having children seven years of age and older, who do not send them to school at the beginning of the term and keep them regularly in school, should be made to feel the full force of the Compulsory Education Law. It is safe to say that to enforce rigorously the Compulsory Education Law in the 1A grade would not only avoid much future trouble with parents, but cure many an incipient case of truancy.

RECOMMENDATIONS

To the end that attendance in the 1A grade may be improved, and that congestion in this grade may be relieved, we recommend:

(1) That a by-law be passed by the Board of Education which prohibits entrance to the 1A grade, after the last day of the fourth week of a school term, to children who will not be seven years old until after the end of the term; and which provides for the exclusion from the school, at the discretion of the principal, of such children when they have been absent forty days, including days lost by late entrance and irregular attendance, during the first half of the term.

(2) That effort be made by the Board of Education to have the Compulsory Education Law so amended that it will apply to children who will be seven years old before the end of a given school term.

(3) That the Permanent Census Board, prior to the beginning of each school term, send to the principal of each school, along with the name and home address of the parent, the names, for the given school district, (a) of all children six years of age who

will not be seven until after the close of the given term; (b) of all children who are six and who will be seven before the end of the given term; and (c) of all children seven years of age, who should enter school at the opening of the given term. In this way each principal will know the number of children that should enter his or her school, and will be able to report at an early date to the attendance officers all children who have not entered and who are subject to the Compulsory Education Law.

(4) That a poster in the several languages of the city be prepared and placed in the several school districts prior to the beginning of each term, which will emphasize the importance of sending children to school at the beginning of the term, and of keeping them regular in attendance, which will state the rules regarding the entrance and attendance of children who will not be seven until after the end of the term, and which will point out the provisions of the Compulsory Education Law.

(5) That a new attendance report be prepared for the 1A grade, which will show for each child the date of entrance, the number of days in attendance during the month, and the cause of each absence, and that a separate report be made for children not amenable to the Compulsory Education Law and for children amenable to it, to the end that definite information may be had on absence in the 1A grade, and on the extent to which the Compulsory Education Law is enforced.

CHAPTER V

THE RATE OF PROMOTION

WITH the exception of the 1A and 8B grades, the rate of promotion, both in the several boroughs and in the Greater City, was, at the end of the February-June term, 1911, as we have seen, uniformly about 90 per cent. The fact that the rate of promotion was uniformly about 90 per cent. gives weight to the statement made to us repeatedly, both by teachers and principals, that they were "unofficially expected" to promote at the end of the February-June term, 1911, approximately 90 per cent. of their pupils, and, hence, that promotions were forced and were made mechanically and without due regard to fitness.

INCREASING THE RATE OF PROMOTION

The City Superintendent of Schools did urge upon principals, during the school year 1910-11, the importance of advancing a large per cent. of pupils. To quote his words: "I have been careful to advise the principals that the *pressure to secure more generous promotions* must not be construed to mean that pupils who are unfitted to do the work of the next higher grade are to be promoted. It means only that every effort is to be made to render every pupil fit for promotion." [1]

Despite the foregoing uniformity in the per cent. of promotion, and the assertion of teachers and principals, referred to above, there is evidence that, on the whole, principals and teachers used discretion in making promotions at

[1] Annual Report of the City Superintendent of Schools for 1910-11, page 83.

the end of the February-June term, 1911, and that promotions were not made on a mere numerical and mechanical basis. To affirm that promotions at the end of the February-June term, 1911, were not made mechanically is not to deny that there was a decided increase in the rate of promotion over corresponding terms of previous years.

Increase in Rate of Promotion

Table XIX gives, by grades, the rate of promotion for the entire February-June term, 1910 (including promotions made during the term and at the end of the term), the rate of promotion for the entire February-June term, 1911, and the increase in the rate of promotion for the entire February-June term, 1911, over the rate for the same term, 1910:

TABLE XIX[1]

Grades	Rate of Promotion for Entire Feb.-June Term		Increase in the Rate of Promotion for the Entire Feb.-June Term, 1911, over the Rate for the Same Term of 1910
	1910	1911	
1A	73.61	78.80	5.19
1B	86.77	90.77	4.00
2A	87.82	91.38	3.56
2B	88.18	92.79	4.61
3A	87.97	92.23	4.26
3B	88.42	92.89	4.47
4A	87.62	91.99	4.37
4B	87.72	92.07	4.35
5A	85.84	91.55	5.71
5B	86.12	92.37	6.25
6A	85.65	91.32	5.67
6B	89.78	91.22	1.44
7A	85.77	89.62	3.85
7B	85.99	91.35	5.36
8A	86.89	91.79	4.90
8B	91.05	94.98	3.93
Total	86.30	90.86	4.56

[1] The figures for this table are exclusive of special classes.

The rate of promotion for the entire February-June term of 1911 was higher in every grade than for the corresponding term of 1910. It was higher by 1.44 per cent. in one grade, by from 3.56 per cent. to 3.93 per cent. in three grades, by 4 per cent. to 4.90 per cent. in seven grades, by from 5.19 per cent. to 5.71 per cent. in four grades, and by 6.25 per cent. in one grade. It will also be observed that the rate of total promotion was higher for the entire February-June term, 1911, by 4.56 per cent., than for the same term of 1910.

An increase of 4.56 per cent. in the rate of promotion, in a single year, is an unusually large increase for the City of New York. Table XX gives by grades the rate of promotion for the entire February-June term of 1906, 1907, 1908, 1909, 1910, and 1911; the increase in the rate of promotion for the entire February-June term, 1910, over the rate for the entire February-June term, 1906; also the increase in the rate of promotion for the entire February-June term, 1911, over the same term, 1910; and, finally, it gives the difference between the increase in the rate of promotion for the entire February-June term of 1911 over the same term of 1910, and the increase for the entire February-June term of 1910 over the same term of 1906. (See page 84.)

There has been, it will be observed, an increase in the rate of promotion in the February-June term, in each of the grades, from 1906 to 1911. The most decided increase was, however, in 1911. So decided was this that the increase in 1911 over 1910 was greater, in eleven of the sixteen grades, than the increase in these grades for the five years prior to 1911. While the increase for 1910, in the rate of promotion, in all grades taken together, over 1906 was, it will be noted, 3.75 per cent., the increase in the rate of total promotion in 1911 over 1910 was 4.56 per cent. Hence, the increase in total promotion for the entire February-June term was .81 of 1 per cent. greater for the single February-June term, 1911, than for the five terms prior to 1911.

This extraordinary increase in the rate of promotion for

TABLE XX [1]

Grades	Rate of Promotion for Entire Feb.-June Term						Increase in Rate of Promotion for		Difference in Increase in Rate of Promotion between the Entire Feb.-June Term, 1911, over 1910 and the Entire Feb.-June Term, 1910, over 1906
	1906	1907	1908	1909	1910	1911	Entire Feb.-June Term, 1910, over Same Term, 1906	Entire Feb.-June Term, 1911, over Same Term, 1910	
1A	68.51	65.49	69.60	71.74	73.61	78.80	5.10	5.19	.09
1B	85.19	82.28	85.26	86.24	86.77	90.77	1.58	4.00	2.42
2A	83.56	82.00	85.98	86.76	87.82	91.38	4.26	3.56	—.70
2B	85.04	83.65	86.50	87.42	88.18	92.79	3.14	4.61	1.47
3A	84.12	81.94	85.73	86.50	87.97	92.23	3.85	4.26	.41
3B	85.85	83.81	86.75	88.07	88.42	92.89	2.57	4.47	1.90
4A	84.38	82.91	85.78	85.94	87.62	91.99	3.24	4.37	1.13
4B	84.62	81.88	85.50	86.58	87.72	92.07	3.10	4.35	1.25
5A	82.93	80.43	83.15	84.62	85.84	91.55	2.91	5.71	2.80
5B	82.75	80.91	83.59	85.01	86.12	92.37	3.37	6.25	2.88
6A	82.85	81.46	83.33	84.12	85.65	91.32	2.80	5.67	2.87
6B	83.11	81.52	85.06	84.69	89.78	91.22	6.67	1.44	—5.23
7A	80.37	79.93	81.01	82.75	85.77	89.62	5.40	3.85	—1.55
7B	82.25	80.79	83.60	84.87	85.99	91.35	3.74	5.36	1.62
8A	81.39	81.93	84.37	85.08	86.89	91.79	5.50	4.90	—.60
8B	82.92	86.81	88.12	88.23	91.05	94.98	8.13	3.93	—4.20
Total	82.56	80.72	83.78	84.98	86.30	90.86	3.75	4.56	.81

[1] These figures are exclusive of special classes.

the entire February-June term, 1911, may have been due either to an increase in promotions during the term, or to an increase at the end of the term, or it may have been due to both an increase during the term and at the end of the term. Table XXI gives, by grades, for the February-June term, 1910, the rate of promotion during the term, and the rate at the end of the term; also the same facts for the February-June term, 1911. It shows, besides, the increase in the rate of promotion during the February-June term, 1911, over the rate during the same term, 1910; also the increase in the rate of promotion at the end of the February-June term, 1911, over the rate at the end of the same term, 1910:

TABLE XXI[1]

Grades	Feb.-June Term, 1910		Feb.-June Term, 1911		Increase in Rate of Promotion Feb.-June Term, 1911, over Feb.-June Term, 1910	
	Rate of Promotion during Term	Rate of Promotion at End of Term	Rate of Promotion during Term	Rate of Promotion at End of Term	Increase during Term	Increase at End of Term
1A..........	2.42	71.19	3.04	75.76	.62	4.57
1B..........	1.64	85.13	2.60	88.16	.96	3.03
2A..........	2.21	85.60	2.66	88.73	.45	3.13
2B..........	1.93	86.26	2.60	90.19	.67	3.93
3A..........	2.28	85.69	2.78	89.45	.50	3.76
3B..........	1.56	86.87	2.45	90.44	.89	3.57
4A..........	1.86	85.76	2.41	89.58	.55	3.82
4B..........	1.52	86.20	2.23	89.83	.71	3.63
5A..........	1.99	83.85	2.75	88.80	.76	4.95
5B..........	1.75	84.37	2.63	89.74	.88	5.37
6A..........	1.98	83.67	2.44	88.88	.46	5.21
6B..........	1.71	88.07	1.77	89.45	.06	1.38
7A..........	3.55	82.22	2.03	87.59	—1.52	5.37
7B..........	2.03	83.96	2.31	89.05	.28	5.09
8A..........	2.00	84.88	2.30	89.49	.30	4.61
8B..........	0.005	91.04	.71	94.28	.705	3.24
Total.......	1.93	84.37	2.44	88.42	.51	4.05

[1] These figures are exclusive of special classes.

There was an increase in the rate of promotion during the February-June term, 1911, over the rate during the same term, 1910, in all grades, except the 7A, where there was a decrease of 1.52 per cent. The rate during the term was higher by from .06 of 1 per cent. to .28 of 1 per cent. in two grades, by from .30 of 1 per cent. to .50 of 1 per cent. in four grades, by from .55 of 1 per cent. to .75 of 1 per cent. in six grades, and by from .88 of 1 per cent. to .96 of 1 per cent. in three grades—while the increase in all grades, taken together, was .51 of 1 per cent.

It will also be observed that there was an increase, in all grades, in the rate of promotion at the end of the February-June term, 1911, over the rate at the end of the same term, 1910. The rate was higher by 1.38 per cent. in one grade, by from 3.03 per cent. to 3.93 per cent. in eight grades, by from 4.57 per cent. to 4.95 per cent. in three grades, and by from 5.09 per cent. to 5.37 per cent. in four grades, while the increase in all grades, taken together, was 4.05 per cent.

Of the 4.56 per cent. increase in the rate of promotion for the entire February-June term, 1911, over the rate for the entire February-June term, 1910, .51 of 1 per cent., or 11.18 per cent., of this increase was, therefore, due to the larger number of promotions during the term, and 4.05 per cent. or 88.82 per cent. of the increase was due to the larger number of promotions at the end of the term.

The fact that the increase in the rate of total promotion for the entire February-June term, 1911, over 1910, was greater than the total increase for the same term from 1906 to 1910 inclusive, and the fact that 88.82 per cent. of the extraordinary increase in the rate of total promotion for the entire February-June term, 1911, was due to the increased number of promotions at the end of the term, raises the question: How was this extraordinary increase in the rate of promotion effected? A part of it was, doubtless, brought about through an increase in the efficiency of the school. The importance of making more liberal promotions having been emphasized, teachers and principals put forth unusual effort to fit pupils for advancement. Yet, when due allowance is made for whatever increase in efficiency there may have been, it must be admitted, by all who are acquainted with school conditions and school work, that the extraordinary increase in the rate of promotion in the February-June term, 1911, was due, in most part, to the "pressure" exercised by the City Superintendent of Schools "to secure more generous promotions."

Increase Justified

The important question, therefore, is: Was the City Superintendent of Schools justified in using "pressure to secure more generous promotions"? In view of the number of over-age pupils, and of the amount of elimination in the elementary schools of the City of New York, we believe the City Superintendent was justified in his endeavor to increase the rate of promotion.

Number of Over-Age Pupils

The course of study in the elementary schools of the City of New York comprises sixteen units, each in theory one-half school year in length. Accordingly, a child, entering school at six or seven, should complete the elementary school by his fourteenth or fifteenth year. If, for any reason, a pupil enters school late or remains a whole year or more in a single grade, such a child becomes over age for his grade.

Table XXII gives the register in regular classes, after promotion June 30, 1911, in the grades of each year, the number of pupils in the grades of each year and among the elementary school graduates of 1910-11, under normal age, normal age, under one year over normal, etc.; it shows, besides, the total number of over-age pupils in the grades of each year and among the elementary school graduates; also the per cent. of the register of each grade and the per cent. of the graduates over age:

TABLE XXII [1]

	First Year Grades	Second Year Grades	Third Year Grades	Fourth Year Grades	Fifth Year Grades	Sixth Year Grades	Seventh Year Grades	Eighth Year Grades	Total All Grades	Elementary School Graduates
Register in Regular Classes after Promotion, June 30, 1911	64,057	87,048	84,650	81,121	75,819	69,236	59,363	44,504	565,798	35,329
Under Normal Age	6,276	12,385	10,050	9,010	6,862	6,365	6,302	5,668	62,918	7,646
Normal Age	52,679	63,294	57,366	49,958	44,980	39,029	35,137	28,579	371,022	13,206
Less Than One Year Over Age	3,639	7,213	10,141	12,260	12,639	14,168	12,291	7,670	80,021	9,708
Between One and Two Years Over Age	947	2,580	4,365	5,706	7,096	6,927	4,620	2,147	34,388	3,862
Between Two and Three Years Over Age	292	991	1,635	2,745	3,004	2,365	878	389	12,299	802
Three and More Years Over Age	224	585	1,093	1,442	1,238	382	135	51	5,150	105
Total Number of Over-Age Pupils	5,102	11,369	17,234	22,153	23,977	23,842	17,924	10,257	131,858	14,477
Per Cent. of Register Over Age	7.96	13.06	20.36	27.31	31.62	34.44	30.19	23.05	23.30	40.98

[1] The data for this table were computed from Tables XXVIII and XXXV, pages 54 and 63 of the Annual Report of the City Superintendent of Schools for 1910–11. The table merely puts in different form the report on the ages of pupils in regular classes of the City Superintendent of Schools for 1911, hence gives the number of over-age pupils when determined by the age-grade standards as fixed by the City Superintendent.

Of the 35,329 graduates in 1910-11, it will be observed that 14,477, or 40.98 per cent., were over age, hence were fifteen years of age and older on completing the elementary school. Despite the fact that the foregoing table has to do only with pupils in regular classes, and despite the fact that age is judged from the point of view of the age limits fixed for being in the grade in which pupils are registered after promotion, there were in the regular classes of all grades,

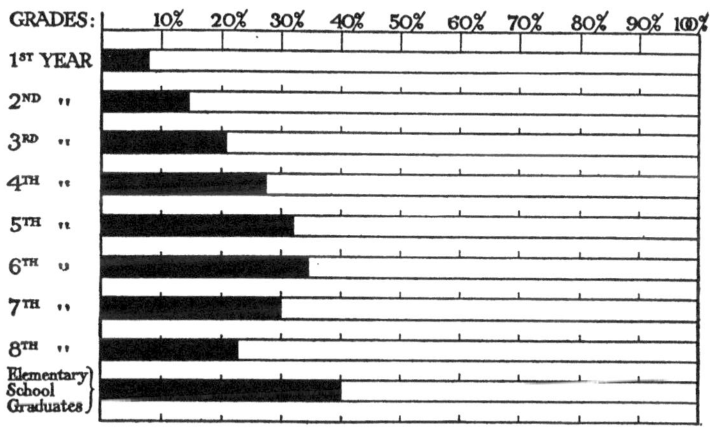

Fig. 1. Black indicates per cent. of over-age pupils in the grades of each year and the per cent. of over-age pupils among the graduates of 1910-11, as reported by the City Superintendent of Schools.

June 30, 1911, according to the City Superintendent of Schools, 131,858 over-age pupils, or 23.30 per cent. of the pupils on register after promotion were behind their grade for their age. The grades of the sixth year show the highest per cent. of over age, 34.44 per cent., and the grades of the first year, the lowest, 7.96 per cent.

Were the foregoing over-age pupils registered in the grade where they should be by reason of their age, these pupils would have been distributed, when distributed according to the age-grade standards as fixed by the City Superintendent of Schools, among the several grades as follows:

TABLE XXIII

Total Number Over-Age Pupils	Present Grade	Grades in Which These Over-Age Pupils in Each Grade Should be Registered by Reason of Their Age; Also the Number That Would be in Each Grade											
		Second	Third	Fourth	Fifth	Sixth	Seventh	Eighth	H. S. First Year	H. S. Second Year	H. S. Third Year	H. S. Fourth Year	College First Year
5,102	First Year......	3,639	947	292	120	59	45	....	....	....	....	....	....
11,369	Second Year....	....	7,213	2,580	991	351	141	93	....	....	....	....	....
17,234	Third Year.....	....	....	10,141	4,365	1,635	705	286	102	....	....	....	....
22,153	Fourth Year....	....	....	....	12,260	5,706	2,745	1,041	350	51	....	....	....
23,977	Fifth Year......	....	....	....	....	12,639	7,096	3,004	1,088	150	....	....	....
23,842	Sixth Year......	....	....	....	....	....	14,168	6,927	2,365	342	40	....	....
17,924	Seventh Year...	....	....	....	....	....	....	12,291	4,620	878	122	13	....
10,257	Eighth Year....	....	....	....	....	....	....	....	7,670	2,147	389	44	7
14,477	Element'y School Graduates....	....	....	....	....	....	....	....	9,708	3,862	802	86	19

There are thousands of pupils in each grade, it will be noted, who are below the grade in which their age entitles them to be. There are pupils in the second grade who, by reason of their age, should be in the eighth grade; pupils in the third, who should be in the high school; and pupils graduating from the elementary school, who should be in college. In the sixth and lower grades alone there are 15,839 pupils who are already fourteen years of age; in the seventh grade, 17,924; and in the eighth grade, 24,597, or a total of 58,360 pupils who, instead of dragging along between the first and eighth grades, should have their elementary education behind them and be either at work or in high school.

The educational significance of over age lies in the fact that just to the degree that pupils in the elementary school are over age, just to that degree do they—particularly those over age because they have failed to receive promotion regularly—tend to fail to complete the elementary school course of study.[1] Hence, of the pupils on register in regular classes June 30, 1911, 34,388, by reason of being over age between one and two years, will probably fail to complete the work of the eighth year; 12,299, by reason of being behind between two and three years, will probably fail to complete the work of the seventh year; and 5,151, by reason of being behind three and more years, will probably fail to complete the grades of the sixth year.

A certain amount of over age in the elementary schools of the city is due to the late entrance of children to the grades of the first year; the major portion of it is, however, due to pupils failing to receive regular promotion after they have once entered school.[2] This fact in itself supplies ample ground for the insistence of the City Superintendent on "more generous promotions."

[1] See page 145.

[2] See Table XXXIII, page 61, Annual Report of the City Superintendent of Schools, 1910-11, and Table XVI, page 69 of this volume.

Amount of Elimination

The dropping out of pupils from the elementary schools before completing the course of study is termed "elimination." It is doubtful whether any large city of this country has, at present, the data at hand to determine with exactness the grades of work completed by the children leaving the elementary school. At all events, such data are not to be had at present in the City of New York.[1]

Following the method pursued by writers on elimination, the per cent. of pupils entering school who continue to the end of each year is estimated by finding what per cent. the pupils in a given grade at the end of a given school year before promotion are of the number of pupils that should be in the grade in view of the first-year beginners for the given school year.

Proceeding in this way,[2] we estimate that, of the pupils entering the elementary schools of the City of New York, the per cent. remaining to the end of each year and the per cent. completing the final grade are as follows:

	Per Cent. Remaining to End of Year	Per Cent. Dropping Out before End of Year
First Year	108.66	......
Second Year	100.73	......
Third Year	99.47	......
Fourth Year	98.57	......
Fifth Year	96.69	3.31
Sixth Year	88.71	11.29
Seventh Year	61.45	38.55
Eighth Year	47.57	52.43
Completing Eighth Grade	41.33	58.67

1 The pupils' record cards, adopted in 1909, will in the near future supply these data.

2 In making this estimate the average of the first-year beginners for 1908-9, 1909-10, and 1910-11 was used as the base. See Annual Report of City Superintendent of Schools, 1909, page 72; 1910, Table XLVII, page 78, and 1911, Table XXXIII, page 61. For the number of pupils remaining to the end of the grades of each year see Annual Report of the City Superintendent of Schools, 1911, Table XXXVII, page 66. The pupils on register June 30, 1911, in special classes were arbitrarily distributed as follows: One-sixteenth to the grades of the second year; one-sixteenth to the grades of the third year; three-sixteenths to the grades of the fourth year; five-sixteenths to the grades of the fifth year, and six-sixteenths to the grades of the sixth year.

It would appear from the foregoing estimates that, of the children entering the elementary schools of the City of New York, practically all remain to the end of the grades of the fifth year, that one pupil out of each eight leaves before the end of the sixth year, four out of each ten fail to remain to the end of the seventh year, less than one in two continues to the end of the eighth year, and but four out of each ten graduate.

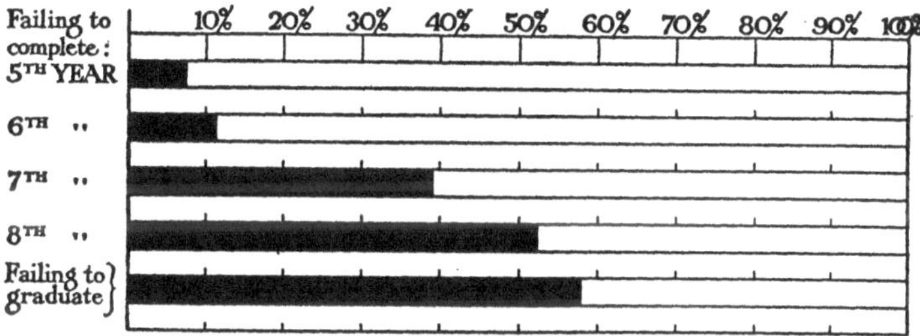

Fig. 2. Black indicates the per cent. of pupils failing to complete the grades of the fifth, sixth, seventh, and eighth years, and the per cent. failing to graduate.

All other conditions remaining the same, the number of grades a pupil is able to complete during the course of his school life is conditioned by standards of promotion. The practical problem confronting the City Superintendent of Schools was, therefore: Is it better for the children of the city to spend their entire time in school in the sixth and lower grades, or would it be better to make the standards of promotion such that pupils in larger numbers may have opportunity to profit by the work of the seventh and eighth grades? The work in the sixth and lower grades is confined primarily to the school arts—reading, spelling, writing, and the fundamentals of arithmetic—and the work of the two higher grades primarily to the giving of information about our industrial, political, and social life which makes for economic insight and personal ideals; hence there can be but one answer to the foregoing question, viz., that it is preferable to make the standards of promotion such that pupils in larger numbers may enjoy the advantages of the work of the seventh and eighth grades.

FORCED PROMOTIONS

While the City Superintendent of Schools was, therefore, justified in his endeavor to increase the rate of promotion, and while principals and teachers used discretion in making promotions, the fact remains that principals and teachers feel that promotions at the end of the February-June term, 1911, were "forced."[1]

No changes were made during this term in the requirements of the elementary school course of study either in the quality of instruction or in the quantity of the subject-matter to be taught. Yet teachers and principals felt constrained to promote more than the usual number of pupils. Teachers and principals were thus placed in a false position —that is, they felt under the necessity of promoting pupils who, when judged by official standards, were not fit for promotion. It is safe to say that many such pupils were promoted, and this accounts not only for the feeling that promotions were "forced," but also for a large part of the extraordinary increase in promotions in the February-June term, 1911, over the corresponding term of 1910.

Teachers and principals should not be put in the position of having to promote pupils who, when judged by official standards, are not prepared for promotion. If the City Superintendent of Schools was convinced that it was desirable to increase the rate of promotion, it was incumbent upon him so to lessen the requirements of the elementary school course of study as to quantity that more pupils could meet its requirements and hence be legitimately promoted in greater numbers.

[1] As already affirmed, this statement is based on the voluntary testimony of many teachers and principals who express themselves freely on the subject.

CHAPTER VI

THE MAXIMUM RATE OF PROMOTION

THE extraordinary increase in the rate of promotion in the elementary schools for the February-June term, 1911, and the fact that this increase was brought about not so much through an increase in the efficiency of the school as through the promotion of pupils who in former terms would not have been advanced, raises the question: What should be the maximum rate of promotion?

THE MAXIMUM RATE ACCORDING TO THE CITY SUPERINTENDENT OF SCHOOLS

The City Superintendent of Schools is inclined to believe that 90 per cent. of promotion on register at the end of the term is the maximum rate for the city as a whole. "It seems probable," to quote from his report, "that little further increase in the general rate of promotion can be expected. A remarkable uniformity is shown in all grades, the rate for the year ranging from 90.4 per cent. to 92 per cent., with the exception of the 8B grade, which should be excluded, because here the unusual incentive of graduation and the more selected group from which the graduates are drawn tend to raise the 8B rate of promotion above what may be normally expected in the grades below. A difference of only 1.6 per cent. in the rate of promotion in the remaining grades shows so little variability as to indicate a close approach to the probable maximum rate." [1]

[1] Annual Report of the City Superintendent of Schools for 1910-11, page 81.

That the rate of promotion in the several grades, exclusive of the 8B, was, for the year 1910-11, uniformly about 90 per cent. does not indicate that 90 per cent. should be regarded as the maximum rate of promotion. The same argument would have placed the maximum rate at approximately 81 per cent. in 1907; at 84 per cent. in 1908; at 85 per cent. in 1909; and at 86 per cent. in 1910.[1] Moreover, while the rate of promotion for the year 1910-11 in the several grades is uniform for both the Greater City and the different boroughs, there were variations in the several districts, ranging from 93 per cent. in District 2 to 98 per cent. in District 24;[2] also in the several schools, ranging from 35 per cent. in Public School Number 25, Richmond, to 110 per cent. in Public School Number 22, Richmond.[3] Further, the rate of promotion at the end of the term in the regular classes of given grades ranged, for the February-June term, 1911, in different schools, from 60 per cent. to 100 per cent. in the 8A grade, from 75 per cent. to 100 per cent. in the 5A grade, and from 57 per cent. to 99 per cent. in the 1A grade. Such variations in the rate of promotion in different grades, in different schools, and in different districts give little support to the thought that the maximum rate has been attained. Indeed, these variations suggest that, even with prevailing standards, there might be a considerable increase in the rate of promotion.

CONDITIONS DETERMINING MAXIMUM RATE OF PROMOTION

However this may be, the present rate of promotion in no wise indicates what the rate of promotion should be. The rate of promotion in the elementary schools of the city

[1] See Table XX, page 84.
[2] Annual Report of the City Superintendent of Schools for 1910-11, Table XL, pages 75-77.
[3] Annual Report of the City Superintendent of Schools for 1910-11, Appendix "C," page 471.

is at present in large part determined by the requirements of its one course of study.

Conditions are favorable to the completion of an elementary school course of study by practically all pupils, hence favorable to a maximum rate of promotion—

(1) When the requirements of the elementary school are adapted to the varying abilities and educational needs of different groups of pupils, and are such that all normal children in regular attendance are able to complete the course of study; hence, when there are as many elementary school courses of study of varying requirements as there are groups of normal children of different abilities and educational needs.

(2) When the total length of each of the different elementary school courses of study is determined (a) by the length of the period pupils may with profit be kept under the régime of the elementary school, and (b) by the length of time pupils may reasonably be expected to be in attendance during this period.

DISREGARD OF CONDITIONS FAVORABLE TO A MAXIMUM RATE OF PROMOTION

These conditions favorable to a maximum rate of promotion have, to a considerable extent, been disregarded in the development and administration of the present elementary school course of study.

Disregard of the Proper Length of the Elementary School Period

The length of the period children can with profit be kept under the régime of the elementary school is determined, on the one hand, by the age at which children may well enter the elementary school, and, on the other, by pubescence. While custom sanctions children entering the elementary school at six, and while children entering at this age probably make on the whole better progress than those entering at any other age,[1] no one actually knows whether the best age of entrance is five, six, seven, or older.[2] In the present state of our knowledge, the best, therefore, that can be done is to follow the custom of admitting children to the elementary school at six, and make six the lower age limit of the elementary school period. This can at least be done until the question of the best age at which to admit children to the elementary schools is determined by experimental investigation.

Pubescence [3] is, as a rule, accompanied by certain physical vigor and mental and emotional development which make pubescent children susceptible to different materials of instruction, different methods of teaching, a different kind of discipline, school organization, and life, than are prepubescent children. Hence, there is general agreement that children cannot be kept with profit under the régime of the elementary school much beyond the beginning of pubescence.[4]

The age at which pubescence begins varies among normal children and the length of the period ranges from one to three years. In consequence, in an age group above twelve years of age, there will be prepubescent (immature) children; pubescent (maturing) children; and postpubescent (mature) children. The per cent. of immature, maturing, and mature boys in different age groups are shown in Table XXIV.

It appears from Table XXIV that no one age can be designated as *the age of the beginning of pubescence.* Dr. Crampton found, however, from a study of 3,835 cases

[1] Ayres: *The Relation between Entering Age and Subsequent Progress among School Children.*

[2] See Table XXXIX, page 149.

[3] Pubescence denotes a process covering a period of time. Puberty or physiological maturity is the point of time when the ability to procreate is established. A pubescent is an individual who is maturing, and hence in the period of pubescence.

[4] Hall: *Adolescence,* Vol. II, Ch. VII.

(high school boys), that "for the ending of prepubescence and the beginning of pubescence, the middle of the mean years is 14.00 years, the average date is 13.44 years, with a variability of, more or less, 1.51 years." [1] No similar data for girls, so far as we know, are available. The average age of puberty (maturity) is, however, well established by

TABLE XXIV [2]

Age in Years	Physiological Age Groups		
	Immature, Per Cent.	Maturing, Per Cent.	Mature, Per Cent.
12.50 to 13.00	69	25	6
13.00 to 13.50	55	26	18
13.50 to 14.00	41	28	31
14.00 to 14.50	26	28	46
14.50 to 15.00	16	24	60
15.00 to 15.50	9	20	70
15.50 to 16.00	5	10	85
16.00 to 16.50	2	4	93
16.50 to 17.00	1	4	95
17.00 to 17.50	0	2	98
17.50 to 18.00	0	0	100

Foster, who found the average age to be fourteen for 4,000 American girls.

While there is need of further data pertaining to both boys and girls with respect to the number of prepubescent, pubescent, and postpubescent children in different age groups, there is still greater need for data concerning what time during pubescence there appear the physical vigor and the mental and emotional development which make neces-

[1] *American Physical Education Review,* 1908, page 146.

[2] This table was taken from "Anatomical or Physiological Age," *Pedagogical Seminary,* June, 1908, an article by C. Ward Crampton, M.D., Supervisor of Physical Training, New York City, and is based on the records of 4,800 boys in a New York high school.

sary a change of school methods and régime. Are these concomitant, as a rule, with the beginning, the middle, or the end of the period? The general impression is that they more often appear at the beginning of the period; yet it must be confessed that but little data have been collected on this point.

Making the data at hand the basis of judgment, it appears that children, as a class, cannot, with profit, be kept under the régime of the elementary school much, if any, beyond fourteen. In fixing on fourteen as the upper age limit for the work of the elementary school we do no violence to educational practice, except in a few large cities,[1] and are in accord with the Compulsory Education Laws of New York and of other states; also in accord with a recent declaration of the National Education Association.[2] *Even if fourteen is accepted as the upper age limit for attendance on the elementary school, this age limit should be subjected to an experimental test and raised or lowered according as experience dictates.* Further, the organization and the administration of the school should be made so flexible that children maturing before fourteen may continue their elementary education under conditions other than those ordinarily found in the elementary school,[3] and that children maturing after fourteen may, on completing their elementary education, continue their schooling under conditions other than those generally found in the high school. For neither should the child be kept under the régime of the elementary school after maturity,[4] nor be placed in the high school before maturity;[5] the one is as detrimental as the other. In a word, fourteen may be taken as the upper age limit for

[1] See Strayer: *Age-Grade Census of Schools and Colleges,* United States Bureau of Education, 1911.

[2] Proceedings of the National Education Association, 1911, page 32.

[3] See pages 55-59.

[4] See results of an experiment in a public school of New York City; Crampton, *Journal of Education,* Boston, April 25 and May 2, 1912.

[5] See results of an experiment in a high school of New York City; Crampton, "The Influence of Physiological Age upon Scholarship," *Physiological Clinic,* June, 1907.

the period of elementary education, but each child should be made the subject of consideration; and, so far as possible, the organization and régime of the school should be adapted to the physiological age of each child.

Little regard is paid in New York City to the limits (six to fourteen) of the elementary school period, for thousands of children are subjected to the régime of the elementary school long after their fourteenth birthday. Of the children thirteen to fourteen years old on the register each year, June 30, after promotion, from 1905 to 1908 inclusive, 64.81 per cent. continued in school one additional year; 27.41 per cent. continued two additional years; and 7.95 per cent. continued three and more additional years. (See Table XXV.[1]) In consequence, an elementary school in the City of New York, from the point of view of the age of its pupils, is not an elementary school, but an elementary school, a high school, and a college, all within the elementary schools.

The practice of holding pupils in the elementary schools of the City of New York long after they are fourteen years of age[2] should be discontinued and attendance should be limited to the period between six and fourteen. To be sure, the education of children fourteen years of age who are still floundering in the fourth or fifth grade is not to be considered complete; but the further education of such children should not be regarded as the legitimate work of the ordinary elementary school.

Late entrance to school is one reason why children continue in the elementary schools of the city long after they are fourteen years old, but there are other factors, such as

[1] Table XXV, on page 102, shows for each of the years 1905 to 1908, inclusive, the number of children on register June 30, after promotion, thirteen to fourteen; the number one year later, fourteen to fifteen; the number two years later, fifteen to sixteen, and the number three years later, sixteen and over; also the total number for the period in each age group and the per cent. of those thirteen to fourteen continuing one, two, and three or more years.

[2] Annual Report of the City Superintendent of Schools for 1911, Table XXVIII, page 54.

absence, inability to use the English language, retardation, crowded classrooms, and poor teaching,[1] which, together with the requirements of the course of study, make it impossible for the great majority of children to complete the elementary school within the limits of the period (six to fourteen). That children need to remain one, two, three, and even four years after becoming fourteen to complete the course of study—and some of them do not complete it even then—shows to what extent the proper length of the

TABLE XXV[2]

Year 13–14	Age				Year 16 and Over
	13–14	14–15	15–16	16 and Over	
1905	51,511	31,951	12,203	3,752	1908
1906	53,959	34,124	14,465	4,526	1909
1907	58,653	38,444	17,133	4,933	1910
1908	60,235	40,885	17,692	4,624	1911
Total	224,358	145,404	61,493	17,835	....
Per Cent. 13–14 Continuing ...		64.81	27.41	7.95	.....

[1] See McMurry: *Elementary School Standards,* likewise in School Efficiency Series; World Book Company.

[2] The data for this table were computed from the annual reports of the City Superintendent of Schools for the years 1905-11.

Few children enter the elementary school at fourteen to fifteen or older (for those entering the 1A grade, fourteen and above, see Annual Report of the City Superintendent of Schools for 1911, page 61), so the only children fourteen to fifteen there can be on register after promotion, June, 1906, are the children thirteen to fourteen on register after promotion June, 1905, who remain in school; the same is true of each later age group. Hence the children in each later age group are the same children that are in the thirteen-to-fourteen-year-old age group. Also there may be a few pupils leaving school at thirteen to fourteen who return at fifteen to sixteen, but it is unreasonable to suppose that the number of such children is large enough to affect the per cent. of the children thirteen to fourteen remaining in school thereafter one, two, and three years.

period of elementary education has been disregarded, and to what extent, considering the conditions under which children have to work, their progress is retarded by the excessive requirement that all of them shall complete the same course.

Disregard of the Length of Attendance within the Limits of the Elementary School Period

If six is made the age of entrance to the elementary school—the present legal age of entrance—and the fourteenth birthday is made the upper age limit of the elementary school period—practically the present upper age limit of the Compulsory Education Law—children will actually be in school within the limits of this period somewhat less than eight years. In consequence, the actual total length of the elementary school course of study should be somewhat short of eight school years.

There are no data at hand to show how long children are actually in attendance on the elementary schools of the city by their fourteenth birthday. This can, however, be estimated with reasonable accuracy. Children enter the elementary schools of the city at twelve to thirteen years of age and even older; the number of such children is, however, so small that they do not materially add to the number of pupils in the twelve-to-thirteen-year-old age group, or to the number of pupils in any other age group.[1] There are also children entering under six years of age, but the number is relatively small, and, for this reason, these pupils may be included among those entering at six. Hence, in estimating the actual length of attendance by fourteen, children may be regarded as entering the elementary schools of the City of New York at from six up to twelve years of age.

Table XXVI shows for each of the years 1904-1906, inclusive, the number of children on register, June 30, six

[1] Working papers showing this have been filed with the Committee on School Inquiry.

years old and under; the number one year later, seven to eight; two years later, eight to nine; three years later, nine to ten; four years later, ten to eleven; and five years later, eleven to twelve; also the total number for the period in each age group, the total number entering at each age, and the per cent. entering at each age:

TABLE XXVI [1]

Year Entering	Age						Year
	6 and Under	7–8	8–9	9–10	10–11	11–12	
1904	33,310	55,074	62,070	66,500	66,318	68,436	1909
1905	36,686	54,185	62,335	64,354	65,919	66,638	1910
1906	39,364	57,294	64,424	67,119	69,709	70,155	1911
Total of Each Age Group	109,360	166,553	188,829	197,973	201,946	205,229	....
Number Entering at Each Age	109,360	57,193	22,276	9,144	3,973	3,283	....
Per Cent. Entering at Each Age	53.29	27.87	10.85	4.46	1.93	1.60	....

It appears from Table XXVI that 53.29 per cent. of the children in the elementary schools of the city enter at six to seven; 27.87 per cent. at seven to eight; 10.85 per cent. at eight to nine; 4.46 per cent. at nine to ten; and 1.93 per cent. at ten to eleven; and 1.60 at eleven to twelve. Some of the children entering at an advanced age have undoubtedly been in the elementary schools of other places, but it is

[1] The figures for this table were compiled from the annual reports of the City Superintendent of Schools for 1904-11. The only way, of course, for the number of children six years of age to be larger in 1905 than in 1904 is for children seven years of age to enter school during 1905. To find, therefore, the number of children entering at a given age, i. e., at eleven to twelve, subtract from the number of pupils of the given age the number in the next lower age group and the remainder will be the number entering at the given age. The per cent. entering at a given age is determined by finding what per cent. the number entering at a given age is of the eleven-to-twelve-year-old group.

equally true that some of these over-age pupils are entering the elementary school for the first time.[1]

Using these per cents. as the basis of judgment, we estimate that, out of each hundred pupils thirteen to fourteen years old in the elementary schools of the city, fifty-three will have been in attendance eight years by their fourteenth birthday; twenty-eight, seven years; eleven, six years; four, five years; two, four years; and two, three years—the equivalent of an attendance per pupil of 7.2 years.[2]

There are three ways in which the time pupils are in attendance by fourteen on the elementary schools of the city may be lengthened: (1) by decreasing the amount of irregular attendance; (2) by enforcing the Compulsory Education Law with a rigorous hand, thereby compelling pupils living in the city to enter school at seven; and (3) by educating the people of the city to the importance of sending their children to school at six. There are, however, factors that seriously militate against children entering at six, notably, traffic conditions. Yet it ought to be possible to increase materially the number entering at this age; the further development of the kindergarten alone would contribute much to this end. It is apparent, however, that, after all has been done that it is possible to do, the attendance of pupils by fourteen would, on the average, be probably considerably less than eight years.

In view of the age limits for the work of the elementary school, six to fourteen, and in view of the estimated actual average attendance during this period of New York City children, the elementary schools of the city are face to face with the problem of giving children an elementary education in from 7.2 years to something less than eight years. Hence, if children are to be able to complete their elemen-

[1] Annual Report of the City Superintendent of Schools, 1911, Table XXXIII, page 61.

[2] This estimate takes no account of the time that may have been lost by irregular attendance, or of the time pupils entering late may have been in the elementary schools of other places.

tary education by fourteen, the actual total length of the course of study in the elementary schools of the city should be somewhat short of eight school years.

But, in determining the actual total length of the elementary school course of study for the city, little attention has been given to the actual length of time children are in attendance on school by fourteen, or to the number of years it actually takes pupils to complete the present course of study.[1] While pupils are, as we have seen, probably in attendance by fourteen on the average 7.2 years, 64.81 per cent. of all pupils thirteen to fourteen, exclusive of those graduating, continue in school between 7.2 and 8.2 years; 27.41 per cent. between 8.2 and 9.2 years; and 7.95 per cent. between 9.2 and 10.2 years.[2] Yet less than 42 per cent. of the pupils entering the elementary schools of the city ever complete the course of study.[3]

Further, of those graduating during the last six years but 23.36 per cent. were under fourteen; 36.68 per cent. were from fourteen to fifteen; 27 per cent. from fifteen to sixteen; 10.62 per cent. from sixteen to seventeen; and 2.34 per cent. were seventeen and over, or 76.64 per cent. were fourteen years old and over. (See Table XXVII on page 109.) On the assumption that these graduates were in attendance on the average of 7.2 years by fourteen, it therefore took 36.68 per cent. of them from 7.2 to 8.2 years to complete the course; 27 per cent. from 8.2 to 9.2 years; 10.62 per cent. from 9.2 to 10.2 years; and 2.34 per cent. from 10.2 to 11.2 years. Hence, on the foregoing assumption, the actual total length of the elementary school course of study exceeds, by from one to four years, the actual time 76.64 per cent. of pupils are in attendance by their fourteenth birthday.

[1] The only data ever collected in the city on the number of years it takes pupils to complete the present elementary school course of study were those collected by Dr. Leonard P. Ayres of the Russell Sage Foundation. While these data were presented to the educational authorities of the city, they have never been published in detail.

[2] See pages 101 and 102. [3] See table, page 92.

Disregard of Varying Abilities and Educational Needs of Different Groups of Children

The difference between children may be characterized as internal and external. Among the internal differences are those of interest and capacity. Arithmetic is of interest to some children; the heroic and human, in literature and history, to others; whereas music, drawing, and manual training appeal strongly to others. Some children do well in literature; others in mathematics and science; while others are gifted with artistic ability and mechanical skill. The interests and ability of certain children incline them toward the professions; of others toward administrative and managing vocations; and of others toward industrial pursuits and commercial activities. Present methods of determining interest and capacity are, to be sure, crude; yet it is possible to group children with reasonable accuracy on the basis of inclination and ability.

Among the external differences influencing the educational needs of children are the immediate conditions without the home and within the family. It is obvious that the educational needs of a child in a district where the streets are clean, where the homes are spacious, where the language of the child's playfellows is pure, and where life in general is permeated with the spirit and ideals of America —it is obvious that the educational needs of such a child are different from those of a child who lives in a foreign and tenement section. It is equally obvious that the educational needs of a child from a home where a foreign tongue is the prevailing language, where the parents are foreign born, and ignorant of American customs, institutions, and ideals, are different from the educational needs of the child who is born of American parentage and who absorbs from birth the spirit of our institutions and life.

Equally influential, with the cultural conditions without and within the family, in determining the educational needs of children is the financial status of the home, because it is the financial status of the home which determines for a majority of children whether the elementary school will be the only school they will ever attend or whether they will also go to high school, to college, or to the university. So great is the economic pressure on the larger number of homes that the school life of the majority of children must end at the time when they can legally join the ranks of wage-earners. In a word, the majority of children, by reason of the economic status of the home, will attend the elementary school only. This being true, it should be apparent that the educational needs of such children are very different from the needs of children who are so situated that they may continue their education in higher institutions.

New York City not only has the largest elementary school population in the world, but this population is also the most heterogeneous. In the elementary schools of the city there are children of each of at least fifty-four[1] nationalities; these children represent the very widest differences in inclination and in native ability, in cultural influences without and within the family, and in the financial status of the home. Yet these differences have been very largely disregarded in the development of the present elementary school course of study and in the determination of its requirements. There is but one course of study for all children in regular classes, whether their ability be of a low or of a high order, whether they are of foreign-born or of American-born parentage, whether they live on the lower East Side or in Queens, whether they will stop school as soon as the law permits or will continue in school, whether on graduating from the elementary school they purpose to go to work or purpose to go to an academic, technical, or commercial high school. Whatever the inclination, the ability, the particular educational need of the child, each must meet the same requirements and pursue the same course of instruction.

The effect of disregarding the varying abilities and edu-

[1] See Report on Races in the Different High Schools, 1908, on file at the office of the City Superintendent of Schools.

TABLE XXVII

Year Graduated	Age at Graduation from Elementary School										
	Total	Under 13	13 to 14	14 to 15	15 to 16	16 to 17	17 to 18	18 to 19	19 to 20	20 to 21	Over 21
1906	19,353	779	4,396	7,134	4,971	1,740	300	32	1	.....	.....
1907	21,111	663	4,667	7,794	5,475	2,070	392	41	5	3	1
1908	23,509	722	4,821	8,626	6,377	2,459	442	53	8	.....	1
1909	27,152	730	5,444	9,811	7,496	3,014	558	82	9	5	3
1910	31,341	716	6,279	11,313	8,578	3,607	764	77	4	3	.....
1911	35,329	743	6,903	13,206	9,708	3,862	802	86	over 19 19	.....	.....
Total of Each Age	157,795	4,353	32,510	57,884	42,605	16,752	3,258	371	46	11	5
Per Cent. Graduating at Each Age	.....	2.76	20.60	36.68	27.00	10.62	2.06	.24	.03	.007	.003

cational needs of different groups of children and of the failure to provide a number of different elementary school courses of study of varying quantitative requirements is revealed in the fact that, of the pupils in regular classes thirteen to fourteen years old on register after promotion June 30, for the five years, 1907-11, inclusive, but 20.82 per cent. had attained the eighth grade; 29.92 per cent. the seventh; 25.57 per cent. the sixth; 15.44 per cent. the fourth; and 2.19 per cent. were still lingering in the third and lower grades. (See Table XXVIII on page 112.[1])

The effect is also revealed by the fact that, of all the pupils on register in regular classes June 30, 1911, after promotion, 23.30 per cent., or practically each fourth child, was behind his grade for his age;[2] and further, despite the fact that many pupils remain in the elementary schools of the city one, two, and three years after they are fourteen, of all those entering but 88.71 per cent. reach the sixth grade; 61.45 per cent. the seventh grade; 47.57 per cent. the eighth grade, and only 41.33 per cent. are ever able to complete the course.[3]

Summary

It is evident, in view of the foregoing, that the present elementary school course of study has been developed and is administered, first, without due regard to the length of the elementary school period, i. e., to the age limits within which children may with profit be subjected to the régime of the elementary school; second, without due regard to the actual length of time children are in attendance by fourteen, hence to the actual length of time the school has in which to give children an elementary education; and, third, without due regard to the varying abilities and educational

[1] The table on page 112 shows for each of the years 1907-11, inclusive, the number of children thirteen to fourteen years old in each grade from the first to the eighth, inclusive; also the total number for the period in each grade, the total in all grades, and the per cent. of the total number in each grade.

[2] See Table XXII, page 88.

[3] See table, page 92.

needs of different groups of children, hence to the number able to complete the course; all of which has reacted to keep the rate of promotion below what it might have been under more favorable conditions.

CHANGES NEEDED TO ATTAIN THE MAXIMUM RATE OF PROMOTION

From the foregoing it is apparent that the changes needed in order to attain in the elementary schools of the city the maximum rate of promotion are:

(1) That the actual total length of each of the different elementary school courses of study be made to correspond (a) with the length of the period between six [1] and fourteen,[2] i. e., to the period children may with profit be kept under the régime of the elementary school, and (b) with the length of time pupils may reasonably be expected to be in actual attendance during this period.

(2) That the requirements of the elementary school be adapted to the varying abilities and educational needs of different groups of children, and such that all normal [3] children in regular attendance are able by fourteen to complete an elementary school course of study; hence as many courses of study of varying requirements as there are distinct groups of children of different abilities and educational needs. A brief discussion of each of these suggested changes follows.

Adjusting the Length of the Different Courses of Study

While the elementary school course of study is, in theory, as a rule, eight years in length, what its actual total length is has seldom been taken into account. The course of study

[1] Probably the best age of entrance.

[2] Probably the beginning of pubescence and the age when children need a régime different from that of the elementary school.

[3] Among normal children are included all pupils other than those physically and mentally defective, for whom special classes and special instruction should be provided.

TABLE XXVIII [1]

Year Ending June 30	Number of Children 13–14 by Grades								Total
	1st Grade	2nd Grade	3rd Grade	4th Grade	5th Grade	6th Grade	7th Grade	8th Grade	
1907	58	268	1,185	3,728	9,929	14,307	15,210	9,758	54,443
1908	51	274	1,240	3,961	9,618	14,359	16,089	10,526	56,118
1909	42	150	1,065	3,796	9,416	15,305	17,340	12,055	59,169
1910	38	136	859	3,099	8,122	15,017	18,413	13,001	58,685
1911	45	141	705	2,745	7,096	14,168	18,552	14,239	57,691
Total	234	969	5,054	17,329	44,181	73,156	85,604	59,579	286,106
Per Cent. of Total in Each Grade	.08	.34	1.77	6.06	15.44	25.57	29.92	20.82	......

[1] The data for this table were computed from the annual reports of the City Superintendent of Schools for 1907–11.

is prescribed and pupils wishing to complete it must remain in school until its requirements are met, whether this takes eight years, ten years, or twelve and more years. The course of study could easily be made so long that to complete it would hold pupils in the elementary school until they were twenty-one and older. But it is obviously unwise educationally to make the elementary course of study actually longer by one, two, or three years than the length of time the rank and file of children may be expected to be in attendance—between six and fourteen—because, by such a procedure, not less than 42 per cent. of all the children who enter would ever complete the elementary school. If, however, all normal children in regular attendance are to be able to finish an elementary course of study by fourteen, it should be evident that the actual length of each of the different courses offered must approximate closely the time children may with profit be held under the régime of the elementary school. Hence, instead of the length of the course of study determining the time children must remain in the elementary school, as is now the case, it is the time children may reasonably be expected to be in school between six and fourteen that must determine the actual total length of the course of study pursued.

The present course of study, with slight modifications, has been operative in the elementary schools of the city since 1905. Yet no one knows with exactness how long it is. The actual length of this course can only be determined as data are collected year by year with reference to length of time taken by normal pupils completing a given grade to do the work of that grade, and as these data are used to determine the actual length of each grade and of the entire course. Until this is done no one will know whether the present course of study is eight, nine, ten, or more years in length. Yet this course of unknown length is set up to be completed by the children who wish to graduate from the elementary school.

Likewise, no data have ever been collected on how long

children are actually in attendance. The only way to determine this is to collect data, year by year, on the length of time children entering have been in attendance on the elementary schools of other places and of the city; and to collect data on the length of time children entering school for the first time in the city actually remain. Until such data are collected no one will know definitely how long children are actually in the elementary schools of the city, or how long they are in school between six and fourteen; consequently, it is impossible to determine what the actual total length of the courses of study should be.

It therefore appears that two sets of data fundamental to the proper adjustment and administration of a course of study in the City of New York are wholly lacking: (a) of how long they are in school between six and fourteen; consequently, it is impossible to determine what the actual total length of the courses of study should be.

Adjusting the Requirements and Determining the Number of Different Courses

The actual length of the elementary school course of study has been determined, in large measure, not in view of what the rank and file of children are able to accomplish within the limits of the time they may reasonably be expected to be in school by fourteen, but in view of certain assumptions of what is required of children entering high school and of the equally arbitrary assumptions of what pupils graduating from the elementary schools ought to know.

Experience has shown that it is impossible to make these academic and arbitrary standards real; and investigation[1] has shown that there is no uniformity in such standards even within the same system. In consequence, these stand-

[1] See *Non-Promotion and Failures by Studies*, Board of Education, Cleveland, 1909.

ards vary, within the system, with the school; within a school, with the grade; also with the study. Indeed, there are practically as many academic standards in a given system as there are principals and teachers multiplied by the number of grades and by the number of studies in the curriculum.

Investigation shows also that these standards have been developed without regard to their effect. Their effect on the elementary schools of the city is revealed by the fact as stated above that, although pupils remain in school one, two, and three years after they are fourteen. less than 42 per cent. of those entering graduate; by the fact that, of those graduating between 1906-11, inclusive, 74.46 per cent. were fourteen and above; and also by the fact that, of the pupils thirteen to fourteen years old, exclusive of those in special classes, on register June 30, after promotion, for the five years 1907-11, inclusive, but 20.82 per cent. had attained the eighth grade; 29.92 per cent. the seventh; 25.57 per cent. the sixth; 15.44 per cent. the fifth; 6.06 per cent. the fourth; and 2.19 per cent. were still lingering in the third and lower grades.

It is obviously unwise educationally for children to pursue a course of study which is out of proportion to their capacities and out of proportion to the time they will remain in school, and such that, at fourteen, they find themselves still in the fifth, sixth, seventh, or eighth grade. The best results can be achieved when children are permitted to pursue a course of study which they can complete within the time they will be in the elementary school between six and fourteen.

Children can be expected, as we have seen, to have been in the elementary schools of the City of New York, between six and fourteen, at least 7.2 years. Hence, if children are to pursue an elementary school course of study which they will be able to finish, there must be as many courses of study, each complete in itself, in the elementary schools of the city as there are considerable groups of children of different abilities and educational needs; and the quantitative requirements of each of these courses must be determined, not in view of the demands of higher institutions, or in view of what may arbitrarily be thought desirable for children graduating from the elementary school to know, but in view of what the given group of children can accomplish between six and fourteen. In a word, instead of the quantitative requirements of the course of study determining the progress of children through the school, the actual progress of children through the school should determine the quantitative requirements of the course of study pursued.

Making the actual completion of an entire elementary school course of study by all normal children in regular attendance the basis of determining the requirements of the course of study in no way does away with the need of academic standards. It does, however, make these standards depend upon the actual progress of children through the school, and hence supplies an objective measure of whether the prevailing standards are too high or too low.

The adjustment of the course of study to the abilities and needs of different groups of children so that all normal children, regular in attendance, are able to cover a complete course of study between six and fourteen may be done in one of two ways: First, there may be one course for all schools in which there are both minimum and optional requirements, the minimum requirements being such as can be met by all normal pupils in regular attendance by fourteen, the optional requirements providing additional work for pupils able to do more than the minimum requirements. Second, there may be a number of distinct and complete courses, each with minimum and optional requirements, corresponding to the different groups of children of varying abilities and educational needs—at the very least, three such courses would probably be needed—one for bright pupils, one for pupils of medium ability, and one for dull pupils.[1] The development of different courses of study is, we believe, the preferable way of making the necessary adjustments.

The number of different courses of study needed in the elementary schools of the city can, to be sure, only be determined as data are collected on the abilities and educational needs of different groups of children. Similarly, the requirements of each of the different courses—that is, the character and quantity of subject-matter and the quality of the work demanded of pupils—can only be finally determined as data are collected on the time taken in each course by normal pupils to complete each grade and used to modify the requirements so that all normal children in the given course in regular attendance are able to complete the course by fourteen.

THE MAXIMUM RATE OF PROMOTION

Pupils are generally promoted or not promoted according as they have or have not met certain academic standards.[2] When the right to promotion is thus determined, as has already been pointed out, the rate of promotion varies with the school system; within the system, with the school; and within the school, with the grade and teacher. Such variations in rate of promotion do injustice to the child, because work that is rewarded with advancement in one school is not so rewarded in another; hence the number of grades a pupil is able to complete depends largely on the teacher he has and on the school he attends. Nor is there any hope that this will not be true so long as the rate of promotion is

[1] Demonstrations of the feasibility and effectiveness of providing different courses of study in the same school were made by Superintendent Ettinger when principal of P. S. 147, Manhattan, and as district superintendent in Richmond. Experiments along this line have also been carried on in Cleveland, Ohio.

[2] These academic standards rest on arbitrary assumptions of what is required of pupils entering high school and on equally arbitrary assumptions of what pupils graduating from the elementary school ought to know.

determined by purely arbitrary assumptions of what children graduating from the elementary school ought to know.

However contrary it may be to present ways of thinking and to present school practice, arbitrary high school entrance requirements and arbitrary assumptions of what elementary school graduates ought to know should not determine the rate of promotion in the elementary school. The purpose of the elementary school is not to give a few pupils favored either by inheritance or by home surroundings, or by both, an arbitrarily assumed amount of knowledge, or to give 42 per cent. of its pupils a complete elementary school course of instruction and to permit the other 58 per cent. to flounder about in the lower grades until they finally drop from school. The elementary school should give each normal child in regular attendance, within the period children may with profit be kept under the régime of the elementary school, a complete elementary school course, the course completed by each child varying with his ability and educational needs. In view of this conception of the time limits on its work, and of this conception of the purpose of the elementary school, the rate of promotion can only be determined in view of the rapidity with which normal children in regular attendance must advance in order to finish an entire elementary school course of study. Courses of study, to be most effective, must be planned with reference to the entire elementary school period. Hence, the rate of promotion in the elementary school ought ultimately to be uniformly about 100 per cent.

The maximum rate of promotion will be about 100 per cent., and not 100 per cent., because there are always a number of pupils in a system who are not in attendance during a given term sufficiently long to enable them to complete the work of any course that may be offered; but there are also a number of pupils who, by reason of beginning their school work at an advanced age, or by reason of being improperly classified, will be able to cover two terms of work in one term; in this way the terms of work lost will tend to balance the terms of work gained, and the rate of promotion thus maintained at about 100 per cent.

The maximum rate of promotion cannot be secured, however, by one school promoting 150 per cent.[1] of its pupils and another school 50 per cent., or, as in the City of New York, by one school promoting 110 per cent. and another 35 per cent., or by the promotion of 98 per cent. of the pupils in one grade of a school and 57 per cent. in another grade of the same school. Such a procedure, on the one hand, enables children to complete the elementary school course of study before the beginning of pubescence, which is unwise; and, on the other hand, holds children in the elementary school beyond this period, and only permits part of the pupils ever to complete a course, hence defeats the very purpose of the elementary school. Consequently, the rate of promotion in each grade and in each school of a system should be uniformly about 100 per cent.

If it is found that a number of normal pupils in regular attendance are unable to do the work of a given grade in a given course, the remedy is not the non-promotion of these pupils. These pupils should either be reclassified with respect to the course they should pursue or the requirements of the course they are following should be lowered. Similarly, if it is found that children in regular attendance are able to do more than is required by the course they are in, the remedy is not double promotion and the completion of the elementary school before the beginning of pubescence. These children should either be put in a more difficult course or the requirements of the course they are in should be raised. For the constant factors in the elementary school are (1) the actual total length of each of the several courses of study, and (2) the rate of promotion; the variable factors are (1) the abilities and needs of children, and (2) the

[1] The rate of promotion for a term in a school is 150 per cent., when during the term 50 per cent. of the pupils of the school complete one term's work and 50 per cent. by receiving double promotion complete two terms' work.

particular courses of study that should be offered and the requirements of these courses. Hence, it is not the rate of promotion, and, in consequence, the actual total length of the courses of study, that should constantly vary, but the particular courses of study that should be offered and the requirements of these courses. It is these that must be constantly adjusted to the abilities and needs of the children with which each school has to do. Consequently, while the actual total length of the courses of study and the rate of promotion should be practically the same in all the schools of a system, the particular courses of study offered and the requirements of these courses may, and generally should, vary with the school.[1]

CONCLUSIONS

That each normal child in regular attendance between six (probably the best age of entrance) and fourteen (probably the beginning of pubescence and the age when children need a régime different from that of the elementary school) may be able to complete an entire elementary school course of study, hence that conditions may be favorable to a maximum rate of promotion in the elementary schools of the city, we recommend:

(1) That data be collected—
- (a) On the best age of entrance to the elementary school.
- (b) On the age at which children need a régime different from that of the elementary. school.

(2) That data be collected—
- (a) On the number of normal children entering and completing the present course of study.
- (b) On the actual total length of the present course of study.

[1] See McMurry's *Elementary School Standards.*

(c) On the length of time normal children remain in attendance (including attendance on the schools of other places); also on the length of time children are in attendance between six and fourteen.

(d) On the groups of children of different abilities and educational needs.

(3) That there be as many different courses of study as there are groups of children having different abilities and educational needs.

(4) That the actual total length of these different courses of study and hence their requirements be made such that each normal child in regular attendance between six and fourteen is able to complete some one of these courses.

(5) That the actual total length of each of these different courses of study and hence the requirements of each be continuously revised in view of data [suggested in (2)] collected by terms.[1]

[1] Lack of time prevents us from including in this volume a study of Methods of Making Promotions. Such a study should, however, be made.

CHAPTER VII

SIZE OF CLASS AND NON-PROMOTION

ONE of the most important working conditions of any school is the size of class—the number of children one teacher is expected to instruct. When classes contain from fifty to sixty or more pupils it is impossible for the teacher to give to each child adequate personal attention and direction. Hence, the efficiency of the school may be materially reduced by the presence of over-size classes.

MAXIMUM SIZE OF REGULAR CLASSES

The maximum size of a regular elementary school class [1] is fixed, by the Board of Education of the city, at fifty. Principals, under the By-laws of the Board, are free to organize classes up to fifty, but, if it becomes necessary, as is often the case, to put more than fifty pupils in a class, such a class cannot be formed without the permission of the Board of Superintendents.[2] Fifty is, therefore, recognized as the maximum beyond which the number of pupils in a class cannot be increased without reducing the efficiency of the school. While fifty is fixed as the maximum, and while the continued lack of adequate school accommodations makes it necessary to put tens of thousands [3] of chil-

[1] Regular classes are to be distinguished from special classes,—that is, from classes for backward, defective, crippled, blind, deaf, and anæmic children, all of which are smaller than regular classes. This report has to do only with regular classes.

[2] Manual of the Board of Education, Sec. 45-7, page 56.

[3] Annual Report of the City Superintendent of Schools for 1910, pages 94-95.

dren annually in classes having fifty and above, there is a strong feeling among the school officials of the city that, if the school is to do its work efficiently, the number of pupils per class ought not to exceed forty.[1] We share this feeling.

NUMBER OF PUPILS IN CLASSES OF EACH SIZE

What the actual size of class was in New York City and how the children were distributed at the end of the February-June term, 1911, among the classes of different sizes is shown by Table XXIX. This table gives, by grades, the number of pupils in regular classes on register before promotion June 30, 1911, in classes under thirty-five, thirty-five to forty, etc.; also the per cent. of the total register of each grade in the classes of each size.[2]

The 73,991 pupils in over-size classes—classes having fifty-one to fifty-five, fifty-six to sixty, and over sixty—were distributed as follows:

					Cumulative Per Cent.
15,025	or 20.31	per cent. were in the	1A	Grade........	20.31
9,760	" 13.19	" " " " "	1B	"	33.50
7,343	" 9.92	" " " " "	2A	"	43.42
8,245	" 11.14	" " " " "	2B	"	54.56
7,261	" 9.81	" " " " "	3A	"	64.37
6,703	" 9.06	" " " " "	3B	"	73.43
5,234	" 7.07	" " " " "	4A	"	80.50
4,886	" 6.60	" " " " "	4B	"	87.10
2,555	" 3.45	" " " " "	5A	"	90.55
2,701	" 3.65	" " " " "	5B	"	94.20
1,494	" 2.02	" " " " "	6A	"	96.22
1,150	" 1.56	" " " " "	6B	"	97.78
433	" .59	" " " " "	7A	"	98.37
332	" .45	" " " " "	7B	"	98.82
259	" .35	" " " " "	8A	"	99.17
610	" .83	" " " " "	8B	"	100.00

[1] Annual Report of the City Superintendent of Schools for 1904, page 98.

[2] See page 124.

TABLE XXIX

Grades	Total Register	Register by Grades in Regular Classes as of June 30, 1911						Per Cent. of Total Register of Each Grade in Classes of Each Size					
		Classes Under 35	35 to 40	41 to 50	51 to 55	56 to 60	Over 60	Classes Under 35	35 to 40	41 to 50	51 to 55	56 to 60	Over 60
1A..	43,012	3,014	4,603	20,370	8,060	4,340	2,625	7.01	10.70	47.36	18.74	10.09	6.10
1B..	49,832	2,487	8,204	29,381	7,530	2,230	.....	4.99	16.46	58.96	15.11	4.48	.....
2A..	39,607	2,876	5,786	23,602	5,461	1,759	123	7.26	14.61	59.59	13.79	4.44	.31
2B..	44,608	2,726	6,800	26,837	6,755	1,429	61	6.12	15.24	60.16	15.14	3.20	.14
3A..	40,180	2,916	7,303	22,700	6,122	1,017	122	7.26	18.17	56.50	15.24	2.53	.30
3B..	42,911	3,195	6,726	26,287	5,588	1,054	61	7.45	15.67	61.26	13.02	2.46	.14
4A..	38,573	3,249	7,255	22,835	4,434	800	.....	8.42	18.81	59.20	11.50	2.07	.....
4B..	39,909	3,330	7,863	23,830	4,429	457	.....	8.34	19.70	59.72	11.09	1.15	.....
5A..	36,823	3,388	7,827	23,053	2,212	343	.....	9.20	21.26	62.60	6.01	.93	.....
5B..	36,035	4,164	8,850	20,320	2,528	173	.....	11.56	24.56	56.38	7.02	.48	.....
6A..	32,873	4,556	9,714	17,109	1,378	116	.....	13.86	29.55	52.05	4.19	.35	.....
6B..	31,134	5,294	11,072	13,618	1,038	112	.....	17.00	35.56	43.73	3.35	.36	.....
7A..	27,667	5,476	10,166	11,592	373	60	.....	19.79	36.74	41.90	1.35	.22	.....
7B..	24,791	6,007	9,137	9,315	332	.....	.....	24.23	36.86	37.57	1.34	.....	.....
8A..	21,112	5,834	7,324	7,695	259	.....	.....	27.64	34.68	36.45	1.23	.....	.....
8B..	19,545	5,632	5,109	8,194	610	.....	.....	28.82	26.14	41.92	3.12	.....	.....
Total	568,612	64,144	123,739	306,738	57,109	13,890	2,992	11.28	21.76	53.94	10.04	2.44	.53

Twenty and thirty-one one-hundredths (20.31) per cent., or one-fifth, of all the pupils in over-size classes at the end of the February-June term, 1911, it will be observed, were in the 1A grade; 54.56 per cent. in the 1A-2B grades; 87.10 per cent. in the grades 1A-4B; and 97.78 per cent. in the grades 1A-6B. In short, over-size classes were confined, at the end of the February-June term, 1911, to the 6B and lower grades.

If comparison is made, grade by grade, between the pupils within each grade in the classes of each of the several sizes (see Table XXIX) it will be noted that the per cent. of pupils in small classes gradually increases from the lowest to the highest grade. In classes under thirty-five the per cent. increases from 7.01 per cent. in the 1A to 28.82 per cent. in the 8B, and, in classes having thirty-five to forty, from 10.70 per cent. to 26.14 per cent. A corresponding decrease will be noted from the 1A to the 8B grades in the per cent. of pupils in over-size classes. In classes having fifty-one to fifty-six the per cent. decreases from 18.74 per cent. in the 1A to 3.12 per cent. in the 8B; in classes having fifty-six to sixty from 10.09 per cent. to zero; and in classes having over sixty from 6.10 per cent. to zero.

It, therefore, appears that the size of a class varies with the grade; that the 1A has the smallest number of small classes and the largest number of large classes, and the 8B has practically the largest number of small classes and the smallest number of large classes.

The presence of large classes in the grades 1A-6B and of small classes in the grades 7A-8B is due partly to policy and partly to necessity. There is a feeling among the school officials of the city that classes in the upper grades should be smaller than in the lower grades. Hence, in schools where there are ample accommodations for all pupils, classes in the 7A-8B grades are so organized as to have from thirty-five to forty pupils, whereas, in the grades 1A-6B, classes range from forty to forty-five. In most cases, small classes in the upper grades and large ones in the lower grades are, however, due to necessity. In many districts, so many pupils leave school in the 6B grade and before that the numbers remaining in the 7A-8B grades are small. Unless these pupils are transferred to a central school, it is impossible to do otherwise than to have small classes. In contrast, the lower grades are crowded. To care for all the pupils in these grades, it is necessary to make the classes large.

RATE OF PROMOTION IN CLASSES OF EACH SIZE

The rate of promotion at the end of the February-June term, 1911, in the classes of each of the several sizes is shown by Table XXX. This table gives, by grades, the per cent. of the register in each size of class promoted at the end of the February-June term, 1911; also the per cent. not promoted. (See page 128.)

When the several grades are considered as a whole it will be observed that the highest per cent. of promotion was in classes under thirty-five, the rate being 89.36 per cent. The rate of promotion in classes of thirty-five to forty was, however, only .22 of 1 per cent. less, and, in classes of forty-one to fifty, only .41 of 1 per cent. less than in classes under thirty-five. Hence, for practical purposes, the rate of promotion was the same in all classes having fifty and under. But the rate of promotion in classes of fifty-one to fifty-five was lower than in classes under thirty-five by 1.68 per cent., in classes of fifty-six to sixty by 5.91 per cent., and in classes over sixty by 18.17 per cent. The major part of the difference in the rate of promotion, at least in classes of fifty-six to sixty, and in classes over sixty, in comparison with the rate of promotion in classes under thirty-five, was, however, due to the fact that pupils in the classes of these two sizes are principally in the lower grades, where the rate of promotion is relatively low. No such differences, it will be observed, appear, if comparison is made, grade by grade, between the rate of promotion in the classes of the several sizes.

The differences, such as they are, in the rate of promotion within each grade, in these different-size classes, become clearer, if all classes of fifty and under are combined and all classes of over fifty, and comparison is made between the rate of promotion in classes of these two sizes only. Table XXXI gives by grades the per cent. of promotion in classes of fifty and under, in classes of over fifty, and the per cent. of promotion in classes of fifty and under, above or below the per cent. of promotion in classes over fifty; also the increase in number of pupils that would have been promoted in classes of over fifty at the rate of promotion in classes of fifty and under. (See page 129.)

In nine out of sixteen grades the higher rate of promotion at the end of the February-June term, 1911, was in classes of fifty and under; in seven the higher rate was in classes of over fifty. The rate of promotion was higher in classes of over fifty in the 1B by .29 of 1 per cent.; in the 4B by .59 of 1 per cent.; in the 5A by 1.29 per cent.; in the 5B by .09 of 1 per cent.; in the 6B by 1.58 per cent.; in the 7B by 3.09 per cent.; and in the 8B by 2.18 per cent. But the difference in the rate of promotion was either so small or the pupils in the given grade were so few that the higher rate of promotion in classes above fifty in these seven grades is found to make a difference of only 134 promotions.

In each grade of the grades 1A-4A—containing 80 per cent. of all pupils in over-size classes[1]—the rate of promotion, with the exception of the 1B grade, was higher in classes of fifty and under. But, with the exception of the 1A grade, the differences in the rate of promotion are too small materially to affect the number of promotions. Thus, although the higher rate of promotion is found, in the majority of grades, in classes of fifty and under, this higher rate is so small that, had promotions in each of the several grades been the same for classes of over fifty as for classes of fifty and under, there would have been, in classes

[1] See table, page 123.

TABLE XXX

Grades	Per Cent. of Register by Grades in Each Size of Class Promoted						Per Cent. of Register by Grades in Each Size of Class Not Promoted					
	Classes Under 35	35 to 40	41 to 50	51 to 55	56 to 60	Over 60	Classes Under 35	35 to 40	41 to 50	51 to 55	56 to 60	Over 60
1A	75.35	80.32	77.04	74.94	73.66	68.57	24.65	19.68	22.96	25.06	26.34	31.43
1B	87.82	88.26	88.87	89.23	88.12	.....	12.18	11.74	11.13	10.77	11.88	.....
2A	91.45	87.94	89.09	90.08	85.05	88.62	8.55	12.06	10.91	9.92	14.95	11.38
2B	91.97	90.56	90.69	89.95	89.01	91.80	8.03	9.44	9.31	10.05	10.99	8.20
3A	90.98	90.55	89.59	89.25	88.89	89.34	9.02	9.45	10.41	10.75	11.11	10.66
3B	90.64	89.40	91.22	90.35	89.47	91.80	9.36	10.60	8.78	9.65	10.53	8.20
4A	89.75	90.20	90.20	89.26	85.25	.....	10.25	9.80	9.80	10.74	14.75	.....
4B	92.04	90.82	89.60	90.77	89.93	.....	7.96	9.18	10.40	9.23	10.07	.....
5A	88.37	89.28	88.65	89.78	91.84	.....	11.63	10.72	11.35	10.22	8.16	.....
5B	89.72	89.50	89.83	89.99	87.28	.....	10.28	10.50	10.17	10.01	12.72	.....
6A	89.11	89.26	88.92	87.81	92.24	.....	10.89	10.74	11.08	12.19	7.76	.....
6B	88.74	89.05	89.90	90.66	93.75	.....	11.26	10.95	10.10	9.34	6.25	.....
7A	88.75	87.99	87.82	82.84	71.67	.....	11.25	12.01	12.18	17.16	28.33	.....
7B	88.95	88.34	89.89	92.17	.....	.....	11.05	11.66	10.11	7.83	.....	.....
8A	89.70	89.45	89.72	81.85	.....	.....	10.30	10.55	10.28	18.15	.....	.....
8B	93.64	93.87	95.20	96.56	.....	.....	6.36	6.13	4.80	3.44	.....	.....
Total	89.36	89.14	88.95	87.68	83.45	71.19	10.64	10.86	11.05	12.32	16.55	28.81

TABLE XXXI

Grades	Per Cent. of Promotion in Classes of 50 and Under	Per Cent. of Promotion in Classes of Over 50	Per Cent. of Promotion in Classes of 50 and Under above or below the Per Cent. of Promotion in Classes Above 50	Increase in Number That Would Have Been Promoted in Classes Over 50 at Rate in Classes of 50 and Under
1A.......	77.40	73.46	3.94	592
1B.......	88.68	88.97	—.29	—29
2A.......	89.10	88.85	.25	19
2B.......	90.76	89.80	.96	79
3A.......	89.92	89.20	.72	52
3B.......	90.83	90.23	.60	40
4A.......	90.15	88.65	1.50	78
4B.......	90.10	90.69	—.59	—29
5A.......	88.77	90.06	—1.29	—33
5B.......	89.73	89.82	—.09	—2
6A.......	89.06	88.15	.91	14
6B.......	89.38	90.96	—1.58	—18
7A.......	88.07	81.29	6.78	29
7B.......	89.08	92.17	—3.09	—10
8A.......	89.62	81.85	7.77	20
8B.......	94.38	96.56	—2.18	—13
Net Increase		.....	....	789

of over fifty, a net increase of only 789 promotions out of a total of 73,991 pupils—the equivalent of one additional promotion to each ninety-four pupils in classes of over fifty.

OVER-SIZE CLASSES AS A FACTOR IN NON-PROMOTION AND CONGESTION

There were, as we have seen, only 789 fewer promotions among the 73,991 pupils in over-size classes than there would have been had these pupils been promoted at the rate for classes of fifty and under. But, in the 1A grade alone, by reason of the lower rate, the promotions were, as we have seen, fewer by 592—the equivalent of one less promotion to each twenty-five 1A pupils in over-size classes.

Hence, as promotions were made at the end of the February-June term, 1911, over-size classes were no material factor, except in the 1A grade, in increasing the number of non-promotions.

It is reasonable to assume that the small number of non-promoted children (197) caused by the slightly lower rate of promotion prevailing in the grades above the 1A was absorbed in the classes already found in these grades, and that, to care for the non-promotions (592) caused by the decidedly lower rate of promotion in the 1A grade, it would be necessary to form only a few, if any, additional 1A classes. Hence, as promotions were made at the end of the February-June term, 1911, over-size classes contributed but slightly, if at all, to congestion.

CONCLUSIONS

The foregoing discussion may be summarized thus:

(1) There were, at the end of the February-June term, 1911, 73,991 pupils in over-size classes—that is, in classes having fifty and above. The greater number of over-size classes was in the grades 1A-6B.

(2) The size of class varies with the grade; the 1A grade has the smallest number of small classes and the largest number of large classes, while the 8B grade has the largest number of small classes and the smallest number of large classes.

(3) The rate of promotion for all grades, with the exception of the 1A grade, at the end of the February-June term, 1911, was practically the same in the classes of the several sizes.

(4) As promotions were made at the end of the February-June term, 1911, over-size classes were no material factor, except in the 1A grade, in increasing the number of non-promotions, and contributed but slightly, if at all, to congestion.

(5) Although there was only a very slight difference, with the exception of the 1A grade, in the rate of promotion at the end of the February-June term, 1911, for classes under fifty and for classes over fifty, and although data derived from tests of the educational achievements of children are not at hand to prove to what extent classes having over fifty offer less favorable opportunities for work than smaller classes, teachers and school officials are a unit in the opinion that classes having over fifty pupils should be eliminated and that all classes should be reduced to at least not more than forty-five pupils.

CHAPTER VIII

ABSENCE AND NON-PROMOTION

THE school year in the City of New York is forty weeks in length, divided into two terms of twenty weeks each. Holidays reduce the actual length of a term to somewhat less than one hundred days. Any considerable absence, due either to irregular attendance or to late entrance, naturally affects the educational progress of children.

NUMBER OF CHILDREN ABSENT FOR CERTAIN INTERVALS

For the purpose of studying the effect of absence [1] on the educational progress of children, pupils have been grouped on the basis of their being absent a given number of days during the February-June term, 1911. Table XXXII gives by grades the number of pupils on register in regular classes June 30, 1911, absent ten days and less, eleven to twenty, twenty-one to thirty, etc.; also the per cent. of the total register of each grade absent ten days and less, eleven to twenty, etc. (See page 133.)

Of the 568,612 pupils on register in regular classes June 30, 1911, 382,406, or 67.25 per cent., were absent during the February-June term, 1911, ten days and less; 97,512, or 17.15 per cent., eleven to twenty days; 39,391, or 6.93 per cent., twenty-one to thirty days; 19,297, or 3.39 per cent., thirty-one to forty days; and 30,006, or 5.28 per cent., forty-one days and above.

[1] It is impossible to distinguish in this report between absence due to irregular attendance and absence due to late entrance.

TABLE XXXII

Grades	Total Register as of June 30, 1911	Register in Regular Classes as of June 30, 1911					Per Cent. of Total Register in Each Grade				
		Absent 10 Days and Less	11 to 20	21 to 30	31 to 40	41 and Above	Absent 10 Days and Less	11 to 20	21 to 30	31 to 40	41 and Above
1A	43,012	17,215	8,708	5,010	3,188	8,891	40.02	20.25	11.65	7.41	20.67
1B	49,832	28,342	10,800	4,938	2,489	3,263	56.88	21.67	9.91	4.99	6.55
2A	39,607	24,826	7,743	3,240	1,612	2,186	62.68	19.55	8.18	4.07	5.52
2B	44,608	29,970	8,063	3,130	1,572	1,873	67.19	18.08	7.02	3.52	4.19
3A	40,180	27,841	6,865	2,690	1,190	1,594	69.29	17.09	6.69	2.96	3.97
3B	42,911	30,157	7,146	2,684	1,257	1,667	70.28	16.65	6.25	2.94	3.88
4A	38,573	26,943	6,445	2,494	1,194	1,497	69.85	16.71	6.47	3.09	3.88
4B	39,909	28,057	6,575	2,552	1,159	1,566	70.31	16.47	6.39	2.91	3.92
5A	36,823	25,420	6,285	2,424	1,148	1,546	69.03	17.07	6.58	3.12	4.20
5B	36,035	25,312	5,958	2,293	1,083	1,389	70.24	16.54	6.36	3.01	3.85
6A	32,873	23,144	5,396	2,069	944	1,320	70.41	16.41	6.29	2.87	4.02
6B	31,134	22,530	4,974	1,783	780	1,067	72.36	15.98	5.73	2.50	3.43
7A	27,667	20,537	4,088	1,501	666	875	74.23	14.76	5.43	2.42	3.16
7B	24,791	18,854	3,655	1,167	514	601	76.05	14.74	4.72	2.07	2.42
8A	21,112	16,638	2,828	925	318	403	78.81	13.40	4.38	1.51	1.90
8B	19,545	16,620	1,983	491	183	268	85.03	10.14	2.52	.94	1.37
Total	568,612	382,406	97,512	39,391	19,297	30,006	67.25	17.15	6.93	3.39	5.28

The Compulsory Education Law operates primarily on children between the ages of seven and fourteen; according to its provisions, children between these ages must be in attendance the entire time school is in session. The great majority of the children in the grades 2A-6B are between these age limits. It is, therefore, astonishing that 65,450, or 17.10 per cent., of all the children in these grades should be absent during the February-June term, 1911, eleven to twenty days; 25,359, or 6.63 per cent., absent twenty-one to thirty days; 11,939, or 3.12 per cent., absent thirty-one to forty days; and 15,705, or 4.10 per cent.—the equivalent of one in each twenty-five—absent forty-one days and above.

If comparison is made grade by grade between the per cent. of all pupils within a grade absent each of the several periods, it will be observed that the per cent. of children absent ten days and less is the lowest in the 1A grade and the highest in the 8B, increasing from 40.02 per cent. in the 1A to 85.03 per cent. in the 8B. With each of the less favorable periods of absence, the reverse is true. Absence eleven to twenty days decreases from 20.25 per cent. in the 1A to 10.14 per cent. in the 8B; twenty-one to thirty days from 11.65 per cent. to 2.52 per cent.; thirty-one to forty days from 7.41 per cent. to .94 per cent.; and absence forty-one days and above from 20.67 per cent. to 1.37 per cent. Hence, the largest amount of absence is in the 1A grade; this gradually decreases to the 8B, in which grade there is the least amount of absence.

The difference in the amount of absence in the several grades and the gradual decrease from the 1A to the 8B become clearer if the pupils on register June 30, 1911, are grouped according to (1) absence twenty days and less, and (2) absence twenty-one days and more. Table XXXIII gives the per cent. of the register of each grade in regular classes as of June 30, 1911, absent twenty days and less and absent twenty-one days and more.

TABLE XXXIII

Grades	Per Cent. of Total Register as of June 30, 1911, Absent Twenty Days and Less	Per Cent. of Total Register as of June 30, 1911, Absent Twenty-one Days and More
1A	60.27	39.73
1B	78.55	21.45
2A	82.23	17.77
2B	85.27	14.73
3A	86.38	13.62
3B	86.93	13.07
4A	86.56	13.44
4B	86.78	13.22
5A	86.10	13.90
5B	86.78	13.22
6A	86.82	13.18
6B	88.34	11.66
7A	88.99	11.01
7B	90.79	9.21
8A	92.21	7.79
8B	95.17	4.83
Total	84.40	15.60

The amount of absence in the two lowest grades, and especially in the 1A, is particularly large, because pupils in these grades are young; the amount of sickness among them is greater than among older children; they have not as yet acquired the school-going habit, and parents generally do not feel it necessary to keep such young children in school regularly. From the 2A to the 6A grade, absence is checked to a greater or less extent by the enforcement of the Compulsory Education Law. The further decrease in the 6B and later grades is probably due to the withdrawal of larger numbers of pupils who were more or less irregular in attendance,[1] and to the more steady habits and fixed purposes of those remaining. But the amount of absence in all grades is large; whether it cannot be greatly reduced is a question worthy of earnest and immediate consideration by the school authorities.

[1] See tables on pages 146 and 188.

RATE OF PROMOTION IN EACH OF THE SEVERAL PERIODS OF ABSENCE

The effect of absence on the progress of children is shown by Table XXXIV. This table gives by grades and for each period of absence the per cent. of the register as of June 30, 1911, promoted; also the per cent. not promoted.

When the several grades are considered together the highest rate of promotion at the end of the February-June term, 1911, was among children absent ten days and less, the rate of promotion being 93.16 per cent. The rate of promotion was lower for pupils absent eleven to twenty days than for pupils absent ten days and less by 5.56 per cent.; lower for pupils absent twenty-one days to thirty days by 11.01 per cent.; lower for pupils absent thirty-one to forty days by 18.62 per cent.; and lower for pupils absent forty-one days and above by 40.34 per cent.

The same relative effect of absence on promotion is to be observed in each of the grades. The promotions out of each hundred pupils on register ranged in the several grades from—

89 to 97 for pupils absent ten days and less
82 to 90 for pupils absent eleven to twenty days
75 to 86 for pupils absent twenty-one to thirty days
60 to 81 for pupils absent thirty-one to forty days
40 to 67 for pupils absent forty-one and above

The highest rate of promotion at the end of the February-June term, 1911, in every grade, was, therefore, for pupils absent ten days and less; the rate decreased in every grade with each succeeding period of greater absence; and the lowest rate of promotion in every grade was for pupils absent forty-one days and above.

The difference in the effect of absence on the rate of promotion in the several grades becomes more apparent if pupils are grouped according as they were absent twenty days and less, and twenty-one days and more, and the rate of promotion for the two groups is given by grades. (See Table XXXV, page 138.)

TABLE XXXIV

Grades	Per Cent. of Register as of June 30, 1911, Promoted					Per Cent. of Register as of June 30, 1911, Not Promoted				
	Absent 10 Days and Less	11 to 20	21 to 30	31 to 40	41 and Above	Absent 10 Days and Less	11 to 20	21 to 30	31 to 40	41 and Above
1A	89.47	85.75	79.02	71.01	40.56	10.53	14.25	20.98	28.99	59.44
1B	92.80	89.02	85.52	80.31	63.84	7.20	10.98	14.48	19.69	36.16
2A	92.19	88.94	84.78	78.97	67.56	7.81	11.06	15.22	21.03	32.44
2B	93.26	89.73	86.01	81.36	66.84	6.74	10.27	13.99	18.64	33.16
3A	92.77	88.27	83.31	80.60	63.24	7.23	11.73	16.69	19.40	36.76
3B	93.62	89.69	84.24	78.20	63.05	6.38	10.31	15.76	21.80	36.95
4A	93.27	88.19	84.32	75.12	58.98	6.73	11.81	15.68	24.88	41.02
4B	93.75	88.29	84.01	74.80	55.49	6.25	11.71	15.99	25.20	44.51
5A	93.00	87.37	80.45	71.34	52.85	7.00	12.63	19.55	28.66	47.15
5B	93.88	88.00	80.59	71.00	51.33	6.12	12.00	19.41	29.00	48.67
6A	93.60	86.12	79.60	68.96	49.62	6.40	13.88	20.40	31.04	50.38
6B	93.57	87.05	79.81	68.08	45.08	6.43	12.95	20.19	31.92	54.92
7A	92.30	84.15	75.15	68.62	40.69	7.70	15.85	24.85	31.38	59.31
7B	93.07	84.02	77.89	60.89	42.27	6.93	15.98	22.11	39.11	57.73
8A	92.65	85.15	77.51	61.95	40.45	7.35	14.85	22.49	38.05	59.55
8B	97.12	82.15	74.95	77.60	67.16	2.88	17.85	25.05	22.40	32.84
Total	93.16	87.60	82.15	74.54	52.82	6.84	12.40	17.85	25.46	47.18

TABLE XXXV

Grades	Rate of Promotion among Pupils Absent 20 Days and Less	Rate of Promotion among Pupils Absent 21 Days and More	Rate of Promotion among Pupils Absent 20 Days and Less above the Rate of Promotion among Pupils Absent 21 Days and More
1A	88.22	57.52	30.70
1B	91.76	77.69	14.07
2A	91.42	78.10	13.32
2B	92.51	79.44	13.07
3A	91.88	76.58	15.30
3B	92.87	76.59	16.28
4A	92.29	74.89	17.40
4B	92.71	73.53	19.18
5A	91.89	70.07	21.82
5B	92.76	69.88	22.88
6A	92.18	68.15	24.03
6B	92.39	67.08	25.31
7A	90.95	63.81	27.14
7B	91.60	64.68	26.92
8A	91.56	65.43	26.13
8B	95.52	73.25	22.27
Total	92.03	70.57	21.46

The effect of absence on the rate of promotion is greatest, it appears, in the 1A grade, being more than twice as great as in the 1B. From the 1B on, the seriousness of absence becomes increasingly greater practically to the 8B. That is, in case a pupil has been absent twenty-one days and more, his chance of promotion decreases with each grade from the 1B to the 8B.

It therefore appears, as promotions were made at the end of the February-June term, 1911, with the exception of the 1A grade, absence affected more seriously the rate of promotion in the higher than in the lower grades, and that, in all grades, the rate of promotion varies inversely with the amount of absence.

ABSENCE AS A FACTOR IN NON-PROMOTION AND CONGESTION

In the group of pupils having the highest per cent. of promotion absence varied from zero to ten days.[1] Hence, so far as our data go, the effect of absence on promotion is least among pupils absent from zero to ten days, and any difference in the rate of promotion in groups absent a longer period may be attributed to the effect of the longer absence.[2] Hence, by making the rate of promotion among children absent from zero to ten days the normal, the effect of absence on promotion may be estimated within reasonable limits.

Table XXXVI gives the actual number of non-promotions among pupils absent eleven days and above, the number of non-promotions there would have been at the rate of non-promotion for pupils absent from zero to ten days, the decrease in number and also the per cent. of decrease in the number of non-promotions at the rate of non-promotion for pupils absent from zero to ten days. (See page 140.)

There were, it will be observed, 38,194 non-promotions at the end of the February-June term, 1911, in all grades among pupils absent eleven days and above. Had the same rate of non-promotion prevailed for such pupils as among pupils absent from zero to ten days there would have been but 13,637 non-promotions, a decrease of 24,557, or 64.30 per cent. The largest numerical reduction would have been in the 1A, 5,785; the smallest in the 8B, 522. The lowest per cent. of decrease would have been in the 2A, 51.86 per cent.; the highest in the 8B, 86.14 per cent. Hence, from 51.86 per cent. to 86.14 per cent. of the non-promotions in

[1] See table on page 137.

[2] In attributing differences in rate of promotion to absence, the assumption is, of course, that all other conditions were the same in the several groups of pupils. While this assumption is evidently not exact, the results based on it are significant. Only additional data not now available and further study can determine exactly the precise effect of absence among the other factors determining non-promotion. In any case, it is obvious that prolonged or frequent absence of children from school must affect their promotion unfavorably.

the several grades and 64.30 per cent. of all non-promotions among pupils absent eleven days and above may be attributed to the effect of absence.

When judged solely in view of promotions as made at the end of the February-June term, 1911, absence appears to be a very large factor in increasing the number of non-promotions, and hence in increasing congestion. The effect of absence is, then, that tens of thousands of children are left back to go over the same work again, to congest the already overcrowded lower grades, to increase the amount and degree of retardation, and to add to the cost of the elementary school.

TABLE XXXVI

NON-PROMOTIONS AMONG PUPILS ABSENT ELEVEN DAYS AND ABOVE

Grades	Actual Number of Non-Promotions	Number of Non-Promotions at Rate of Promotion for Pupils Absent Zero to Ten Days	Decrease in Number of Non-Promotions at Rate of Promotion for Pupils Absent Zero to Ten Days	Per Cent. of Decrease in Non-Promotions at Rate of Promotion for Pupils Absent from Zero to Ten Days
1A......	8,501	2,716	5,785	68.05
1B......	3,571	1,547	2,024	56.68
2A......	2,397	1,154	1,243	51.86
2B......	2,180	987	1,193	54.72
3A......	2,087	892	1,195	57.26
3B......	2,050	814	1,236	60.29
4A......	2,063	783	1,280	62.05
4B......	2,167	741	1,426	65.81
5A......	2,326	798	1,528	65.69
5B......	2,150	656	1,494	69.49
6A......	2,129	623	1,506	70.74
6B......	1,839	553	1,286	69.93
7A......	1,749	549	1,200	68.61
7B......	1,390	411	979	70.43
8A......	989	329	660	66.73
8B......	606	84	522	86.14
Total...	38,194	13,637	24,557	64.30

CONCLUSIONS

The foregoing discussion may be thus summarized:

(1) The greatest amount of absence during the February-June term, 1911, was in the 1A grade; this gradually decreased to the 8B, in which grade there was the least absence.

(2) The amount of absence in all grades is large; whether it cannot be greatly reduced is a question worthy of immediate and earnest attention.

(3) With the exception of the 1A grade, absence affected more seriously the rate of promotion in the higher than in the lower grades; and, in all grades, the rate of promotion varies inversely with the amount of absence.

(4) Absence is a very large factor in increasing the number of non-promotions, and hence in increasing congestion.

(5) In view of the effect of absence on the child's progress through the school, the first duty of teachers and principals should be to keep children regular in attendance, and the corresponding responsibility of the department of school attendance is, therefore, very great.

CHAPTER IX

OVER AGE AND NON-PROMOTION

INVESTIGATIONS carried on within the last five years have established two facts: (1) That children in large numbers, either from inclination or from necessity, on becoming fourteen years of age drop out of school permanently; (2) that many of the children leaving the elementary school permanently have not advanced farther in the course of study than the fifth or sixth year.

These facts have led to the question of the grade a child of a given age should have completed, providing he is to finish the entire elementary school course of study by a given age. Accordingly, certain age limits have been fixed for entering and for completing each of the grades of the elementary school. Children finishing a grade before the age limit fixed for completing the given grade are termed "under age." Children finishing a grade at the age limit fixed for completing the given grade are termed "normal age." Children finishing a grade at an older age than the age limit fixed for completing the given grade are termed "over age"—that is, are behind the grade for their age.

In determining the number of over-age pupils in a school system and the degree of over age—that is, the length of time children are behind their grade—much depends on the age-grade standards adopted and on the method employed in making the estimate. It is impracticable at this point to consider the many problems involved in an accurate estimate of over age;[1] and it was impossible, with the data

[1] See pages 199-266 of this volume for a discussion of over age and method of determining over age.

at hand, to do otherwise than to adopt the age-grade standards fixed by the City Superintendent of Schools,[1] and to determine over age, without regard to whether pupils were advanced or not advanced, by the age fixed for being in the grade in which pupils were registered before promotion at the end of the term, the method of estimating over age most commonly used. The ages of children are as of June 30, 1911.[2]

NUMBER OF OVER-AGE PUPILS IN REGULAR CLASSES[3]

The number of over-age pupils in the regular classes of elementary schools of the city at the end of the February-June term, 1911, is shown by Table XXXVII. This table gives by grades the number of pupils on register June 30,

[1] Annual Report of the City Superintendent of Schools for 1904, page 47.

[2] While the age-grade standards and the ages of the children are the same in both estimates, our estimate of over age at the end of the February-June term, 1911, differs radically from that of the City Superintendent of Schools for the same term. (See table on page 88 for his estimate.) Our estimate is much higher than his. Even our estimate is somewhat too low, because the over age of pupils not promoted is determined by the ages fixed for being in the grade in which such pupils were registered rather than by the ages fixed for completing the grade last finished. The estimate of the City Superintendent of Schools for promoted pupils is based on the ages fixed for being in the grades of the several years to which such children have just been advanced, and, for non-promoted pupils, on the ages fixed for being in the grades of the several years in which such pupils were registered during the term, but from which they failed to be promoted. In a word, the over age, if any, of all children is judged by him as if they had completed the grade which they have just entered. (Non-promoted pupils have, of course, been in the grade for the term, but for practical purposes are just entering it.) To judge over age by the method of the City Superintendent is to lessen the recorded number of pupils over age, and to reduce the length of time pupils are over age by from a half to an entire school year; to estimate over age in this way is clearly wrong.

[3] We are concerned here with over age in regular classes only. We are not concerned with over age among the 31,430 pupils in special classes at the end of the February-June term, 1911. See Annual Report of the City Superintendent of Schools for 1911, page 67.

1911, before promotion, under normal age, of normal age, and over normal age; also the per cent. of the total register of each grade under normal age, of normal age, and over normal age.

TABLE XXXVII

REGISTER IN REGULAR CLASSES AS OF JUNE 30, 1911, BEFORE PROMOTION

Grades	Number Under Normal Age	Number Normal Age	Number Over Normal Age	Per Cent. of Total Register		
				Below Normal Age	Of Normal Age	Over Normal Age
1A..........	414	36,882	5,716	.96	85.75	13.29
1B..........	516	40,114	9,202	1.03	80.50	18.47
2A..........	828	27,967	10,812	2.09	70.61	27.30
2B..........	835	31,361	12,412	1.87	70.31	27.82
3A..........	1,219	24,339	14,622	3.03	60.57	36.40
3B..........	885	25,839	16,187	2.06	60.22	37.72
4A..........	1,264	19,253	18,056	3.28	49.91	46.81
4B..........	1,029	20,652	18,228	2.58	51.74	45.68
5A..........	1,195	16,981	18,647	3.24	46.12	50.64
5B..........	1,019	17,380	17,636	2.83	48.23	48.94
6A..........	1,352	14,169	17,352	4.11	43.11	52.78
6B..........	1,202	14,515	15,417	3.86	46.62	49.52
7A..........	1,460	12,393	13,814	5.28	44.79	49.93
7B..........	1,168	12,658	10,965	4.71	51.06	44.23
8A..........	1,504	10,660	8,948	7.12	50.49	42.39
8B..........	1,461	10,765	7,319	7.48	55.07	37.45
Total.......	17,351	335,928	215,333	3.05	59.08	37.87

Of the 568,612 pupils on register June 30, 1911, in regular classes, 17,351, or 3.05 per cent., were under normal—ahead of their grade; 335,928, or 59.08 per cent., were normal—up to grade; and 215,333, or 37.87 per cent., were over normal—behind their grade. The smallest number of over-age children was in the 1A grade, 5,716; the number is largest in the 5A, 18,647; while from the 5A the number gradually decreases to 7,319 in the 8B. Correspondingly, the lowest per cent. of over age is in the 1A, 13.29 per cent.; and the highest 52.78 per cent., in the 6B; then there is a gradual decrease to 37.45 per cent. in the 8B grade.

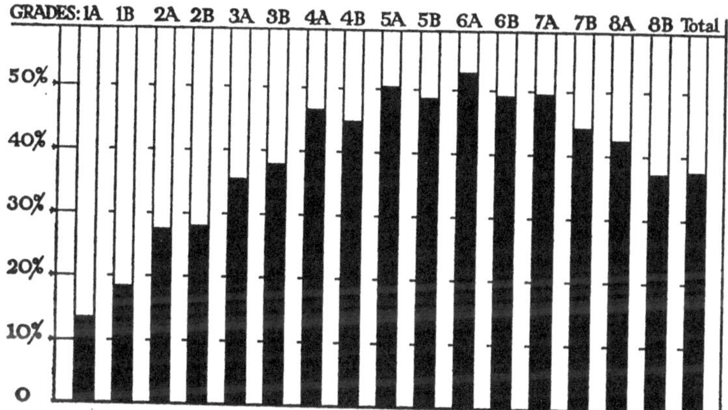

Fig. 3. Black indicates the per cent. of pupils in each grade over age. (Compare with estimate of City Superintendent of Schools, Figure 1, page 89.)

THE DEGREE OF OVER AGE

The fact that there were at the end of the February-June term, 1911, in regular classes 215,333 over-age pupils is in itself significant, but the full significance of this fact becomes apparent only in view of the length of the period these pupils are behind their grades. Table XXXVIII gives by grades the number of pupils over age under one year, between one and two years, between two and three years, and three years and more; also the per cent. of the total number of over-age pupils in each grade under one year over age, between one and two years, etc. (See page 146.)

Of the 215,333 over-age pupils, 120,618, or 56.01 per cent., are less than one year behind their grade, 62,247, or 28.91 per cent., between one and two years; 22,547, or 10.47 per cent., between two and three years; and 9,921, or 4.61 per cent., three years and more.

TABLE XXXVIII

Grades	Total Number Over Age	Number Over Age				Per Cent. of Total Number Over Age			
		Under 1 Year	Between 1 and 2 Years	Between 2 and 3 Years	3 Years and More	Under 1 Year	Between 1 and 2 Years	Between 2 and 3 Years	3 Years and More
1A	5,716	3,942	1,224	305	245	68.96	21.41	5.34	4.29
1B	9,202	6,333	1,892	614	363	68.82	20.56	6.67	3.95
2A	10,812	6,999	2,407	879	527	64.73	22.26	8.13	4.88
2B	12,412	7,641	3,003	1,124	644	61.56	24.19	9.06	5.19
3A	14,622	8,257	4,034	1,402	929	56.47	27.59	9.59	6.35
3B	16,187	8,753	4,405	1,814	1,215	54.07	27.21	11.21	7.51
4A	18,056	9,629	4,894	2,234	1,299	53.33	27.10	12.37	7.20
4B	18,228	9,148	5,300	2,451	1,329	50.19	29.07	13.45	7.29
5A	18,647	8,855	5,910	2,731	1,151	47.49	31.69	14.65	6.17
5B	17,636	8,520	5,748	2,416	952	48.31	32.59	13.70	5.40
6A	17,352	8,785	5,934	2,099	534	50.63	34.20	12.09	3.08
6B	15,417	8,393	5,089	1,647	288	54.44	33.01	10.68	1.87
7A	13,814	8,025	4,440	1,182	167	58.09	32.14	8.56	1.21
7B	10,965	6,788	3,336	719	122	61.91	30.42	6.56	1.11
8A	8,948	5,805	2,565	491	87	64.87	28.67	5.49	.97
8B	7,319	4,745	2,066	439	69	64.83	28.23	6.00	.94
Total	215,333	120,618	62,247	22,547	9,921	56.01	28.91	10.47	4.61

The largest number of pupils between one and two years over age is in the 6A grade, 5,934; the number of such pupils decreases with each succeeding grade to 2,066, in the 8B. The largest number of pupils between two and three years over age is in the 5A, 2,731; the number then falls to 439, in the 8B. The largest number of pupils three years and more over age is in the 4B grade, 1,329; the number declines with each succeeding grade until there are but sixty-nine such pupils in the 8B grade. It therefore appears that pupils between one and two years over age drop from school in increasing numbers after the 6B grade; that pupils between two and three years over age leave after the 5A; and that pupils three and more years over age find it increasingly difficult to remain in school after the 4B.

Of the total number of over-age pupils in each grade, the per cent. under one year over age is the highest in the 1A, being 68.96 per cent.; this falls to 47.49 per cent. in the 5A, and then rises to 64.87 per cent. in the 8A. The per cent. between one and two years over age rises gradually from 20.56 per cent. in the 1B to 34.20 per cent. in the 6A, and then falls to 28.23 per cent. in the 8B. The per cent. between two and three years over age is the lowest in the 1A, 5.34 per cent.; this rises to 14.65 per cent. in the 5A; and falls to 5.49 per cent. in the 8A. The per cent. three and more years over age rises from 3.95 per cent. in the 1B to 7.51 per cent. in the 3B, then gradually diminishes to .94 of 1 per cent. in the 8B Judged by the length of the period pupils are over normal, over age is, therefore, the least serious in the 1A grade; grows increasingly serious to the 5A-5B grades; and thereafter gradually declines in seriousness to the 8B, but never becomes less serious than in the 1A grade.

The full significance of 215,333 pupils being over age lies, therefore, in the fact that, of these 215,333 pupils, 120,618 are behind their grade less than one year; 62,247 between one and two years; 22,547 between two and three years; and 9,921 three years and more, and also in the fact that the tendency among these children—especially among those behind their grade because of failure to be advanced regularly—to fail to complete the work of the elementary school keeps pace with the extent to which they are over age.

RATE OF PROMOTION FOR OVER-AGE PUPILS

On the assumption that school conditions were the same for both classes of children, a materially lower rate of promotion at the end of the February-June term, 1911, for over-age children than for children of normal age can be attributed to lack of capacity among over-age children, or to home conditions which prevent them from doing their best work, or to both.

Table XXXIX gives by grades the rate of promotion at the end of the February-June term, 1911, for pupils under normal age, for pupils of normal age, and for over-age pupils.[1] (See page 149.)

The rate of promotion in the 1A grade was lower for children under normal and of normal age than for over-age pupils. The higher rate of promotion for over-age 1A pupils might be due to the fact that, though the native ability of over-age children is less than that of children under normal age and of normal age, the greater maturity of over-age children enables them to do better the work of the 1A. Should investigation prove this to be true, there would be ample grounds for modifying, in favor of children under normal and of normal age, the work of the 1A grade.

In each of the grades 1A-4B, inclusive, with the exception of the 4A, the rate of promotion was higher for normal pupils than for pupils under normal. From the 5B on, however, the higher rate in each grade was for children

[1] With the data at hand it was impossible to distinguish between pupils over age because of late entrance and pupils over age because of slow progress in school.

under normal age. It therefore appears that children under normal age, although they must have greater native ability, do not do as well in the lower grades, as a rule (probably because of immaturity), as pupils of normal age, but that

TABLE XXXIX

RATE OF PROMOTION

Grades	For Pupils Under Normal Age	For Pupils of Normal Age	For Over-Age Pupils	Rate of Promotion for Pupils of Normal Age over Rate of Promotion for Over-Age Pupils
1A.........	53.62	75.69	79.76	—4.07
1B.........	76.36	89.72	85.14	4.58
2A.........	88.04	90.51	85.34	5.17
2B.........	91.02	92.40	85.95	6.45
3A.........	89.42	92.28	85.68	6.60
3B.........	92.09	93.74	85.87	7.87
4A.........	94.62	93.70	85.63	8.07
4B.........	92.91	94.19	85.47	8.72
5A.........	94.91	94.00	83.79	10.21
5B.........	94.70	94.40	84.86	9.54
6A.........	95.56	94.16	84.30	9.86
6B.........	95.76	94.23	84.44	9.79
7A.........	93.56	92.73	83.10	9.63
7B.........	95.12	92.40	84.70	7.70
8A.........	93.68	92.49	85.28	7.21
8B.........	96.92	96.04	91.61	4.43
Total......	92.24	90.84	85.03	5.81

younger pupils (owing doubtless to superior capacity) do better than pupils of normal age in each of the grades from the 5A to the 8B.

With the exception of the 1A grade, the rate of promotion was higher in each grade from 4.43 per cent. to 10.21 per cent. for pupils of normal age than for over-age pupils. By reason of this lower rate of promotion, it would seem that over-age pupils have decidedly less capacity for regular school work than pupils of normal age, or enjoy decidedly less favorable home surroundings, or have both less capacity and less favorable home surroundings. Investigation should be made to determine whether this difference in rate of promotion for normal pupils and for over-age pupils is due to home surroundings or to difference in capacity for regular school work; also to what extent over age is due to late entrance and to what extent it is due to failure to be regularly promoted.

There is no reason to suppose that the lower rate of promotion prevailing among over-age children was exceptional for the February-June term, 1911. Hence, it would appear that the factors, whether late entrance, lack of capacity, or conditions in the home, or in the school, which cause the child to become over age continue to operate, with the result that over-age children tend to fall farther and farther behind. The cumulative effect of over age is shown by Table XL.

Whether the decidedly lower rate of promotion, with the exception of the 1A grade, for over-age pupils, and the decided decrease in the rate of promotion with each increase in the length of the period of over age, are due to lack of capacity, to home conditions, or to conditions in the school, or to all these factors together, this lower rate is evidence of the wisdom of the special classes ("E" classes) in which special attention and direction are given to over-age pupils; also evidence of the need of increased provisions for over-age children. The 9,921 pupils on register June 30, 1911, three and more years over age, the 22,547 between two and three years behind their grades, and the 62,247 between one and two years over age would certainly profit from special attention. It does not follow, however, that these over-age pupils should all be put in "E" classes, which add approximately 50 per cent. to the cost of educating an elementary school pupil. An investigation should be made in each case to determine to what extent over age is due to late entrance and to what extent

TABLE XL

NUMBER PROMOTED JUNE 30, 1911, OUT OF EACH ONE HUNDRED PUPILS ON REGISTER

Grades	Of Normal Age	Under One Year Over Normal	Between 1 and 2 Years Over Normal	Between 2 and 3 Years Over Normal	3 Years and More Over Normal
1A	76	79	81	78	84
1B	90	85	85	85	87
2A	91	86	84	83	84
2B	92	87	85	84	82
3A	92	87	84	82	81
3B	94	88	85	83	82
4A	94	88	85	81	79
4B	94	88	84	81	79
5A	94	88	82	79	74
5B	94	88	84	79	72
6A	94	88	82	78	71
6B	94	88	82	76	79
7A	93	85	81	78	74
7B	92	86	83	81	84
8A	92	87	83	78	79
8B	96	93	90	86	88
Total	91	87	83	80	79

it is due to slow progress, that is, to retardation. For it is obvious that the treatment of a group of pupils over age by reason of late entrance and who have received promotion regularly should be different from the treatment of a group of pupils over age because of failure to be regularly promoted.

Further, earnest consideration should be given to the question of whether or not large numbers of over-age pupils (over age merely because of late entrance) and of retarded pupils (over age because of failure to be promoted) could not be cared for quite as well through segregating them into classes of standard size and adapting the course of study to their abilities and needs, hence without increased expense, as through segregating them into "E" classes as now organized and conducted and increasing the cost by 50 per cent.

OVER AGE AS A FACTOR IN NON-PROMOTION AND CONGESTION

When over age is taken as the expression of certain persistent conditions, the extent to which it is a factor in increasing the number of non-promotions, and hence in increasing congestion, is shown by Table XLI. This table gives the actual number of over-age pupils non-promoted, the number that would have been non-promoted at the rate of non-promotion for pupils of normal age, the decrease

TABLE XLI

NON-PROMOTIONS AMONG OVER-AGE PUPILS

Grades	Actual Number of Non-Promotions	Number of Non-Promotions at Rate of Non-Promotion for Pupils of Normal Age	Decrease in Number of Non-Promotions at Rate of Non-Promotion for Pupils of Normal Age	Per Cent. of Decrease in Non-Promotions at Rate of Non-Promotion for Pupils of Normal Age
1A.......	1,157	1,390	—233	—20.14
1B.......	1,367	946	421	30.80
2A.......	1,585	1,026	559	35.27
2B.......	1,744	943	801	45.93
3A.......	2,094	1,129	965	46.08
3B.......	2,287	1,013	1,274	55.71
4A.......	2,595	1,138	1,457	56.15
4B.......	2,648	1,059	1,589	60.01
5A.......	3,022	1,118	1,904	63.00
5B.......	2,670	988	1,682	63.00
6A.......	2,724	1,013	1,711	62.81
6B.......	2,399	890	1,509	62.90
7A.......	2,335	1,004	1,331	57.00
7B.......	1,678	833	845	50.36
8A.......	1,317	672	645	48.97
8B.......	614	290	324	52.77
Total....	32,236	15,452	16,784	52.07

and also the per cent. of decrease in the number of non-promotions at the rate of non-promotion for pupils of normal age. (See page 152.)

Had the rate of non-promotion been the same for over-age pupils as for normal pupils, there would have been a reduction in each grade, with the exception of the 1A, in the number of over-age pupils not promoted. The reduction would have varied from 30.80 per cent. in the 1B to 63 per cent. in the 5B. While there would have been more non-promotions in the 1A by 233, there would have been a total net reduction in non-promotions of 16,784, or 52.07 per cent.—equivalent to one less non-promotion to each thirteen over-age pupils on register. Over age—as the expression of persistent conditions—is, therefore, an important factor in increasing the number of non-promotions, and hence in increasing the amount of congestion.

CONCLUSIONS

The conclusions from the foregoing discussion may be thus summarized:

(1) There were 215,333 over-age pupils in regular classes at the end of the February-June term, 1911, or 37.87 per cent. of all pupils on register in regular classes were behind the grade for their age.

(2) Of the 215,333 over-age pupils, 120,618, or 56.01 per cent., were less than one year over age; 62,247, or 28.91 per cent., between one and two years; 22,547, or 10.47 per cent., between two and three years; and 9,921, or 4.61 per cent., three years and more.

(3) Pupils between one and two years over age drop from school in increasing numbers after the 6B grade; those between two and three years over age begin to leave after the 5B, and those three years and more over age find

it increasingly difficult to remain in school after the 4B grade.

(4) Judged by the length of the period pupils are over normal, over age is the least serious in the 1A grade; grows increasingly serious to the 5A-5B grades; and thereafter gradually declines in seriousness to the 8B, but never becomes less serious than in the 1A grade.

(5) In each of the grades 1A-4B, inclusive, with the exception of the 4A, the rate of promotion was higher for normal pupils than for pupils under normal age. From the 5B on, however, the higher rate in each grade was for pupils under normal age.

(6) With the exception of the 1A grade, the rate of promotion was higher in each grade from 4.43 per cent. to 10.21 per cent. for pupils of normal age than for over-age pupils.

(7) When over age is viewed as the expression of the lack of ability among children, or of the failure of the school to adapt its requirements to the abilities of pupils, or of unfavorable home conditions, or of these and other factors together, over age is cumulative; that is, over-age children tend to fall farther and farther behind.

(8) Over age is a decided factor in increasing the number of non-promotions, and hence increasing the amount of congestion.

In view of these facts, we recommend:

(1) That classes in which special attention and direction are given to over-age pupils be provided at least for all pupils two and more years behind their grade.

(2) That an investigation be made of the pupils now in "E" classes to determine to what extent the over

age of the pupils in these classes is due to late entrance and to what extent it is due to slow progress or retardation; and to determine to what extent the pupils in the classes are classified and the instruction given is determined according as they are over age because of late entrance or slow progress.

(3) That before additional "E" classes are organized serious consideration be given to the question of whether or not large numbers of over-age children cannot be better provided for through segregating them into classes of standard size (hence causing no increase in cost) and through adapting the course of study to their abilities and needs, than through segregating them into "E" classes as now organized and conducted and increasing the cost.

(4) That data be collected and so reported that it will not only be possible to determine the exact amount of over age, but to determine to what extent over age is due to late entrance and to what extent it is due to slow progress or retardation.

CHAPTER X

INABILITY TO USE THE ENGLISH LANGUAGE AND NON-PROMOTION

THERE are thousands of pupils enrolled in the elementary schools of the City of New York who are foreign born, or who are of foreign-born parentage. To a large proportion of these children the English language is essentially a foreign language. Classes have been organized—"C" classes—to give special help to such children, to the end that they may more quickly acquire a working knowledge of the English language and be prepared, at an early date, to take their place in regular classes. Despite the help given by "C" classes,[1] there are pupils in regular classes who, in the opinion of the teachers, have such difficulty in understanding and in using the English language that this interferes with their progress through the school.

NUMBER OF PUPILS IN REGULAR CLASSES UNABLE TO USE THE ENGLISH LANGUAGE

The number of pupils in regular classes as of June 30, 1911, whose inability to use the English language was, in the opinion of teachers, interfering with their school progress is shown in Table XLII. This table gives by grades the number of pupils unable to use the English language, the per cent. of the register of each grade unable to use the English language, also the per cent. of all such pupils in each grade. (See page 157.)

It will be observed that there were 8,739 pupils, or 1.54

[1] 2,689 pupils were on register in "C" classes June 30, 1911. Annual Report of the City Superintendent of Schools for 1911, page 67.

per cent. of the total register in regular classes, whose inability to use the English language was such, in the opinion of the teachers, as to interfere with their school work. Of these 8,739 pupils unable to use the English language, over one-half—55.87 per cent.—were in the 1A and 1B grades (3,648, or 41.74 per cent., in the 1A and 1,235, or 14.13 per cent., in the 1B); in the 1A-3B grades together there were 6,986, or 79.94 per cent. The remaining 1,753, or 20.06 per cent., were in the grades 4A-8B, ranging from 354, or 4.05 per cent., in the 4A to eleven, or .13 of 1 per cent., in the 8B grade. It will be observed that the per cent. of the total register unable to use the English language is the highest in the 1A grade, being 8.48 per cent., and that the per cent. decreases from 2.48 per cent. in the 1B to .06 of 1 per cent. in the 8B.

TABLE XLII

Grades	Total Register in Regular Classes as of June 30, 1911	Number of Pupils Unable to Use the English Language	Per Cent. of the Register of Each Grade Unable to Use the English Language	Per Cent. of All Pupils Unable to Use the English Language in Each Grade	Cumulative Per Cent.
1A..........	43,012	3,648	8.48	41.74	41.74
1B..........	49,832	1,235	2.48	14.13	55.87
2A..........	39,607	649	1.64	7.43	63.30
2B..........	44,608	556	1.25	6.36	69.66
3A..........	40,180	475	1.18	5.44	75.10
3B..........	42,911	423	.99	4.84	79.94
4A..........	38,573	354	.92	4.05	83.99
4B..........	39,909	404	1.01	4.62	88.61
5A..........	36,823	388	1.05	4.44	93.05
5B..........	36,035	232	.64	2.65	95.70
6A..........	32,873	165	.50	1.89	97.59
6B..........	31,134	46	.15	.53	98.12
7A..........	27,667	48	.17	.55	98.67
7B..........	24,791	85	.34	.97	99.64
8A..........	21,112	20	.09	.23	99.87
8B..........	19,545	11	.06	.13	100.00
Total........	568,612	8,739	1.54	.....	.....

EFFECT OF INABILITY TO USE THE ENGLISH LANGUAGE ON RATE OF PROMOTION

The number of pupils in each grade unable to use the English language is, therefore, relatively small. Hence, whatever the rate of promotion for such pupils, this would affect but slightly the rate of promotion for the grade as a whole. Just what the effect of the presence of such pupils in regular classes was on the rate of promotion for the grade as a whole at the end of the February-June term,

TABLE XLIII

Grades	Rate of Promotion for Pupils Able to Use the English Language	Rate of Promotion in Regular Classes—Includes Both Pupils Able and Unable to Use the English Language	Difference in Rate of Promotion in Regular Classes Due to the Presence of Pupils Unable to Use the English Language
1A	77.56	76.02	1.54
1B	89.16	88.74	.42
2A	89.24	89.04	.20
2B	90.76	90.58	.18
3A	89.92	89.79	.13
3B	90.85	90.74	.11
4A	90.07	89.95	.12
4B	90.30	90.18	.12
5A	88.97	88.86	.11
5B	89.77	89.74	.03
6A	89.08	89.02	.06
6B	89.50	89.44	.06
7A	88.02	87.96	.06
7B	89.20	89.12	.08
8A	89.56	89.52	.04
8B	94.48	94.45	.03
Total	88.99	88.68	.31

1911, is shown by Table XLIII. This table gives by grades the rate of promotion at the end of the February-June term, 1911, for pupils able to use the English language; the rate of promotion in regular classes (includes both pupils able and pupils unable to use the English language); and the difference in the rate of promotion in regular classes due to the presence of pupils unable to use the English language.

Had there been no pupils in regular classes unable to use the English language the rate of promotion at the end of the February-June term, 1911, would have been somewhat higher in every grade. It would have been higher in the 1A by 1.54 per cent.; in the 1B by .42 of 1 per cent.; and higher in the remaining grades by from .03 of 1 per cent. to .20 of 1 per cent. Such differences—even that in the 1A grade—are very small. Hence, the presence of pupils in regular classes unable to use the English language had no material effect on the rate of promotion at the end of the February-June term, 1911, for the grade as a whole.

RATE OF PROMOTION FOR PUPILS ABLE AND FOR PUPILS UNABLE TO USE THE ENGLISH LANGUAGE

Nevertheless, inability to use the English language materially affects the school progress of children. This will be seen, if the rate of promotion for pupils able to use the English language is compared with the rate of promotion for pupils unable to use it.

Table XLIV gives by grades the rate of promotion at the end of the February-June term, 1911, for pupils able to use the English language; the rate of promotion for pupils unable to use the English language; also the difference in the rate of promotion in favor of pupils able to use the English language.

The rate of promotion at the end of the February-June term, 1911, for pupils able to use the English language was higher, it will be observed, in every grade, from 4.49 per cent. to 58.12 per cent., than for pupils unable to use it. The greatest difference in the rate of promotion for these two classes of children was in certain of the higher grades. By reason of the number of pupils affected, the smaller difference in the lower grades is, however, more significant. When measured by the difference in the rate of promotion, inability to use the English language seriously interferes, therefore, in regular classes, with the

TABLE XLIV

Grades	Rate of Promotion for Pupils Able to Use the English Language	Rate of Promotion for Pupils Unable to Use the English Language	Difference in Rate of Promotion in Favor of Pupils Able to Use the English Language
1A	77.56	59.10	18.46
1B	89.16	72.06	17.10
2A	89.24	77.81	11.43
2B	90.76	76.62	14.14
3A	89.92	79.16	10.76
3B	90.85	79.43	11.42
4A	90.07	76.84	13.23
4B	90.30	78.22	12.08
5A	88.97	78.35	10.62
5B	89.77	84.48	5.29
6A	89.08	76.36	12.72
6B	89.50	52.17	37.33
7A	88.02	54.17	33.85
7B	89.20	84.71	4.49
8A	89.56	55.00	34.56
8B	94.48	36.36	58.12
Total	88.99	69.05	19.94

child's chances of promotion, lessening his chances from 4.49 per cent. to 58.12 per cent.

The decidedly lower rate of promotion for pupils unable to use the English language is evidence of the wisdom of special classes ("C" classes) for the instruction of such children; and the number of such children at the end of the February-June term in the regular classes, particularly of the 1A-3B grades—6,986—indicates that the number of "C" classes should be greatly increased. It also emphasizes the necessity of providing a flexible course of study so that, where there is need, additional time may be devoted in regular classes to giving children a working knowledge of the English language.

INABILITY TO USE THE ENGLISH LANGUAGE AS A FACTOR IN NON-PROMOTION AND IN CONGESTION

The actual effect on the number of non-promotions of the lower rate of promotion for pupils unable to use the English language is shown by Table XLV. This table gives by grades the number of non-promotions among pupils unable to use the English language, the number of non-pro-

TABLE XLV

NON-PROMOTION AMONG PUPILS UNABLE TO USE THE ENGLISH LANGUAGE

Grades	Actual Number of Non-Promotions	Number of Non-Promotions at Rate of Non-Promotion for Pupils Able to Use the English Language	Decrease in Number of Non-Promotions at Rate of Promotion for Pupils Able to Use the English Language	Per Cent. of Decrease in Non-Promotion at Rate of Non-Promotion for Pupils Able to Use the English Language
1A.......	1,481	819	662	44.70
1B.......	345	134	211	61.16
2A.......	144	70	74	51.39
2B.......	130	51	79	60.77
3A.......	99	48	51	51.52
3B.......	87	39	48	55.17
4A.......	82	35	47	57.32
4B.......	88	39	49	55.68
5A.......	84	43	41	48.81
5B.......	36	24	12	33.33
6A.......	39	18	21	53.85
6B.......	22	5	17	77.27
7A.......	22	6	16	72.73
7B.......	30	9	21	70.00
8A.......	9	2	7	77.78
8B.......	7	1	6	85.71
Total....	2,705	1,343	1,362	50.35

motions there would have been among such pupils at the rate of non-promotion for pupils able to use the English language, also the decrease and the per cent. of decrease in the number of non-promotions among such pupils at the rate of non-promotion for pupils able to use the English language.

Had the rate of non-promotion been the same as for pupils able to use the English language there would have been, among pupils unable to use the English language, a decrease in every grade in the number of non-promotions. The decrease would have varied from six in the 8B to 662 in the 1A, and the per cent. of decrease would have ranged from 33.33 per cent. to 85.71 per cent.; while, in all the grades together, there would have been 1,362 fewer non-promotions, or a decrease of 50.35 per cent.—the equivalent of one less non-promotion to each six pupils on register unable to use the English language.

When viewed in relation to the number of pupils involved, inability to use the English language is, therefore, a decided factor in increasing the number of non-promotions, but, because of the relatively small number of such children, it contributes very slightly in the lower and probably not at all in the upper grades to congestion.

CONCLUSIONS

The foregoing discussion is summarized in the following conclusions:

(1) The presence of pupils in the regular classes of a grade unable to use the English language had no material effect, at the end of the February-June term, 1911, on the rate of promotion for the grade as a whole.

(2) But the rate of promotion for pupils able to use the English language was higher in each of the grades, from 4.49 per cent. to 58.12 per cent., than for pupils unable to use the English language.

(3) When viewed in relation to the number of pupils involved, inability to use the English language is a decided factor in increasing the number of non-promotions, but, because of the relatively small number of such children, it contributes to congestion only slightly in the lower and probably not at all in the upper grades.

(4) Although the presence of pupils in regular classes unable to use the English language, because of the relatively small number of such pupils, does not affect the rate of promotion for a grade as a whole or add materially to congestion, inability to use the English language does affect decidedly the school progress of those pupils who are unable to use the English language. In view of the conclusions stated above, we recommend:

(1) That "C" classes—classes for the instruction of pupils unable to use the English language—be provided at once, at least for all pupils in the 1A grade unable to use the English language.

(2) That the course of study be made so flexible that, where there is need, additional time may be devoted in regular classes to aiding children to acquire a working knowledge of the English language.

CHAPTER XI

PART TIME AND NON-PROMOTION

MEANING OF WHOLE TIME AND PART TIME

OWING to the chronic lack of sufficient schoolrooms there have developed in the elementary schools of the city two kinds of classes—whole-time classes and part-time classes. Children in whole-time classes are in school the standard day—five hours; hence each whole-time class requires one schoolroom. Children in part-time classes are in school but three hours and three-quarters;[1] hence two part-time classes are accommodated in one room on the same day. By putting large numbers of children on part time it has been possible to provide, in a way, for all the children admitted to the elementary schools of the city.

CONDITIONS GIVING RISE TO PART TIME

In addition to the increase in register, three policies of the Board of Education (all to be highly commended) have contributed to make the number of pupils (68,610) on part time June 30, 1911, larger than the number (35,347) on part time June 30, 1902: (1) The policy inaugurated in 1903 of admitting to school all children of school age. Prior to 1903 when a school was full the principal might, at his discretion, refuse admission. In consequence, there was in nearly every school in crowded districts a waiting list. It was not uncommon for a child to be on this list a half year and even a whole year. (2) The policy of re-

[1] Manual of the Board of Education, Sec. 45, 10; page 59.

ducing "classes of enormous and irrational sizes"—classes having from one hundred to one hundred and fifty pupils; also of reducing the register of all regular classes to fifty and less. (3) The policy of providing special classes for over-age, backward, and defective children.[1] Part time, as it now exists in the city, is, therefore, not only the result of the continued failure to provide adequate school accommodations for the increase in register, but also to provide adequate accommodations to carry into effect the educational policies of the Board of Education.

DIFFERENT ATTITUDES TOWARD PART TIME

The school authorities have, as a rule, looked with favor on part time as a means of doing, under adverse conditions, the most for the greatest number of school children; but have regarded part time in itself as an evil which should be abolished whenever school accommodations became adequate to give each child a full day's schooling of the kind best suited to his needs.

The cost of providing modern school accommodations, the presence at times of part-time classes even in the sixth grade, and differences of opinion among theorists on the proper length of the school day for young children have led some persons to believe that, while part time is an evil in the upper grades, it is preferable to whole time in the two lowest grades; and hence, on both economic and educational grounds, should be made universal in the 1A and 1B grades. That is, it is maintained by some persons that the standard school day for all children in the 1A and 1B grades should be three and a half hours; and the time of attending school so arranged that one schoolroom will accommodate two classes—one class to attend in the forenoon only, the other in the afternoon only.[2]

[1] Annual Report of the City Superintendent of Schools for 1905, pages 53-55; also for 1911, page 47.

[2] See Annual Report of the City Superintendent of Schools, 1904, page 78.

PART TIME AT END OF FEBRUARY-JUNE TERM, 1911

The number of pupils in part-time classes at the end of the February-June term, 1911, and hence the number affected by part time, is given in Table XLVI. This table gives by grades the total register before promotion in the regular classes of the elementary school as of June 30, 1911, the register in whole-time classes, and the per cent. of the total register in whole-time classes; also the register in part-time classes, the per cent. of the total register in part-time classes, and the per cent. of all part-time pupils in the classes of each grade.

TABLE XLVI

Grades	Total Register in Regular Classes as of June 30, 1911	Register in Whole-Time Classes as of June 30, 1911	Per Cent. of the Total Register in Whole-Time Classes June 30, 1911	Register in Part-Time Classes as of June 30, 1911	Per Cent. of the Total Register in Part-Time Classes June 30, 1911	Per Cent. of All Part-Time Pupils in Each Grade	Cumulative Per Cent.
1A	43,012	26,110	60.71	16,902	39.29	24.64	24.64
1B	49,832	34,056	68.34	15,776	31.66	22.99	47.63
2A	39,607	30,377	76.70	9,230	23.30	13.45	61.08
2B	44,608	36,301	81.38	8,307	18.62	12.11	73.19
3A	40,180	34,487	85.83	5,693	14.17	8.30	81.49
3B	42,911	37,868	88.25	5,043	11.75	7.35	88.84
4A	38,573	35,320	91.57	3,253	8.43	4.74	93.58
4B	39,909	37,568	94.13	2,341	5.87	3.41	96.99
5A	36,823	35,624	96.74	1,199	3.26	1.75	98.74
5B	36,035	35,357	98.12	678	1.88	.99	99.73
6A	32,873	32,727	99.56	146	.44	.21	99.94
6B	31,134	31,092	99.87	42	.13	.06	100.00
7A	27,667	27,667	100.00	......	......	......	......
7B	24,791	24,791	100.00	......	......	......	......
8A	21,112	21,112	100.00	......	......	......	......
8B	19,545	19,545	100.00	......	......	......	......
Total	568,612	500,002	87.93	68,610	12.07	......	......

QUESTIONS INVOLVED IN PART TIME

The questions involved in part time may be thus stated: Do the best interests of children demand that each child, in whatever grade, shall enjoy a whole day's schooling? Or can the interests of children be equally well conserved by universalizing part time in the 1A and 1B grades, thereby doing away with it above the 1B grade? Or are the best in-

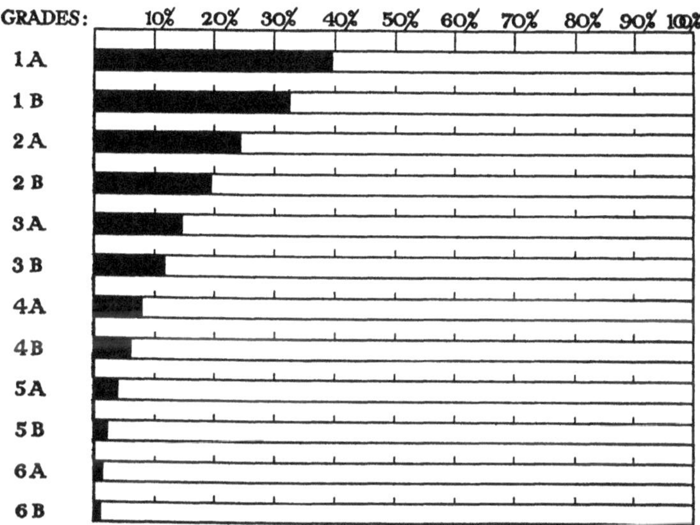

Fig. 4. Black indicates the per cent. of the register of each grade on part time.

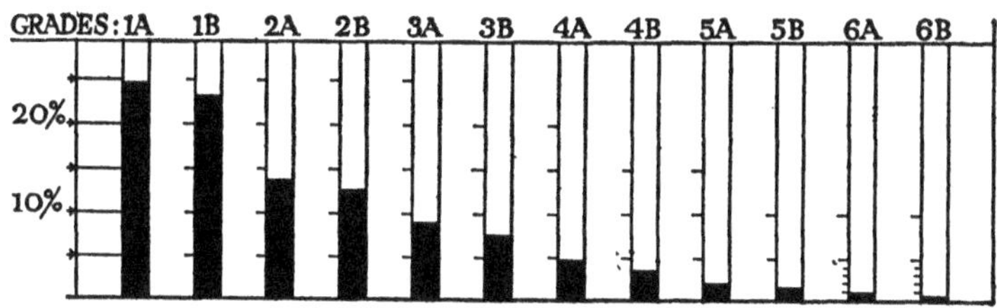

Fig. 5. Black indicates the per cent. of all part-time pupils in each grade.

terests of children conserved by permitting them, as now, to be in part-time classes one or more terms in the grades below 7A? In a word, is part time an evil in all grades? Or is it an evil only above the 1B grade? Or does it do children in the elementary school no harm to be on part time one term or more?

A definite answer to these questions would require an investigation exceeding the means and the time at the disposal of the present inquiry. It would need to consider the problem from at least three points of view—the physical, the educational, and the social or ethical. It would be necessary, among other things, (1) to measure the effect of the two kinds of classes on the health and physical development of children; (2) to examine the school achievements of the children in each kind of class; and (3) to study the differences in the interests, habits, and conduct of children in school the whole day (five hours) and of children in school only a part of the day (three hours and three-quarters).

With the time and means at our disposal it has been possible, in addition to holding conferences with principals and teachers, to collect data on but one phase of the educational aspect of the problem—the rate of promotion in the two kinds of classes.

RATE OF PROMOTION IN WHOLE-TIME AND IN PART-TIME CLASSES

Table XLVII gives by grades, both for whole-time classes and for part-time classes, the per cent. of the register as of June 30, 1911, promoted and the per cent. not promoted; also the per cent. of promotion in whole-time classes over or under the per cent. of promotion in part-time classes. (See page 169.)

In the twelve grades in which there were both whole- and part-time classes it will be observed that the rate of promotion in whole-time classes was higher than in part-time classes in nine and lower in three grades. The rate of promotion was lower in whole-time classes in the 4A, the 4B, and the 6B grades and higher in the 1A-3B, the 5A, the

5B, and the 6A grades. The largest difference was in the 6A, where 4.78 per cent. more pupils were promoted in whole-time classes than in part-time classes. A difference in the rate of promotion in the lower grades is, however, more significant than in the higher grades, because 88.84 per cent of all part-time pupils are in the 1A-3B grades,[1]

TABLE XLVII

Grades	Whole-Time Classes		Part-Time Classes		Per Cent. of Promotion in Whole-Time Classes Over or Under Per Cent. of Promotion in Part-Time Classes
	Per Cent. of Register as of June 30, 1911, Promoted	Per Cent. of Register as of June 30, 1911, Not Promoted	Per Cent. of Register as of June 30, 1911, Promoted	Per Cent. of Register as of June 30, 1911, Not Promoted	
1A......	76.96	23.04	74.56	25.44	2.40
1B......	88.87	11.13	88.45	11.55	.42
2A......	89.29	10.71	88.24	11.76	1.05
2B......	90.86	9.14	89.39	10.61	1.47
3A......	89.87	10.13	89.34	10.66	.53
3B......	90.84	9.16	90.03	9.97	.81
4A......	89.91	10.09	90.32	9.68	—.41
4B......	90.16	9.84	90.43	9.57	—.27
5A......	88.94	11.06	86.32	13.68	2.62
5B......	89.74	10.26	89.38	10.62	.36
6A......	89.03	10.97	84.25	15.75	4.78
6B......	89.45	10.55	90.48	9.52	—1.03
7A......	87.97	12.03	.....	.....	......
7B......	89.12	10.88	.....	.....	......
8A......	89.52	10.48	.....	.....	......
8B......	94.44	5.56	.....	.....	......

and in each of these grades the rate of promotion was lower in part-time than in whole-time classes.

The significance of the higher rate of promotion in whole-time classes than in the part-time classes in nine out of twelve grades is clearly seen if the actual number of pupils promoted in part-time classes is compared with the

[1] See Table XLVI, page 166.

number that would have been promoted had the rate of promotion, grade for grade, been the same in part-time as in whole-time classes.

Table XLVIII gives by grades the register in part-time classes as of June 30, 1911, the number in part-time classes promoted, June 30, 1911, and the number that would have been promoted at the rate in whole-time classes; and also the difference between the last two numbers.

TABLE XLVIII

Grades	Register in Part-Time Classes as of June 30, 1911	Number in Part-Time Classes Promoted, June 30, 1911	Number in Part-Time Classes Who Would Have Been Promoted at the Rate in Whole-Time Classes	Increase in Number That Would Have Been Promoted at the Rate in Whole-Time Classes
1A.........	16,902	12,602	13,008	406
1B.........	15,776	13,954	14,020	66
2A.........	9,230	8,145	8,241	96
2B.........	8,307	7,426	7,548	122
3A.........	5,693	5,086	5,116	30
3B.........	5,043	4,540	4,581	41
4A.........	3,253	2,938	2,925	—13
4B.........	2,341	2,117	2,111	—6
5A.........	1,199	1,035	1,066	31
5B.........	678	606	608	2
6A.........	146	123	130	7
6B.........	42	38	38	0
Total......	68,610	58,610	59,392	782 (Net Increase)

Had the rate of promotion been the same in the part-time classes of the 1A grade as it was in the whole-time classes of this grade the number of part-time promotions would have been increased, it will be observed, by 406; in the 1A-3B grades, which contain 88.84 per cent. of all part-time pupils, by 731; and in part-time classes as a whole there would have been a net increase of 782. That is, the lower rate of promotion prevailing in part-time classes resulted in the 1A grade in one less promotion to each forty-one 1A pupils; in the 1A-3B grades in one less promotion to each eighty-three pupils in these grades; and in part-time classes as a whole in one less promotion to each eighty-seven part-time pupils. Rate of promotion taken by itself is not a satisfactory measure of school achievements; because, as stated above, promotions are at times made for other reasons than that pupils are prepared for the work of the next grade—i. e., because of the crowded conditions of a school. Hence, there is no reason to believe that the school achievements of pupils promoted in part-time classes were higher by reason of the lower rate than the achievements of pupils promoted in whole-time classes. Indeed, since part time indicates congestion, and congestion may tend to "forced" promotions, it is quite probable that the achievements of the pupils promoted in part-time classes were not higher, to say the least, than the achievements of pupils promoted in whole-time classes.

PART TIME AS A FACTOR IN NON-PROMOTION AND CONGESTION

The lower rate of promotion prevailing at the end of the February-June term, 1911, in part-time classes resulted, as we have seen, in but 782 fewer promotions out of a total of 68,610 part-time pupils than would have been the case had the rate of promotion been the same as in whole-time classes.[1] Hence, the *direct effect* of part time on promotions, as promotions were made at the end of the February-June term, 1911, was small. There may, however, be certain important *indirect effects,* such as indifference to school work, bad conduct, and truancy, which affect materially the future progress of children. These possible indirect effects of part time should be thoroughly investigated.

If part time was a small factor in increasing the number

[1] See Table XLVIII, page 170.

of non-promotions at the end of the February-June term, 1911, it was a still smaller factor in contributing to congestion. At most, owing to the lower rate of promotion prevailing in part-time classes, there were but 782 additional pupils left in the several grades to augment the numbers in these grades in September. There is every reason to believe that these 782 additional pupils, distributed as they were among nine different grades, were all absorbed without the formation of a single additional class and without materially adding to the numbers in any one class.

Part time, therefore, when judged solely in view of promotions as they were made at the end of the February-June term, 1911, is but a slight factor in increasing the number of non-promotions, and probably had no effect on increasing congestion.

KINDS OF PART-TIME CLASSES

In the foregoing discussion the rate of promotion at the end of the February-June term, 1911, in part-time classes has been contrasted with the rate of promotion in whole-time classes; hence, part-time classes have been treated as a whole—that is, as if there were but one kind. There are, however, four different kinds of part-time classes: A. M. part-time classes, P. M. part-time classes, alternating part-time classes, and "Ettinger" part-time classes.

In A. M. part-time classes pupils attend school for at least a term in the forenoon only; in P. M. part-time classes for at least a term in the afternoon only; while in alternating part-time classes pupils attend a part of a term in the forenoon only and a part of a term in the afternoon only.

The length of the school day in these three kinds of part-time classes varies from three hours and three-quarters to four hours. When the day is three hours and three-quarters in length, A. M. part-time classes begin work at 8.30 and stop at 12.15; P. M. part-time classes begin at 12.30 and continue to 4.15. When the school day is four hours, the time is divided thus: A. M. part-time classes, 8.15 to 12.15, and P. M. part-time classes, 12.15 to 4.15. The hours are the same for alternating part-time classes, but the forenoon classes alternate with the afternoon classes. These changes from forenoon to afternoon and from afternoon to forenoon are made in some schools at the end of each fourth week, and in others at the end of each ten weeks.

While three hours and three-quarters to four hours is the length of the school day in these three kinds of part-time classes, pupils in each kind, falling behind and in need of special help, are brought back for an hour to an hour and a quarter for individual instruction. Children in A. M. part-time classes return in the afternoon and children in P. M. part-time classes come in the forenoon. Any available nook or corner of the school building is used for this individual work. In this way a considerable number of the children in these three kinds of part-time classes not only receive a whole day's schooling (five hours), but receive a considerable amount of personal attention.[1]

Ettinger part-time classes are distinguished from A. M., P. M., and alternating part-time classes by the fact that in Ettinger part-time classes the school day is practically five hours in length. Children in Ettinger part-time classes are not under actual instruction five hours per day, but they are under the influence of the school for that length of time daily. This is accomplished by alternating each two classes between a classroom and the "yard." [2] When one class is receiving instruction in the classroom the other is in the "yard," where they have play, physical training, and drill —particularly in the three R's. Each class is thus kept under educative direction the whole day (five hours).[3]

[1] Manual of Board of Education, Section 45, Paragraph 12, page 60.

[2] "Yard" is the term used in New York City to designate that portion of the first floor of a school building which serves as an assembly place for children prior to the opening of school and for play and physical training.

[3] As the yard takes the place of a classroom for a part of the school day, it is obvious that Ettinger part-time classes are to be found only in schools having yards.

The following is an illustrative daily time schedule for two Ettinger part-time classes:

First Class		Second Class	
8:30—10	Classroom	9:30—10	Yard
10: —10:45	Yard	10: —10:45	Classroom
10:45—11:45	Classroom	10:45—11:45	Yard
11:45—12:45	Noon Recess	11:45—12:45	Classroom
12:45— 1:45	Classroom	12:45— 1:45	Noon Recess
1:45— 2:30	Yard	1:45— 3:30	Classroom

The reasons why principals prefer one kind of part time to another kind are revealed in the following quotations taken from special reports from principals to this Committee:

> "I do not believe in alternating the time . . . because it leads to irregular habits of living, both in sleeping and eating. The boys are best in the morning, when they come clean and not all tired out with hard play. I find that the mothers let the girls sleep later for the afternoon work, and they, too, come clean and rested."
>
> "Part-time boys are held to better attendance and less truancy, from homes where the mother is employed, by attendance in the morning classes. If on the street during the forenoon it is hard for the mothers to find the boys at 11.30 for luncheon and prepare them for school."
>
> "The mid-term alternation I have tried thoroughly and found impracticable because of the interference with the formation of habits of punctuality. It is almost impossible to secure regular attendance and a habit of being on time if every ten weeks the time to come changes. It also makes serious trouble for the parents."
>
> "We aim to alternate them [classes] each term. Any more frequent change is troublesome to the home domestic arrangements for luncheon, work hours, etc. Many of the mothers are washerwomen or otherwise

employed . . . and frequent changes discommode them very much."

"I believe, in order to be just to every part-time pupil, it is necessary so to distribute the period of instruction that no classes or group of classes will receive instruction during an entire term only in the afternoon, when physical and mental rhythm are at greater or less ebb. Pupils who report in the afternoon are generally tired because of a morning's play on the street. They are less receptive than those who come in the morning."

NUMBER OF PUPILS IN EACH KIND OF PART-TIME CLASS

The distribution at the end of the February-June term, 1911, of part-time pupils among the several kinds of part-time classes is shown by Table XLIX. This table gives by grades the register and the per cent. of all part-time pupils on register June 30, 1911, in Ettinger part-time classes; also the same facts for alternating part-time classes, for A. M. part-time classes, and for P. M. part-time classes.

The 68,610 pupils on part time June 30, 1911, were distributed as follows: 5,723, or 8.34 per cent., in Ettinger part-time classes; 43,939, or 64.04 per cent., in alternating part-time classes; 9,461, or 13.79 per cent., in A. M. part-time classes; and 9,487, or 13.83 per cent., in P. M. part-time classes. The part-time pupils in each of the grades 1A-3B were distributed in about the same proportion among the different kinds of part-time classes. It will be noted also that there were no pupils in Ettinger part-time classes above the 4A grade, that the per cent. of all part-time pupils of each grade in alternating part-time classes decreases in each of the grades above the 4A, and that there is a corresponding increase in the per cent. in these grades in A. M. and in P. M. part-time classes.

If, therefore, the different kinds of part time are arranged in view of the total number of pupils in each kind June 30, 1911, the order would be as follows (page 177):

TABLE XLIX

Grades	Part-Time Classes								
		Ettinger Part-Time Classes		Alternating Part-Time Classes		Morning Part-Time Classes		Afternoon Part-Time Classes	
	Total Register as of June 30, 1911	Register as of June 30, 1911	Per Cent. of Total Number of Part-Time Pupils in Ettinger Classes	Register as of June 30, 1911	Per Cent. of Total Number of Part-Time Pupils in Alternating Classes	Register as of June 30, 1911	Per Cent. of Total Number of Part-Time Pupils in A.M. Classes	Register as of June 30, 1911	Per Cent. of Total Number of Part-Time Pupils in P.M. Classes
1A	16,902	1,526	9.03	10,693	63.26	2,246	13.29	2,437	14.42
1B	15,776	1,755	11.12	10,111	64.09	1,651	10.47	2,259	14.32
2A	9,230	927	10.04	5,836	63.23	1,147	12.43	1,320	14.30
2B	8,307	552	6.64	5,747	69.18	1,155	13.91	853	10.27
3A	5,693	370	6.50	3,765	66.13	850	14.93	708	12.44
3B	5,043	335	6.64	3,389	67.20	771	15.29	548	10.87
4A	3,253	258	7.93	2,056	63.20	559	17.19	380	11.68
4B	2,341	....	.....	1,431	61.13	501	21.40	409	17.47
5A	1,199	....	.....	516	43.04	333	27.77	350	29.19
5B	678	....	.....	291	42.92	205	30.24	182	26.84
6A	146	....	.....	62	42.47	43	29.45	41	28.08
6B	42	....	.....	42	100.00	....	.....	....	.....
Total	68,610	5,723	8.34	43,939	64.04	9,461	13.79	9,487	13.83

Alternating part-time classes
P. M. part-time classes
A. M. part-time classes
Ettinger part-time classes

This same order also holds, with slight exceptions, for each of the grades.

RATE OF PROMOTION IN A. M. AND IN P. M. PART-TIME CLASSES

Principals are generally agreed that better educational results are obtained in A. M. part-time classes than in P. M. part-time classes. Table L gives by grades the rate of promotion in A. M. and in P. M. part-time classes at the end of the February-June term, 1911; also the rate of promotion in A. M. part-time classes over or under the rate of promotion in P. M. part-time classes.

The rate of promotion was higher, it will be observed, in A. M. part-time classes in all grades, with the exception of the 2A, the 2B, and the 5A, than in P. M. part-time

TABLE L

Grades	Rate of Promotion in A.M. Part-Time Classes	Rate of Promotion in P.M. Part-Time Classes	Rate of Promotion in A.M. Part-Time Classes Over or Under Rate of Promotion in P.M. Part-Time Classes
1A.........	78.85	72.34	6.51
1B.........	89.40	88.36	1.04
2A.........	85.79	86.51	—.72
2B.........	87.36	90.50	—3.14
3A.........	90.58	88.70	1.88
3B.........	89.75	88.69	1.06
4A.........	89.62	87.89	1.73
4B.........	90.02	86.80	3.22
5A.........	82.28	86.00	—3.72
5B.........	90.73	87.36	3.37
6A.........	81.40	78.05	3.35
Total.......	86.13	83.99	2.14

classes, varying from 6.51 per cent. in the 1A to 1.04 per cent. in the 1B; also the total rate in A. M. part-time classes was higher than in P. M. part-time classes by 2.14 per cent. It therefore appears that A. M. part-time classes afford more favorable opportunities for advancement than P. M. part-time classes, and hence, on the assumption that conditions of instruction and standards of promotion were the same in the two kinds of part-time classes—a legitimate assumption—A. M. part-time classes are preferable to P. M. part-time classes.

It is thus possible to compare the rate of promotion in A. M. and in P. M. part-time classes and to judge of the relative efficiency of these two kinds of part time; but it is impossible to compare the rate of promotion in A. M. part-time classes and in P. M. part-time classes separately with the rate of promotion in whole-time classes or in alternating and in Ettinger part-time classes.

The conditions which give rise to part time require that one room accommodate two classes. Hence, that there may be classes which attend school for a term in the forenoon only, there must also be classes which attend school for a term in the afternoon only. A. M. and P. M. part-time classes are, therefore, inseparably connected; they are two parts of a whole and one part cannot exist without the other. Consequently, A. M. and P. M. part-time classes must be combined and viewed as one kind of part time if comparisons are made between the relative efficiency of whole-time classes and different kinds of part-time classes.

RATE OF PROMOTION IN WHOLE-TIME AND IN EACH KIND OF PART-TIME CLASS

Table LI gives by grades[1] the number out of each one hundred pupils on register promoted June 30, 1911, in

[1] There were only sixty-two pupils in the 6A and forty-two in the 6B grades in alternating part-time classes, and only eighty-four pupils in the 6A and none in the 6B of A.M. and P.M. part-time classes combined; hence these grades have been omitted from this table. See table on page 176.

whole-time classes, in Ettinger part-time classes, in alternating part-time classes, and in A. M. and P. M. part-time classes combined:

TABLE LI

Grades	Number Promoted June 30, 1911, Out of Each 100 on Register in Whole-Time Classes	Number Promoted June 30, 1911, Out of Each 100 on Register in Ettinger Part-Time Classes	Number Promoted June 30, 1911, Out of Each 100 on Register in Alternating Part-Time Classes	Number Promoted June 30, 1911, Out of Each 100 on Register in A.M. and P.M. Part-Time Classes Combined
1A.......	77	78	74	75
1B.......	89	91	88	89
2A.......	89	92	89	86
2B.......	91	91	89	89
3A.......	90	92	89	90
3B.......	91	95	90	89
4A.......	90	97	90	89
4B.......	90	..	92	89
5A.......	89	..	89	84
5B.......	90	..	90	89

Whole-Time and Ettinger Part-Time Classes

It will be observed that one more pupil out of each hundred was promoted in the 1A grade in Ettinger part-time classes than in whole-time classes; in the 1B two more; in the 2A three more; in the 3A two more; in the 3B four more; and in the 4A seven more. In the 2B the number promoted was the same in the two kinds of classes. With this one exception, more pupils were promoted in Ettinger part-time classes in each grade in which there were such classes than were promoted in whole-time classes in the same grades.

Judged solely by rate of promotion, Ettinger part-time classes appear to be preferable to whole-time classes. But part of the difference in rate of promotion in favor of Ettinger part-time classes may be due to the difference in the number of pupils on register. There were, for example, in 1A whole-time classes, 26,115 pupils and in 1A Ettinger part-time classes 1,526; in 3B whole-time classes 37,868, and in 3B Ettinger part-time classes 370. Also part of this difference in rate of promotion might be due to the influence of congestion. Further, rate of promotion throws no light upon the relative educational superiority of these two kinds of classes. To determine their relative superiority would require an extensive investigation, among other things, of the educational achievements, of the punctuality and regularity of attendance, of the school conduct, and of the health of the children in these two kinds of classes. Hence, Ettinger part-time classes cannot be declared preferable to whole-time classes merely on the ground of a higher rate of promotion for the February-June term, 1911.

Whole-Time and Alternating Part-Time Classes

If the promotions in whole-time and alternating part-time classes are compared, it will be observed (a) that in only one grade, the 4B, was the number of pupils promoted per hundred in alternating part-time classes higher than the number promoted in whole-time classes; (b) that the rate of promotion in the 2A, 4A, 5A, and 5B grades was the same; and (c) that, in each of the grades 1A-3B (with the exception of the 2A, as noted above), containing 90 per cent. of all the children in alternating part-time classes, the number of pupils promoted per hundred was less than in whole-time classes. Hence, when judged solely on the basis of the rate of promotion at the end of the February-June term, 1911, alternating part-time classes afford less favorable opportunities for advancement than whole-time classes.

Whole-Time and A. M. and P. M. Part-Time Classes

Further, it will be observed that in two grades, the 1B and the 3A, the number of pupils promoted per hundred in A. M. and P. M. part-time classes combined is the same as in whole-time classes, but that in all other grades the number promoted per hundred pupils is less. Hence, the opportunities for advancement in A. M. and P. M. classes combined are less favorable than in whole-time classes.

Ettinger Part-Time and Alternating and A. M. and P. M. Part-Time Classes

Since the rate of promotion was higher at the end of the February-June term, 1911, in Ettinger part-time classes than in whole-time classes, and the rate of promotion was lower both in alternating part-time classes and in A. M. and P. M. part-time classes combined, it follows that the rate of promotion was higher in Ettinger part-time classes than in either of the two other kinds of part-time classes. Hence, Ettinger part-time classes afford more favorable conditions for advancement than either alternating or A. M. and P. M. part-time classes.

Considering the higher rate of promotion in Ettinger part-time classes, also the fact that in these classes children are under the influence of the school the whole day (five hours), and the favorable experience of teachers and principals with these classes, we are of the opinion that the Board of Education should insist, when part time is necessary, that principals establish, wherever possible, Ettinger part-time classes.[1] At least this should be done until further investigation into the efficiency of the different kinds of part time affords evidence that it is better to do otherwise.

Alternating and A. M. and P. M. Part-Time Classes

Finally, it remains to consider the relative efficiency of alternating and A. M. and P. M. part-time classes. Table LII gives by grades the register as of June 30, 1911, in

[1] Ettinger part-time classes can, of course, be introduced only in schools having suitable yards.

A. M. and P. M. part-time classes combined, the actual number promoted, the number that would have been promoted had the same rate of promotion prevailed in A. M. and P. M. part-time classes as in alternating part-time classes; also the increase in number that would have been promoted at the rate of promotion in alternating part-time classes:

TABLE LII

Grades	Register as of June 30, 1911, in A.M. and P.M. Part-Time Classes Combined	Actual Number Promoted June 30, 1911, in A.M. and P.M. Part-Time Classes Combined	Number That Would Have Been Promoted at the Rate in Alternating Part-Time Classes	Increase in Number That Would Have Been Promoted at the Rate in Alternating Part-Time Classes
1A.........	4,683	3,534	3,452	—82
1B.........	3,910	3,472	3,434	—38
2A.........	2,467	2,126	2,184	58
2B.........	2,008	1,781	1,797	16
3A.........	1,558	1,398	1,384	—14
3B.........	1,319	1,178	1,184	6
4A.........	939	835	846	11
4B.........	910	806	833	27
5A.........	683	575	609	34
5B.........	387	345	347	2
6A.........	84	67	76	9
Total......	18,948	16,117	16,146	29 (Net Increase)

Table LII shows that, had the rate of promotion been the same in A. M. and P. M. part-time classes as in alternating part-time classes, eighty-two fewer pupils would have been promoted in the 1A grade; thirty-eight fewer in the 1B; and fourteen fewer in the 3A; whereas fifty-eight more would have been promoted in the 2A; sixteen more in the 2B; and eighty-nine more in the grades 3B-6A; or, in all grades combined, there would have been a net increase of only twenty-nine additional promotions out of 18,948 pupils. There is, therefore, no practical difference between the rate of promotion in alternating and in A. M. and P. M. part-time classes combined.

It will, however, be remembered that the rate of promotion in A. M. part-time classes, when considered separately from P. M. part-time classes, was found to be considerably higher in all but two grades than in P. M. part-time classes.[1] Hence, the disadvantages of part time fall most heavily on those pupils who attend school for a term in the afternoon only. A. M. part-time classes and P. M. part-time classes are alternated—that is, pupils who attend one term in the forenoon only attend the following term, as a rule, in the afternoon only. The disadvantages of attending in the afternoon only are thus somewhat equalized. There is, however, no assurance that a pupil on part time one term will be on part time the next; hence, no assurance that the disadvantages suffered by attending school one term in the afternoon only will be equalized by attendance the following term in the forenoon only. In view, therefore, not only of the slight difference in the rate of promotion in favor of alternating part-time classes, but also in view of the probability of a more equitable distribution of the disadvantages of part time in such classes, we are inclined to believe that alternating part-time classes are to be preferred to A. M. and P. M. part-time classes.

CONCLUSIONS

The conclusions from the foregoing discussion may be summarized as follows:

(1) The rate of promotion at the end of the February-June term, 1911, was higher in whole-time classes than in part-time classes in nine out of the twelve grades in which there were both kinds of classes, but, had the higher rate of promotion in whole-time classes prevailed in part-time classes, the number of promotions in part-time classes would have been increased by only 782.

[1] See table on page 176.

(2) Part time, so far as our data go, is but a very slight factor in increasing the number of non-promotions, and probably augments congestion not at all.

(3) The rate of promotion at the end of the February-June term, 1911, was not only higher in Ettinger part-time classes than in whole-time classes, but higher than in any other kind of part-time class. For this reason, and also because pupils in Ettinger part-time classes are under the influence of the school for five hours daily, the Board of Education may well insist, when part time is necessary, that principals establish, wherever possible, Ettinger part-time classes.

(4) The rate of promotion differs little in alternating and in A. M. and P. M. part-time classes combined, but, since the disadvantages of part-time are probably more equally distributed in alternating than in A. M. and P. M. part-time classes, alternating part-time classes are preferable.

(5) Considering the difference in rate of promotion in favor of whole-time classes, the physical, the educational, and the social questions involved in judging of the relative merits of whole-time and part-time classes, the custom in other cities of the country of making every effort to provide accommodations for an all-day schooling for all elementary school pupils, the strong demand in the community that each child, whatever his grade, have a whole day's schooling, and the legal and social right of each child to a whole day's schooling, the Board of Education is justified in attempting to eliminate part time from all the grades. But should the Board of Education request the funds to eliminate part time from all the grades, the Board of Estimate and Apportionment, in view of the differences of opinion and questions involved, would be justified in requesting of the Board of Education an investigation into the relative merits of whole- and part-time classes, to the end that a definite policy with regard to school accommodation may be fixed on and carried out.

CHAPTER XII

THE PROBLEM OF PUPILS WHO LEAVE SCHOOL[1]

IN all the foregoing discussions the pupils on register at the end of the term only have been considered. But the register at the end of the term does not include the thousands of pupils, exclusive of transfers, who have been on register and who have left before the end of the term.

FAILURE TO COLLECT DATA ON PUPILS LEAVING SCHOOL

The By-laws of the Board of Education provide that "the principal of each school shall keep a record which shall contain the names of all pupils dropped from the school register, with a statement of the reason therefor."[2] But no report has ever been made for the city as a whole on the number of pupils leaving the elementary schools during a term or a school year and on the reasons therefor.

NUMBER OF PUPILS LEAVING DURING FEBRUARY-JUNE TERM, 1911

Table LIII[3] gives the number of pupils, by sexes, leaving the regular classes of each grade during the February-June term, 1911; also, by sexes, the per cent. of the total enrollment in the regular classes for each grade leaving:

[1] Leaving is used to include pupils who leave school temporarily and also pupils who leave permanently.

[2] Manual of the Board of Education, Section 45, 2 a, pages 57-58.

[3] These data have to do with pupils leaving regular classes only. Pupils dropping from special classes are not included.

TABLE LIII

Grades	Number of Pupils Leaving Regular Classes Feb.-June Term, 1911			Per Cent. of Total Enrollment in Regular Classes Leaving		
	Boys	Girls	Total	Boys	Girls	Total
1A	1,245	1,219	2,464	5.38	5.46	5.42
1B	1,128	1,066	2,194	4.27	4.16	4.22
2A	816	810	1,626	3.85	4.04	3.94
2B	831	818	1,649	3.56	3.57	3.56
3A	745	732	1,477	3.55	3.55	3.55
3B	703	768	1,471	3.17	3.46	3.31
4A	651	727	1,378	3.22	3.68	3.45
4B	726	725	1,451	3.47	3.54	3.51
5A	788	813	1,601	4.07	4.26	4.17
5B	1,141	1,050	2,191	6.07	5.40	5.73
6A	1,409	1,250	2,659	7.93	7.03	7.48
6B	1,456	1,212	2,668	8.52	7.25	7.89
7A	1,611	1,444	3,055	10.60	9.30	9.94
7B	1,247	1,225	2,472	9.30	8.85	9.07
8A	955	923	1,878	8.52	7.83	8.17
8B	405	356	761	4.05	3.45	3.75
Total	15,857	15,138	30,995	5.26	5.07	5.17

Fifteen thousand eight hundred and fifty-seven (15,857) boys and 15,148 girls, a total of 30,995, or 5.17 per cent. of the total enrollment,[1] dropped from the regular classes of the elementary schools during the February-June term, 1911; or one pupil in each twenty enrolled in regular classes left school before the end of the term. The number leaving the several grades varied from 761, or 3.75 per cent. of the total enrollment, in the 8B grade, to 3,055, or 9.94 per cent., in the 7A.

From the 1A to the 5A the per cent. of boys leaving was slightly lower than the per cent. of girls leaving, whereas, from the 5B on, the reverse was true. Taking the several

[1] Total enrollment is the sum of the register at the end of the term plus all pupils, exclusive of transfers, leaving before the end of the term.

grades together there was, however, little difference between the losses among boys, 5.26 per cent., and the losses among girls, 5.07 per cent., a difference of but .19 of 1 per cent. in favor of girls.

AGES AND GRADES OF PUPILS LEAVING SCHOOL

Whether pupils leaving school are out temporarily or permanently depends largely on the grade they are in and on their age at leaving. Table LIV gives by grades the number of pupils leaving the regular classes at each of the several ages: under six, six to seven, etc.; also the total number leaving at each age, and the per cent. leaving at each age of the total number dropping out. (See page 188.)

The number of pupils leaving the regular classes at each of the several ages from six to seven up to thirteen to fourteen, inclusive, is quite uniform, varying from 1,843 (12 to 13) to 2,515 (7 to 8), or from 5.95 per cent. to 8.11 per cent. of the total number leaving. The losses from fourteen to fifteen were the largest, 6,312, or 20.37 per cent. The number dropping out from fifteen to sixteen was likewise large, 4,571, or 14.75 per cent., as was also the number from sixteen to seventeen, 2,381, or 7.68 per cent.

Seventeen thousand three hundred and twelve (17,312), or 55.84 per cent., of the pupils leaving regular classes, were under fourteen. Of these, 2,190 were less than seven years of age and were, therefore, not of compulsory school age; 15,122 were, however, between seven and fourteen, and, in consequence, were subject to the Compulsory Education Law; 13,683, or 44.16 per cent., were fourteen and above. Of these, 822 were between fourteen and sixteen, and were also in the grades 1A-5A, hence could not qualify for labor certificates; the remaining 12,861 were, however, free, by reason of their age and their grade, to drop from school permanently. 15,944 (15,122 plus 822), or 51.44 per cent. of those leaving regular classes, were, therefore, subject to the Compulsory Education Law, and 2,190 were

TABLE LIV

Age	Grade																Total	Per Cent. of Total Number Leaving at Each Age
	1A	1B	2A	2B	3A	3B	4A	4B	5A	5B	6A	6B	7A	7B	8A	8B		
Under 6 Years	45	5	.....	.....	.....	.....	.....	.....	.....	.....	.....	.....	.....	.....	.....	.....	50	.16
6 to 7	1,512	570	43	12	2	.....	.....	1	.....	.....	.....	.....	.....	.....	.....	.....	2,140	6.90
7 to 8	662	970	550	281	43	9	.....	.....	.....	.....	.....	.....	.....	.....	.....	.....	2,515	8.11
8 to 9	177	430	591	613	397	177	30	8	1	.....	.....	1	.....	.....	.....	.....	2,425	7.82
9 to 10	42	140	262	412	436	445	258	117	41	9	1	1	.....	.....	.....	.....	2,164	6.98
10 to 11	14	45	99	183	294	361	373	374	209	94	35	10	2	.....	.....	.....	2,093	6.75
11 to 12	8	16	48	74	158	235	293	318	313	248	132	75	27	9	1	.....	1,955	6.31
12 to 13	.....	8	19	30	69	107	173	232	249	276	183	121	70	23	23	7	1,843	5.95
13 to 14	1	2	4	22	42	60	106	143	232	293	308	297	237	211	131	38	2,127	6.86
14 to 15	.....	4	4	8	20	36	65	99	243	643	1,038	1,137	1,299	953	593	170	6,312	20.37
15 to 16	1	3	4	6	7	20	45	80	177	420	583	683	930	775	603	234	4,571	14.75
16 to 17	1	1	2	8	8	20	31	72	128	179	262	253	379	378	420	239	2,381	7.68
17 to 18	1	.....	.....	.....	1	1	4	7	8	16	23	26	54	68	87	62	358	1.16
Over 18	.....	.....	.....	.....	.....	.....	.....	.....	.....	13	1	2	6	8	20	11	61	.20
Total	2,464	2,194	1,626	1,649	1,477	1,471	1,378	1,451	1,601	2,191	2,659	2,668	3,055	2,472	1,878	761	30,995	......

under compulsory school age. Hence, of the 30,995 pupils leaving during the February-June term, 1911, 18,134 (15,944 plus 2,190), or 58.51 per cent., will doubtless, in most part, return to school; but that 15,944 pupils of compulsory school age dropped from school during a single term is a serious matter and investigation should be made as to what extent these pupils had legal reasons for being out of school, and to what extent their being out was due to inefficiency on the part of the Department of Compulsory Attendance.

EFFECTS ON REPORTS OF TAKING NO ACCOUNT OF PUPILS LEAVING

The fact that no account is taken of the thousands of pupils leaving school leads to a defect in certain of the reports of the City Superintendent of Schools. A report on the number of pupils in the elementary schools of each of the several ages—under five, five to six, etc.—will illustrate this defect. Table LV gives the number of pupils in the elementary school on register June 30, 1911, of each of the several ages—under five, five to six, etc.; the number of each age, together with the pupils leaving regular classes during the February-June term, 1911; also the number of pupils of each age leaving regular classes. (See page 190.)

The number of pupils of each age given in column (1) is taken from the Annual Report of the City Superintendent of Schools for 1911. Excepting that the number of pupils of each age is given by totals instead of by sexes, this is his entire report on the ages of pupils in the elementary school. This report gives an idea of the number of pupils of each age on register at the end of the term, but gives no idea of the number of pupils of each age on register during the whole term. For this number one must turn to column (2).[1] A report on ages that has to do only with pupils on

[1] Column (2) gives the number of pupils of each age on register during the February-June term, 1911, with the exception of pupils leaving school from special classes.

register at the end of the term is, therefore, a partial report, and, unless supplemented by the ages of all pupils on register during the term as a whole, is incomplete.

What is true of the foregoing report of the City Superintendent of Schools is true of all of his reports, when made only in view of conditions at the end of the term or at the end of the school year; they are incomplete and to that ex-

TABLE LV

Ages	Elementary Schools		
	(1)[1] Number of Pupils of Each Age on Register June 30, 1911	(2)[2] Number of Pupils of Each Age on Register, June 30, 1911, Including Pupils Leaving Regular Classes during the Feb.-June Term, 1911	(3) Number of Pupils of Each Age Leaving Regular Classes Not Accounted for in Column (1)
18 and Over.....	104	165	61
17 to 18.........	636	994	358
16 to 17.........	3,884	6,265	2,381
15 to 16.........	18,086	22,657	4,571
14 to 15.........	42,163	48,475	6,312
13 to 14.........	63,369	65,496	2,127
12 to 13.........	66,806	68,649	1,843
11 to 12.........	70,155	72,110	1,955
10 to 11.........	68,864	70,957	2,093
9 to 10.........	67,860	70,024	2,164
8 to 9.........	70,934	73,359	2,425
7 to 8.........	66,652	69,167	2,515
6 to 7.........	51,707	53,847	2,140
5 to 6.........	6,358	6,408	50
Total...........	597,578	628,573	30,995

[1] Data for column (1) were taken from Table XXVII, page 52, Annual Report of the City Superintendent of Schools for 1911.

[2] Data for column (2) were taken from the foregoing table and also from the reports made to the Committee on School Inquiry, June, 1911.

tent misleading. This is particularly true of the reports on promotion and on over age.[1]

REDUCING THE NUMBER LEAVING SCHOOL

There is no reason to assume that the fact that 30,995 pupils left the regular classes alone during the February-June term of 1911 is exceptional. There is every reason to believe that a similar number drop from school every term. Since, if pupils leave school prematurely, the very purpose for which the school exists is defeated, the problem of reducing the total number leaving and particularly of reducing the number leaving who are subject to the Compulsory Education Law demands immediate and earnest attention.

Though principals and teachers may be doing much to keep down the number leaving, so long as the reports of the several schools on pupils leaving and on the reasons therefor are not tabulated, it is impossible for District Superintendents, Associate Superintendents, and the City Superintendent to give the help in the solution of this problem that they should give. As a preliminary step in the reduction of school losses, we, therefore, recommend that the reports from the several schools on pupils leaving and on the reasons therefor be collected and tabulated, term by term, for the Greater City, to the end that the number dropping from school and the reasons therefor may be known and that the causes of their leaving, in so far as these lie within the school, may be eradicated.

CONCLUSIONS

The foregoing discussion may be thus summarized:

(1) Thirty thousand nine hundred and ninety-five (30,995) pupils, or 5.17 per cent. of the total enrollment, in regular classes dropped from the elementary school dur-

[1] See Annual Report of the City Superintendent of Schools for 1911, Table XXVIII, page 54, and Table XXXVII, pages 66-67.

ing the February-June term, 1911; or one pupil out of each twenty in regular classes left school before the end of the term.

(2) Taking the several grades together, there was little difference between the losses among boys, 5.26 per cent., and the losses among girls, 5.07 per cent.—a difference of but .19 of 1 per cent. in favor of girls.

(3) The number of pupils leaving regular classes at each of the several ages from six to seven up to thirteen to fourteen, inclusive, was quite uniform, varying from 1,843 (12 to 13) to 2,515 (8 to 9), or from 5.95 per cent. to 8.11 per cent. of the total number leaving. The losses from fourteen to fifteen were the largest, 6,312, or 20.37 per cent. The number dropping out from fifteen to sixteen was likewise large, 4,571, or 14.75 per cent., as was also the number from sixteen to seventeen, 2,381, or 7.68 per cent.

(4) Of the 30,995 leaving regular classes during the February-June term, 1911, 15,944, or 51.44 per cent., were subject to the Compulsory Education Law.

(5) Because no account is taken of the number of pupils leaving school, certain of the reports of the City Superintendent of Schools are incomplete.

(6) The reduction of the number dropping from school and particularly the reduction of the number leaving who are subject to the Compulsory Education Law demand immediate and earnest attention.

(7) To the end that the number leaving and the reasons therefor may be known, and that the causes of their leaving, in so far as they lie within the school, may be eradicated, we recommend that the reports from the several schools on the number dropping out and the reasons therefor be collected and tabulated term by term for the Greater City.

CHAPTER XIII

CONCLUSIONS AND RECOMMENDATIONS AS TO NON-PROMOTION AND PART TIME

A SUMMARY of conclusions and recommendations is given at the end of each of the several sections of the foregoing report. It will, therefore, be necessary to bring together only certain of our conclusions and the more important of our recommendations.

THE CHIEF CAUSES OF NON-PROMOTION

Among the chief causes of non-promotion assigned by the eight committees appointed in the fall of 1909 by the City Superintendent of Schools were Part Time, Excessive Size of Classes, Irregular Attendance, Late Entrance to School, Sluggish Mentality, and Ignorance of the English Language.

Basing our conclusions on the rate of promotion at the end of the February-June term, 1911, we find, when each of these assigned causes is considered apart from the others:

(1) That part time and excessive size of classes are responsible for the non-promotion of relatively few pupils.

(2) That irregular attendance is a decided factor in increasing the number of non-promotions.

(3) That late entrance to school and sluggish mentality, as expressed in over age, are material factors in causing non-promotion.

(4) That inability to use the English language increases decidedly, in the relatively small group of pupils affected, the number of pupils failing of promotion.

SIZE OF CLASSES

Considering the slightly lower rate of promotion at the end of the February-June term, 1911, for over-size classes, but more particularly the acknowledged educational disadvantages of over-size classes, and the prevailing practice in other cities of the country, we recommend that whenever practicable all classes having more than fifty pupils be reduced to classes of forty-five pupils.

INABILITY TO USE THE ENGLISH LANGUAGE

Basing our judgment on the decidedly lower rate of promotion at the end of the February-June term, 1911, for over-age pupils, and for pupils unable to use the English language, we recommend:

(1) That classes in which special attention and direction are given to over-age pupils be provided at least for all pupils two and more years behind their grade.

(2) That "C" classes—classes for the instruction of pupils unable to use the English language—be provided at least for all pupils in 1A classes unable to use the English language.

FURTHER DATA NEEDED

In this report certain of our conclusions and recommendations—for example, our recommendation to reduce all classes having above fifty pupils to forty-five pupils—do not rest so much on the facts presented as on educational opinion. Educational opinion, to have proper weight, should be supported by facts. To determine, on the basis of fact, the relative worth of whole-time and part-time classes, the proper size of class, and to answer, on the basis of fact, other questions raised in this report, such as the actual length of the present course of study, the actual length of time pupils are in school between six and fourteen, inclusive, etc., further data are needed. To collect some of the needed data it will be necessary to conduct special investigations; other data can be collected from the current and cumulative records of the schools.

Among the more important special investigations we recommend are investigations to determine:

(1) The relative educational achievements of pupils in whole-time and part-time classes.

(2) The relative educational worth of classes of each of the several sizes.

(3) The proper limits of the period of elementary education.

(4) The different groups of pupils of varying abilities and educational needs.

(5) The extent to which pupils now in "E" classes are classified and instructed according as their over age is due to late entrance or to slow progress—retardation.

The Blank Form Recommended for the Collection of Further Data

The more important items of the data we recommend to be collected, at least for a time, by terms from the current and cumulative records of the school, are shown in the blank following page 198.

All the items called for in this blank are not now both matters of current and cumulative school record. The causes of absence due to late entrance, for example, are not now a part of the current record. Further, owing to the fact that the pupil's record card (a cumulative record) was not introduced until June, 1909, it is impossible to give for all pupils now in school, who entered the 1A grade, the date of entrance and the total number of days in school from entrance in the 1A grade to June 28, 1912. These facts could be given only for pupils entering the 1A grade in the February-June term, 1909, and thereafter. Similarly, with regard to pupils entering later than the 1A grade. It is also impossible to give the total number of terms a pupil has been on part-time since entrance to school. But the current and cumulative records of the school are such, or can easily be made such, that all the items called for in the blank could, in due time, be supplied, and it is possible even now to supply the major part of them.

If the recommended blank is adopted and those data which can now be supplied are collected and tabulated, data will be at hand similar to those presented in this report, and additional data as follows:

(1) Data on the actual ages of children (Item 2), and these data, in connection with the data on grade (Item C) and on promotion and non-promotion (Items 11 and 12), will make possible for the first time an accurate estimate of the amount and degree of over age in the entire system (exclusive of classes for the deaf, the blind, and crippled and defective children).

(2) Data to show the amount of absence due to late entrance ("(1)" of "a" of Item 3). These data, together with data on absence due to irregular attendance ("b" of Item 3), will make it possible for the first time to determine the actual total amount of absence. Should teachers and principals be notified, at the beginning of a term, it would be possible at the end of the term to collect data on the causes of late entrance. With a knowledge of the causes of late entrance, it would be possible to de-

termine to what extent such absence is due to home and other conditions, and to what extent it is due to failure to enforce the Compulsory Education Law.

(3) The data supplied on tardiness, conduct, and truancy (Items 4, 5, and 6), along with the data on absence (Item 3), will go far to substantiate or to disprove the prevalent belief that part time has an unfavorable effect on the attendance, punctuality, and conduct of children.

(4) The data on pupils leaving school (Item 7), and the causes thereof (Item 8), will not only make it possible to make a complete report on register, absence, promotion, non-promotion, and over age, etc., which is not now done, but the knowledge of the causes of leaving might make it possible to reduce greatly the number dropping from school.

(5) Data will also be at hand (Item 14) to determine the number of beginners in the 1A grade, hence will supply the basis of estimating what portion of all pupils entering the school continue to the end of each grade.

(6) Data (Items 10, 11, and 12) to determine, with accuracy, the actual rate of promotion and of non-promotion, also the number of pupils receiving double promotion.

(7) Data (Item 13) to determine the actual length of time it takes pupils to complete each of the grades.

(8) Data (Items 14 and 15) to determine:

(a) The actual total time pupils are in school between six and fourteen; also the total length of time they are in school.

(b) The actual total length of the elementary school course of study, also the actual total length of time it takes to complete a given number of grades, e. g., the 1A-6B grades, inclusive. (c) The best age of entering the 1A grade, when judged solely in view of progress through the school.

Although it is impossible, as suggested above, to supply now the data called for in Items 14 and 15 for all pupils, the data that can be supplied now will answer for practical purposes.

(9) Should provision be made to collect the data called for in Item 16, some light will be thrown on the question whether part time affects unfavorably the school progress of children.

(10) From Items 17 and 18, data will be at hand to determine whether the transfer of pupils from school to school affects unfavorably their advancement.

The blank is drawn so that the data called for can be tabulated by a general tabulating machine. This method of tabulation deprives teachers and principals of the value to be derived from tabulating the data for their own school, but it minimizes the work imposed on them, and makes possible a larger use of the data than when the reports of the several teachers are summarized on a principal's blank.

Should the data called for in this blank be collected, as we recommend, these data would not only supply a reliable basis for answering certain of the questions raised in this report, but would also supply currently a reliable basis for various kinds of administrative action in relation to them. Should data also be collected currently, as we would recommend, on deficiencies in the several studies of the curriculum, these would supply the basis of adjusting the qualitative and quantitative requirements of the course of study to the varying abilities and needs of different groups of children.

CHAPTER XIV

THE SIGNIFICANCE OF OVER AGE

THE Educational Laws of the State of New York not only make it obligatory on financial and school officials to provide such facilities that the children of the state may have free opportunity to secure a complete elementary education, but these laws also seek to guarantee this opportunity to each child of the state.

THE AGE STANDARD SET BY LAW FOR THE SCHOOLS OF NEW YORK

The Compulsory Education Law, which seeks to guarantee to the child free opportunity to secure a complete elementary education, requires, under certain conditions, that children attend school regularly until they are sixteen years of age. But it is clearly indicated in this law that normal children, who attend school regularly, should be able to complete their elementary education by the time they are fourteen years old.[1] Hence, the state considers the attainment of the fourteenth birthday the normal age to complete the elementary school.

How impossible it is for children to complete the work of the elementary school of the City of New York by their fourteenth birthday is revealed by the fact that of the pupils, exclusive of those in special classes, thirteen to fourteen years old, on the register after promotion June 30th for the five years 1907-1911 inclusive, only 20.82 per cent.

[1] See Compulsory Education Law of the State of New York, Section 622.

had attained the eighth grade; 29.92 per cent., the seventh; 25.57 per cent., the sixth; 15.44 per cent., the fifth; 6.06 per cent., the fourth, and 2.19 per cent. were still in the third and lower grades.[1] That is, if these thirteen-to-fourteen-year-old pupils remained in school and progressed regularly, 20.82 per cent. would be between fourteen and fifteen years old on completing the elementary school; 29.92 per cent. between fifteen and sixteen; 25.57 per cent. between sixteen and seventeen; 15.44 per cent. between seventeen and eighteen, and 8.25 per cent. eighteen and older.

Pupils in considerable numbers remain in the elementary schools of the City of New York from one to three years after they are fourteen in order to complete the course.[2] Still larger numbers on becoming fourteen or on receiving employment certificates drop from school permanently, irrespective of the grade they have attained. It is estimated that of all the pupils entering the elementary schools of the City of New York, 3.31 per cent. drop out before completing the work of the fifth year; 11.29 per cent. before completing the work of the sixth year; 38.55 per cent. before completing the work of the seventh year, and only 41.33 per cent. ever remain to complete the eighth or final year.[3]

The fact that thousands of children remain in the elementary schools of the City of New York until they are sixteen, seventeen, and eighteen years of age in order to complete the course of study and that tens of thousands of children, though remaining until they are fourteen and older, drop from school permanently without having been able to advance beyond the work of the sixth or seventh year, leads to the question of the grade a child of a given age should be entering or should be completing by a given age.

DEFINITION OF AGE LIMITS

Certain age limits have been fixed for entering and for completing each of the several grades of the elementary

[1] See page 112. [2] See page 109. [3] See page 92.

school. Children entering a grade before the age fixed for entering, or completing a grade before the age fixed for completion, are termed *under age;* children entering a grade at the age fixed for entrance, or completing a grade at the age fixed for completion, are termed *normal age;* children entering the grade older than the age fixed for entrance, or completing the grade older than the age fixed for completion, are termed *over age;* that is, are behind the grade for their age.

Had children an indefinite length of time in which to secure an education, the fact that they were behind the grade for their age would have no educational significance. But over age has educational significance, because the state only directly secures to the child the opportunity of attending school until he is fourteen, and because children in large numbers on becoming fourteen, either from necessity or choice, drop from school permanently. Hence, for children to fall behind their grade one or more years, means that they will probably drop from the elementary school without completing one or more of the upper grades, and in consequence enter on some practical pursuit with only a sixth or seventh grade education.[1]

OVER AGE AS A TEST OF EFFICIENCY OF A SCHOOL SYSTEM

Since over-age children tend to fail to complete the work of the elementary school, just to the extent that they are behind their grade for their age, over age becomes one of the primary standards of judging the efficiency of a school system. When judged in view of the purpose of the elementary school, viz., to give each normal child a complete elementary education, that system of schools is the most efficient—all things considered—which has the smallest per cent. of over-age pupils, because a large proportion of its pupils will continue until they complete the entire elementary school course of study; whereas that system is

[1] See pages 92 and 188.

the least efficient which has the highest per cent. of over-age pupils, because a small proportion of its pupils will continue until they complete the entire course.

The number of over-age pupils in a school system and the length of time these pupils are over age are therefore questions of the highest practical importance. The number of pupils over age is an index to the probable number of children who will drop permanently from school before completing the course of study, and the length of time these pupils are over age is an index to the extent these over-age children will probably fail to complete the course.[1] Hence, definite knowledge by grades of the number of over-age children in a system and definite knowledge of the length of time these pupils are over age, supply the basis of judging to what extent the system is succeeding or not succeeding in giving to each normal child a complete elementary education, and also of judging of the efficiency or inefficiency of the organization and administration of the particular system of schools.

FINANCIAL SIGNIFICANCE OF THE OVER-AGE PROBLEM

The question of over age has, however, not only great social and educational significance, but also financial significance. With the recognition of the tendency among over-age pupils to drop from school, without having completed the entire elementary school course of study, provisions have been made by school authorities to give over-age pupils special attention, to the end that they may be able to advance farther in the course of study than it would be possible for them to advance were they left in regular classes. There were in the elementary schools of the City of New York, for example, May 31st, 1912, 888

[1] Over age is much more serious in the upper grades than in the lower grades, because, by the proper classification and instruction of pupils a considerable portion of the pupils in the lower grades will be able to reduce the length of time they are over age by the time they reach the upper grades.

such classes, with an average register of thirty-two pupils per class and a total register of 28,083 pupils. In regular classes, one classroom accommodates and one teacher instructs forty-five pupils; special classes for over-age pupils are, however, organized, as a rule, on the basis of thirty pupils per classroom and teacher. Hence, to organize special classes for over-age pupils is to increase the cost of educating such pupils beyond what it would cost to instruct them in regular classes. The presence of a large number of over-age pupils in a system of schools and the consequent necessity of providing special classes for the instruction of such children, if they are to advance much, if any, beyond the fifth grade before dropping from school permanently, add, therefore, materially to the cost of the elementary school; whereas in a system having a small number of over-age pupils there is need of but few, if any, special classes for such pupils, and hence the ordinary cost of the elementary school is increased but little, if at all.

Further, over-age pupils, by failing to advance during their entire school life beyond the lower grades, instead of advancing regularly through the school, congest these grades. In consequence, the classrooms in the lower grades are crowded, whereas those in the upper grades have empty seats. In a system of schools having a large number of over-age pupils, more classrooms are therefore required to accommodate a given school population than are required to care for the same number of pupils in a system of schools having few over-age pupils. Hence, the financial significance of over age.

THE DETERMINATION OF THE NUMBER OF OVER-AGE PUPILS

It is not an easy matter to determine accurately the number of over-age pupils in a system of schools. To determine accurately the number of over-age pupils and the length of time these pupils are over age, or to make an age-grade report, it is necessary to have clearly in mind:

(1) the age-grade standards to be used; (2) the time to make the report—whether for the beginning or for the end of the official school year; (3) when to take the ages of the children—whether at the end or at the beginning of the official school year, or at the close or the opening of the schools for instruction; (4) how to take the ages of the children; and, finally, (5) what children to include. We shall consider each of these points in turn.

CHAPTER XV

AGE-GRADE STANDARDS TO USE IN AGE-GRADE REPORTS

I. AGE-GRADE STANDARDS FOR BEING IN A GRADE

WRITERS on over age and superintendents in making age-grade reports have been none too careful in determining the proper age-grade standards to be used in judging whether or not a pupil is under age, normal age, or over age. The age-grade standards given in the following quotations are typical of those in use:

"Normal age in this study is defined as follows: Children who are 6 or 7 years of age in the first grade, 7 or 8 years of age in the second grade, 8 or 9 years of age in the third grade, and so on, are normal." [1]

"NORMAL AGES OF CHILDREN IN THE GRADES

Grade	*Age*
First Grade	6 to 8
Second Grade	7 to 9
Third Grade	8 to 10
Fourth Grade	9 to 11
Fifth Grade	10 to 12
Sixth Grade	11 to 13
Seventh Grade	12 to 14
Eighth Grade	13 to 15" [2]

"Counting 7 years as standard age for first year, 8 years for second, 9 years for third, 10 years for fourth, etc." [3]

[1] Strayer: *Age-Grade Census of Schools and Colleges*, page 12.
[2] Ayres: *Laggards in Our Schools*, page 35.
[3] Annual Report of the Board of Education of Newark, N. J., 1910-11, page 161.

It will be observed that the age-grade standards of the foregoing quotations are in each case the normal ages for "being in the grade" and that in not one of these quotations is there an intimation that to determine accurately whether or not a pupil is under age, normal age, or over age, there is need of age-grade standards fixing the normal age limits for entering and for completing each of the several grades of the elementary school. What is true of the age-grade standards in these quotations is, with but one or two exceptions, true of those given in all articles written up to the present time on over age and in all school reports on over age, viz., the age-grade standards are for "being in the grade."

The Right Basis for Age-Grade Reports

"Being in the grade" has to do only indirectly with whether or not a child is under age, normal age, or over age. To make the age-grade standards for "being in a grade" the basis of determining whether or not a pupil is under age, normal age, or over age is to use a wrong basis, and in consequence to make unreliable and inaccurate age-grade reports.

A child is under age, or normal age, or over age in view of the task in hand, viz., completing the entire elementary school course of study by a given age. When the whole task is subdivided, as it is, into several units or grades, a child is under age, or normal age, or over age as he progresses through the school, according as he is younger or older on finishing a given grade than the normal age limits fixed for completing the respective grade. To be sure, when the normal age-grade standards for completing each of the several grades are determined, these standards may in turn be employed as the basis of fixing the normal age limits for entering each of the several grades. With these age-grade standards in hand, it is possible to determine under age, normal age, and over age from the point of view of entering a grade with the same accuracy as from the point of view of completing a grade. Hence, to determine accurately whether or not a child is under age, or normal age, or over age, involves fixing on the normal age limits for entering and on the normal age limits for completing each of the several grades—which has not as yet been done.

The following illustrations will suffice to show that age-grade standards for "being in the grade" supply an inexact basis for age-grade reports.

The Case of "A"

The normal ages for being in the seventh grade, according to Dr. Ayres, are 12 up to 14. (See quotation, page 205.) Were a boy "A," 13 years and 11 months old June 30th, in the 7th grade at the close of the year, when an age-grade report was made, such a boy judged by the age-grade standards for "being in the grade" would ordinarily be *recorded and reported as of normal age.* As a matter of fact, whether or not "A" is actually of normal age depends (a) on whether the age-grade report is made *before* or *after* promotion and (b) on whether "A" is to be promoted or is not to be promoted.

When the Age-Grade Report Is Made before Promotion

When the age-grade report is made at the end of the year *before promotion,* pupils are "in" the respective grades where they have been registered during the whole or a part of the year ending. Hence, were "A" 13 years and 11 months old in the seventh grade to be *promoted,* it would be correct to record and report him as of normal age. But were "A" *not to be promoted,* it is obvious that it will probably be necessary for him to remain an entire year in the seventh grade in order to complete it; that is, until he is 14 years and 11 months old. Instead, therefore, of "A" being of normal age, he is, in fact, one year over age.

Hence, to report "A" of normal age is to give him the advantage of the time it will probably take him to complete the grade, an entire year.

What is true of "A" when age-grade reports are made *before promotion* on the basis of the age-grade standards for "being in the grade" is true, within limits, of all children whose ages are near the upper age limit for "being in the grade." That is, to determine under age, normal age, and over age *before promotion* on the basis of the age-grade standards for "being in the grade" is practically to subtract one year from the ages of all *non-promoted* children or is to give *such pupils* an age advantage of the time it takes to complete a grade, an entire year.[1] In consequence, pupils are reported as of normal age who are actually over age, and this results in an increase in the reported number of pupils of normal age and decrease in the reported number of over-age pupils. (See tables on pages 213 and 214.)

When the Age-Grade Report Is Made after Promotion

When the age-grade report is made at the end of the year *after promotion, non-promoted pupils* are "in" the respective grades where they have been registered during a whole or a part of the year ending, whereas *promoted pupils* are "in" the respective grades to which they have just been advanced. Hence, were "A," 13 years and 11 months

[1] In a system where promotions are made semi-annually, and an age-grade report is made, at the end of each term, *before promotion*, on the basis of the age-grade standards for "being in the grade" for each of the sixteen grades, non-promoted pupils are given the advantage of only a half year, the time to complete a grade. But in a system having semi-annual promotions, where an age-grade report is made *before* promotion on the basis of the age-grade standards for "being in the grade" and for the grades of each of the several years, at the end of the year only, in such a case *non-promoted pupils* in the classes of all *A grades* are given the advantage of an entire year, while *non-promoted pupils* in the classes of all *B grades* and the *promoted pupils* in the classes of all *A grades* are given the advantage of a half year. (See tables on pages 213 and 220.)

old, *not promoted,* and in the seventh grade, it is obvious that although he has been "in" the seventh grade for a whole or part of the year ending, for all practical purposes he is just entering the seventh grade. To complete this grade, it will probably be necessary for him to remain "in the grade" an entire year, that is, until he is 14 years and 11 months old. Instead, therefore, of "A" being of normal age as he would be recorded and reported when the age-grade report is made on the basis of the age-grade standards for "being in the grade," he is actually one year over age, and to report him as of normal age is to give him the advantage of an entire year, the time it will probably take him to complete the grade.

Finally, were "A," 13 years and 11 months old, and *promoted* from the sixth grade to the seventh grade, to complete the seventh grade it will probably be necessary for him to remain "in" the grade an entire year; that is, until he is 14 years and 11 months old. Instead, therefore, of "A" being of normal age as he would be reported when the age-grade report is made *after promotion* and on the basis of the age-grade standards for "being in the grade," he is in reality one year over age, and to report him as of normal age is equivalent to subtracting one entire year from his age.

What is true of "A" when age-grade reports are made *after promotion* on the basis of age-grade standards for "being in the grade" is true within limits of all children whose ages are near the upper age limit for "being in the grade"; that is, to determine under age, normal age, and over age *after promotion* on the basis of the age-grade standards fixed for "being in the grade" is to give to *non-promoted and also to promoted children,* hence *to all children,* an age advantage of the time it takes to complete a grade, an entire year, and is equivalent to subtracting an entire year from the ages of all children.[1] In consequence

[1] In a system where promotions are made semi-annually and an age-grade report is made at the end of each term, *after promotion,* on

pupils are reported as of normal age, who are actually over age, and this results in an increase in the reported number of pupils of normal age and a decrease in the reported number of over-age pupils.[1]

The Case of "B"

The age-grade standards for being in the seventh grade are, according to Dr. Ayres,[2] 12 to 14, and for being in the eighth grade, 13 to 15. Were a boy "B," 12 years and 1 month old, in the seventh grade at the end of a year, whether such a boy was reported as of normal age or as under age, would depend on whether or not the age-grade report was made *before* or *after* promotion, that is *before* or *after* the grades and classes were reorganized for the new year, and on whether or not he was promoted or not promoted. Were "B," 12 years and 1 month old, in the seventh grade at the end of the year, and the age-grade report made *before promotion,* "B" would be recorded as of normal age, whereas were "B" promoted, and the age-grade report made *after promotion,* and were "B" reported from the eighth grade, the grade to which he has just been advanced, he would be recorded as being under age. What is true of "B" is true, within limits, of all children whose ages are near the lower age limit for "being in a grade." That is, when the age-grade report is made *before promotion* pupils are recorded of normal age, who, when the age-

the basis of the age-grade standards for "being in the grade," for each of the sixteen grades, all pupils are given the advantage of a half year. But in a system having semi-annual promotions, where an age-grade report is made *after promotion* on the basis of the age-grade standards for "being in the grade" for the grades of the several years, at the end of the year only, in such a case *promoted* pupils in the classes of all *A grades* and *non-promoted* pupils in the classes of all *B grades* are given the advantage of a half year, while *non-promoted* pupils in the classes of all *A grades* and *promoted* pupils in the classes of all *B grades* are given the advantage of an entire year. (See tables on pages 213 and 214.)

[1] See pages 214 and 218.

[2] See page 205.

grade report is made *after promotion,* are recorded as under age. In consequence, to make age-grade reports on the basis of the age-grade standards for being in the grade, *before promotion,* is to increase the recorded number of pupils of normal age and to decrease the recorded number of pupils under age, and to make such reports *after promotion* is to increase the recorded number of pupils under age and to decrease the recorded number of pupils of normal age. (See tables on pages 213 and 214.)

To summarize: to make an age-grade report, either before promotion or after promotion, on the basis of the age-grade standards for being in the grade, is to increase the reported number of pupils of normal age and to decrease the reported number of pupils over age. Obviously age-grade standards which permit such arbitrary changes in the recorded number of pupils under age, normal age, and over age, are inexact age-grade standards, and it is equally obvious that age-grade reports made on the basis of such age-grade standards are inexact.

Reports Based on Age Grade Standards Used in New York City in 1904 and 1905

The age-grade standards proposed in 1904 by the City Superintendent of Schools of the City of New York, and used by him now as the basis of his age-grade reports, are given below:

"The normal ages of children in the several grades are as follows:

"First-year grades	6 to 8 years
Second-year grades	7 to 9 years
Third-year grades	8 to 10 years
Fourth-year grades	9 to 11 years
Fifth-year grades	10 to 12 years
Sixth-year grades	11 to 13 years
Seventh-year grades	12 to 14 years
Eighth-year grades	13 to 15 years"[1]

[1] Annual Report of the City Superintendent of Schools for 1904, page 47; also for 1911, pages 53 ff.

The age-grade standards proposed and used by the City Superintendent of Schools as the basis of his age-grade reports are, it will be observed, for "being in the grade." Hence, in view of the foregoing, the age-grade standards employed by the City Superintendent of Schools supply an inexact basis of determining whether or not a pupil is under age, or normal age, or over age, and age-grade reports made on the basis of such age-grade standards are not as exact as such reports should be.

In 1904, the year in which the City Superintendent of Schools proposed the foregoing age-grade standards for "being in the grade," he made his age-grade report *before* promotion, that is, before the classes and grades were reorganized for the new year. There were included in this age-grade report only the children on register June 30th, when the schools closed for instruction.[1] His age-grade report for 1905 was made in the same way as the report for 1904, with one exception, the age-grade report for 1905 was made *after promotion,* that is, after the classes and grades were organized for the new year.[2] The effect of this change from making his age-grade report *before promotion* to making it *after promotion,* on the reported number and per cent. of under-age, normal-age, and over-age pupils, is shown in Table LVI.[3] (See pages 213-214.)

Age-grade Table LVI-1 conforms in every respect to the age-grade report of the City Superintendent of Schools for

[1] Annual Report of the City Superintendent of Schools for 1904, pages 42 ff.

[2] Annual Report of the City Superintendent of Schools for 1905, pages 58 ff.

[3] In order to make clear the several points of this report, age-grade data were collected for all the pupils on the register during the course of the February-June term, 1910-11, in five elementary schools of the City of New York. These five schools, having a total or net enrollment of 8,249 pupils, were selected at random from the schools having all grades, one school from each of the several boroughs. The data used in all the illustrative tables of this report are for the same children. Consequently any differences that appear are due to differences in method of determining under age, normal age, and over age, or in making age-grade reports.

TABLE LVI

SHOWS THE NUMBER AND PER CENT. OF UNDER-AGE, NORMAL-AGE, AND OVER-AGE PUPILS, WHEN AN AGE-GRADE REPORT IS MADE ON THE BASIS OF AGE-GRADE STANDARDS FOR "BEING IN THE GRADE"

(1) REPORT BEFORE PROMOTION, AS MADE BY THE CITY SUPERINTENDENT OF SCHOOLS IN 1904

Grades	Register as of June 30 before Promotion	Under Age		Normal Age		Over Age	
		Number Under Age	Per Cent. of Register Under Age	Number Normal Age	Per Cent. of Register Normal Age	Number Over Age	Per Cent. of Register Over Age
1st Year.........	956	17	1.78	836	87.45	103	10.77
2nd Year.........	907	3	.33	715	78.83	189	20.84
3rd Year.........	920	20	2.17	658	71.52	242	26.31
4th Year.........	936	17	1.82	568	60.68	351	37.50
5th Year.........	952	13	1.36	515	54.10	424	44.54
6th Year.........	892	27	3.03	460	51.57	405	45.40
7th Year.........	1,121	44	3.92	647	57.72	430	38.36
8th Year.........	816	43	5.27	499	61.15	274	33.58
Total............	7,500	184	2.45	4,898	65.31	2,418	32.24

1904; Table LVI-2 conforms in every respect to his age-grade report for 1905. Consequently, Table LVI shows what the effect was on the reported per cent. of under-age, normal-age, and over-age pupils, of the City Superintendent of Schools making his age-grade report in 1905 *after promotion.*

Table LVI-1, in which under age, normal age, and over age are determined *before promotion,* shows that of the pupils on register *before promotion,* June 30th, in the five schools in question, 2.45 per cent. were under age, 65.31 per cent. of normal age, and 32.24 per cent. over age. Table LVI-2, in which under age, normal age, and over age are determined *after promotion,* shows that for the same pupils, with the one exception noted, and for the same

TABLE LVI (*Continued*)

(2) REPORT AFTER PROMOTION, AS MADE BY THE CITY SUPERINTENDENT OF SCHOOLS IN 1905[1]

Grades	Register as of June 30 after Promotion	Under Age		Normal Age		Over Age	
		Number Under Age	Per Cent. of Register Under Age	Number Normal Age	Per Cent. of Register Normal Age	Number Over Age	Per Cent. of Register Over Age
1st Year.....	525	17	3.24	476	90.67	32	6.09
2nd Year.....	904	147	16.26	663	73.34	94	10.40
3rd Year.....	938	122	13.01	662	70.57	154	16.42
4th Year.....	934	106	11.35	603	64.56	225	24.09
5th Year.....	889	73	8.21	549	61.76	267	30.03
6th Year.....	1,010	102	10.10	561	55.54	347	34.36
7th Year.....	1,013	108	10.66	578	57.06	327	32.28
8th Year.....	915	131	14.32	575	62.84	209	22.84
Total........	7,128	806	11.31	4,667	65.47	1,655	23.22

schools 11.31 per cent. of the pupils were under age, 65.47 per cent. of normal age, and 23.22 per cent. over age.[2] To make an age-grade report *before promotion*, on the basis of age-grade standards for being in the grade, is, therefore, in contrast to making it *after promotion*, to decrease the recorded number of pupils under age and to increase the recorded number of pupils over age; whereas, to make such a report *after promotion* is, in contrast to making it *before promotion*, to decrease the recorded number of pupils over age and to increase the recorded number of pupils under age and normal age.

[1] It will be observed that in the five schools in question the register, as of June 30th in Table LVI-1, is given as 7,500, whereas, as in Table LVI-2, the register as of June 30th is given as 7,128. This difference in register is due to the fact that when an age-grade report is made *after promotion* 8B promoted pupils are necessarily excluded.

[2] How typical these five schools are of the system as a whole is indicated by the fact that the reported per cent. of over-age pupils in the grades of the several years was 23.3 per cent. Annual Report of the City Superintendent of Schools for 1911, page 59.

In a word, by a change in statistical method, that is, by making his age-grade report in 1905 *after promotion,* instead of, as in 1904, *before promotion,* the City Superintendent was able to report for the elementary schools of the city, when judged on the basis of Table LVI-2, 8.86 per cent. more pupils under age and 9.02 per cent. fewer pupils over age, than he would have been able to report had he made his report for 1905, as in 1904, *before promotion.*

This being true, there is little wonder that the City Superintendent of Schools was able to report in 1905 as follows:

"The next table shows the number in each year grade above normal age, on June 30th, 1905, and the percentage of this number on the whole number of children in the grade, together with the corresponding percentage in 1904:

Grades	Number of Pupils	Number above Normal Age	Per Cent. of Whole Number	Corresponding Per Cent. in 1904
First Year	58,330	9,707	16.6	23.2
Second Year	83,881	21,508	25.6	38.1
Third Year	84,364	28,733	34.1	45.0
Fourth Year	81,114	32,577	40.1	49.2
Fifth Year	72,277	30,998	42.9	49.0
Sixth Year	54,910	20,660	37.6	42.0
Seventh Year	39,982	11,201	28.0	32.8
Eighth Year	27,176	5,165	19.0	25.3
Total	502,034	160,549	32.0	39.0

"This table shows a considerable improvement over the conditions which obtained when I first brought the facts to light as to the ages of the pupils in the grades in my report for 1904." [1]

[1] Annual Report of the City Superintendent of Schools for 1905, page 63.

The City Superintendent of Schools points to the improved conditions with respect to the number of pupils over age in 1905 over 1904, his table showing that the per cent. of over-age pupils in the grades was reduced from 39 per cent. in 1904 to 32 per cent. in 1905, a reduction of 7 per cent. The City Superintendent of Schools was undoubtedly unaware of the effect of making his age-grade report in 1905 *after promotion* instead of, as in 1904, *before promotion,* on the reported per cent. of pupils under age, normal age, and over age. At all events, he failed to call attention to the change in the time of making his age-grade report and to point out that this change alone reduced the reported per cent. of over-age pupils approximately 9.2 per cent. In a word, had his age-grade report for 1905 been made as in 1904, the reported per cent. of over-age pupils would have been approximately 41.2 per cent. instead of 32 per cent., or approximately 2 per cent. higher than in 1904 instead of, as reported, 7 per cent. lower. Consequently, the reported reduction in the per cent. of over age in 1905 over 1904 was not an actual reduction due to improved conditions in the schools, but probably a reduction due solely to a change in statistical method, viz., making his age-grade report before instead of after promotion.

Reports Based on Age-Grade Standards Used in New York City since 1905

There are, in the elementary schools of the City of New York, sixteen grades. The City Superintendent of Schools, however, does not make a separate age-grade report for each of these sixteen grades, the 1A grade, 1B grade, etc., but he makes his age-grade report for the grades—the A and B grades, of each of the several years, first year grades, etc. The effect on the reported number of pupils under age, normal age, and over age of the City Superintendent of Schools, making his age-grade report for the grades of each of the several years, instead of for each of the several grades, is shown by Table LVII-1 and Table LVII-2.

TABLE LVII

SHOWS THE NUMBER AND PER CENT. OF UNDER-AGE, NORMAL-AGE, AND OVER-AGE PUPILS, WHEN AN AGE-GRADE REPORT IS MADE AFTER PROMOTION, ON THE BASIS OF AGE-GRADE STANDARDS FOR "BEING IN THE GRADE" (AS MADE BY THE CITY SUPERINTENDENT OF SCHOOLS SINCE 1905)

(1) FOR THE GRADES OF THE SEVERAL YEARS

Grades	Register as of June 30 after Promotion	Under Age		Normal Age		Over Age	
		Number Under Age	Per Cent. of Register Under Age	Number Normal Age	Per Cent. of Register Normal Age	Number Over Age	Per Cent. of Register Over Age
1st Year.........	525	17	3.24	476	90.67	32	6.09
2nd Year.........	904	147	16.26	663	73.34	94	10.40
3rd Year.........	938	122	13.01	662	70.57	154	16.42
4th Year.........	934	106	11.35	603	64.56	225	24.09
5th Year.........	889	73	8.21	549	61.76	267	30.03
6th Year.........	1,010	102	10.10	561	55.54	347	34.36
7th Year.........	1,013	108	10.66	578	57.06	327	32.28
8th Year.........	915	131	14.32	575	62.84	209	22.84
Total............	7,128	806	11.31	4,667	65.47	1,655	23.22

Age-grade Table LVII-1 conforms in every respect to the age-grade reports as made by the City Superintendent since 1905.[1] Age-grade Table LVII-2 conforms in every respect to the age-grade reports as made by the City Superintendent since 1905; with one exception, the report is for each of the grades separately. Consequently, Table LVII shows what the effect was, on the reported number of un-

[1] See Annual Report of the City Superintendent of Schools for 1905, pages 58 ff.; and for 1911, pages 53 ff.

TABLE LVII (*Continued*)

(2) FOR EACH OF THE SEVERAL GRADES SEPARATELY

Grades	Register as of June 30 after Promotion	Under Age		Normal Age		Over Age	
		Number Under Age	Per Cent. of Register Under Age	Number Normal Age	Per Cent. of Register Normal Age	Number Over Age	Per Cent. of Register Over Age
1A	131	4	3.05	106	80.92	21	16.03
1B	394	129	32.74	240	60.91	25	6.35
2A	486	144	29.63	292	60.08	50	10.29
2B	418	73	17.46	278	66.51	67	16.03
3A	486	106	21.81	298	61.32	82	16.87
3B	452	81	17.92	265	58.63	106	23.45
4A	477	89	18.66	271	56.81	117	24.53
4B	457	73	15.97	230	50.33	154	33.70
5A	473	63	13.32	256	54.12	154	32.56
5B	416	45	10.82	210	50.48	161	38.70
6A	548	84	15.33	255	46.53	209	38.14
6B	462	59	12.77	204	44.16	199	43.07
7A	436	74	16.97	188	43.12	174	39.91
7B	577	80	13.86	287	49.74	210	36.40
8A	515	101	19.61	265	51.46	149	28.93
8B	400	68	17.00	214	53.50	118	29.50
Total	7,128	1,273	17.86	3,859	54.14	1,996	28.00

der-age, normal-age, and over-age pupils, of the City Superintendent of Schools making his age-grade reports for the grades of the school year instead of for each of the several grades.

Table LVII-1, in which the number of pupils under age, normal age, and over age is reported for the grades of the several years, shows that 11.31 per cent. of the pupils on register June 30th after promotion in the five schools in question were under age, 65.47 per cent. normal age, and 23.22 per cent. over age, whereas Table LVII-2, in which the number of pupils under age, normal age, and over age is reported for each of the grades, shows that, of the same pupils on register June 30th, after promotion in the same schools, 17.86 per cent. were under age, 54.14 per cent. were normal age, and 28 per cent. were over age. In a word, the City Superintendent of Schools, by making his age-grade reports for the grades of the several years, is able to report, judged on the basis of Table LVII, 4.78 per cent. fewer over-age pupils in the elementary schools of the City

TABLE LVIII

SHOWS THE NUMBER AND PER CENT. OF UNDER-AGE, NORMAL-AGE, AND OVER-AGE PUPILS, WHEN AN AGE-GRADE REPORT IS MADE AFTER PROMOTION, ON THE BASIS OF AGE-GRADE STANDARDS FOR "BEING IN THE GRADE" (AS MADE BY THE CITY SUPERINTENDENT OF SCHOOLS SINCE 1905)

(1) FOR THE GRADES OF THE SEVERAL YEARS

Grades	Register as of June 30 after Promotion	Under Age		Normal Age		Over Age	
		Number Under Age	Per Cent. of Register Under Age	Number Normal Age	Per Cent. of Register Normal Age	Number Over Age	Per Cent. of Register Over Age
1st Year.........	525	17	3.24	476	90.67	32	6.09
2nd Year.........	904	147	16.26	663	73.34	94	10.40
3rd Year.........	938	122	13.01	662	70.57	154	16.42
4th Year.........	934	106	11.35	603	64.56	225	24.09
5th Year.........	889	73	8.21	549	61.76	267	30.03
6th Year.........	1,010	102	10.10	561	55.54	347	34.36
7th Year.........	1,013	108	10.66	578	57.06	327	32.28
8th Year.........	915	131	14.32	575	62.84	209	22.84
Total............	7,128	806	11.31	4,667	65.47	1,655	23.22

of New York than if he made his age-grade report for each of the several grades.

The combined effect, on the reported number of under-age, normal-age, and over-age pupils of the City Superintendent of Schools making his age-grade reports *after promotion* and for the grades of the several years, instead of making them *before promotion* and for each of the grades separately, is shown by Table LVIII. (See page 219.)

TABLE LVIII (*Continued*)

(2) FOR EACH OF THE GRADES

Grades	Register as of June 30 before Promotion	Under Age		Normal Age		Over Age	
		Number Under Age	Per Cent. of Register Under Age	Number Normal Age	Per Cent. of Register Normal Age	Number Over Age	Per Cent. of Register Over Age
1A	481	17	3.53	402	83.58	62	12.89
1B	475	5	1.05	393	82.74	77	16.21
2A	405	3	.74	294	72.59	108	26.67
2B	502	5	1.00	363	72.31	134	26.69
3A	448	18	4.02	275	61.38	155	34.60
3B	472	11	2.33	312	66.10	149	31.57
4A	459	17	3.70	234	50.98	208	45.32
4B	477	7	1.47	263	55.13	207	43.40
5A	424	10	2.36	175	41.27	239	56.37
5B	528	16	3.03	255	48.30	257	48.67
6A	462	18	3.90	188	40.69	256	55.41
6B	430	19	4.42	195	45.35	216	50.23
7A	583	35	6.00	232	39.80	316	54.20
7B	538	35	6.50	272	50.56	231	42.94
8A	436	33	7.57	200	45.87	203	46.56
8B	380	32	8.42	202	53.16	146	38.42
Total	7,500	281	3.75	4,255	56.73	2,964	39.52

Age-grade Table LVIII-1 conforms in every respect to the age-grade reports as made by the City Superintendent of Schools since 1905. Age-grade Table LVIII-2 conforms in every respect to the age-grade reports as made by the City Superintendent of Schools since 1905, with two exceptions, whether or not pupils are under age, normal age, or over age is determined *before promotion*,[1] and the age-grade table is for each of the several grades. Consequently, Table LVIII shows what the effect was, on the reported number of under-age, normal-age, and over-age pupils, of the City Superintendent making his age-grade reports *after promotion* and for the grades of the several years.

Table LVIII-1, in which the number of pupils under age, normal age, and over age is reported *after promotion* and for the grades of the several years, shows that 11.31 per cent. were under age, 65.47 per cent. normal age, and 23.22 per cent. over age. Table LVIII-2, in which the number of pupils under age, normal age, and over age is reported *before promotion* and for each of the several grades, shows, for the same pupils (with the one exception noted) and for the same schools, that 3.75 per cent. were under age, 56.73 per cent. of normal age, and 39.52 per cent. were over age. In a word, the City Superintendent of Schools is able to report when judged on the basis of Table LVIII, 7.56 per cent. more pupils under age, 8.74 per cent. more pupils normal age, and 16.30 per cent. fewer pupils over age, than if he made his age-grade reports *before promotion* and for each of the sixteen grades separately.

The age-grade reports of the City Superintendent of Schools are, therefore, not only inexact, by reason of the inexact basis thereof—age-grade standards for being in the grade—but they are rendered still more inexact by being for the grades of the several years instead of, as they should be, for each of the several grades.

[1] That is, before the classes and grades are organized for the new year.

2. AGE-GRADE STANDARDS FOR ENTERING AND FOR COMPLETING EACH OF THE SEVERAL GRADES

What the normal-age limits for entering and for completing each of the several grades of the elementary schools are, when determined, depends on the age accepted for completing the entire elementary school course of study.

Fourteen as the Upper Age Limit

One group of writers and school officials rest their case on the following facts: (1) that the legal age of entering the elementary school is six; (2) that children entering at six years of age have the best chance of advancing regularly and completing their elementary education prior to their fourteenth birthday[1]; (3) that the state only directly guarantees the child to the school up to his fourteenth birthday[2]; (4) that children in large numbers, either from necessity or from choice, drop permanently from school on becoming fourteen years old; (5) that, under present methods of school administration and organization, children dropping from school have not advanced much beyond the grade of the sixth or the seventh year; and (6) that children cannot, with the greatest profit, be held under the régime of the elementary school much, if any, beyond their fourteenth birthday. Resting their case on these facts and also on the belief that a democratic school must serve equally all the children and all the people of the community, this group of writers and school officials fixes the upper normal-age limit for completing the elementary school just prior to the attainment of the fourteenth birthday.[3]

The elementary school course of study of the City of New York is divided into sixteen units or grades, each in

[1] Ayres: *The Relation between Entering Age and Subsequent Progress among School Children.*

[2] Compulsory Education Law of the State of New York, Section 621.

[3] Report of Committee on Uniform Reports, National Education Association Proceedings, 1911, pages 288-291.

theory one-half year in length. When just prior to the attainment of the fourteenth birthday is made the upper normal-age limit for completing the elementary school, the normal age for entering and the normal age for completing each of the several grades is respectively as follows:

TABLE LIX

SHOWS THE NORMAL AGE TO ENTER AND THE NORMAL AGE TO COMPLETE EACH OF THE GRADES OF THE ELEMENTARY SCHOOL, WHEN UP-TO-FOURTEEN IS ACCEPTED AS THE UPPER NORMAL-AGE LIMIT FOR COMPLETING THE ELEMENTARY SCHOOL COURSE OF STUDY

Grades	Normal Age to Enter	Normal Age to Complete
1A	6 (Sixth Birthday)	up to 6½
1B	6½	up to 7
2A	7	up to 7½
2B	7½	up to 8
3A	8	up to 8½
3B	8½	up to 9
4A	9	up to 9½
4B	9½	up to 10
5A	10	up to 10½
5B	10½	up to 11
6A	11	up to 11½
6B	11½	up to 12
7A	12	up to 12½
7B	12½	up to 13
8A	13	up to 13½
8B	13½	up to 14

By reason of the date of birth and the date of the opening of the school term, it is obviously impossible for all children to enter school on their sixth birthday. But it is possible, so far as the date of birth and the date of the opening of the school term are concerned, for all children to enter school between their sixth birthday and the time just prior to becoming six and a half years old. Accordingly, even when just prior to fourteen is accepted as the upper normal-age limit to complete the elementary school, for the foregoing practical reasons, a range of a half year is allowed for entering and for completing each of the several grades. Hence, the normal-age limits for entering and the normal-age limits for completing each of the several grades are respectively:

TABLE LX

SHOWS THE NORMAL-AGE LIMITS FOR ENTERING AND THE NORMAL-AGE LIMITS FOR COMPLETING EACH OF THE GRADES OF THE ELEMENTARY SCHOOL WHEN UP-TO-FOURTEEN-AND-A-HALF IS ACCEPTED AS THE UPPER NORMAL-AGE LIMIT FOR COMPLETING THE ELEMENTARY SCHOOL COURSE OF STUDY

Grades	Normal-Age Limit for Entering	Normal-Age Limit for Completing
1A	6 up to 6½	6½ up to 7
1B	6½ up to 7	7 up to 7½
2A	7 up to 7½	7½ up to 8
2B	7½ up to 8	8 up to 8½
3A	8 up to 8½	8½ up to 9
3B	8½ up to 9	9 up to 9½
4A	9 up to 9½	9½ up to 10
4B	9½ up to 10	10 up to 10½
5A	10 up to 10½	10½ up to 11
5B	10½ up to 11	11 up to 11½
6A	11 up to 11½	11½ up to 12
6B	11½ up to 12	12 up to 12½
7A	12 up to 12½	12½ up to 13
7B	12½ up to 13	13 up to 13½
8A	13 up to 13½	13½ up to 14
8B	13½ up to 14	14 up to 14½

These are the normal-age limits for entering and for completing each of the several grades which, we believe, conform most closely to the actual working conditions and to the real purpose of the elementary school, viz., to give each normal child of the community a complete elementary education. Hence, these are the age-grade standards according to which under age, normal age, and over age can be most accurately determined, and, therefore, the age-grade standards which should be used in determining the number of pupils in a school system under age, normal age, and over age.

Fifteen as the Upper Age Limit

A second group of writers and school officials rest their case on the following facts: (1) that, notwithstanding the legal age of entrance, six, children in large numbers do not enter school until they are seven years of age and older [1]; (2) that the child is not directly guaranteed by the state to the school until he is seven years old; and (3) that to give the child a full eight years' elementary school course of instruction the school must have eight years in which to do its work, hence the upper normal-age limit for completing the course must be eight years higher than the lower age limit of the Compulsory Education Law; resting their case on these facts, this second group of writers and school officials fixes the upper normal-age limit for completing the elementary school just prior to the attainment of the fifteenth birthday. If up to fifteen years of age is accepted as the upper normal-age limit for completing the elementary school, the normal-age limits for entering and the normal-age limits for completing each of the several grades are respectively as shown in Table LXI.

If comparison is made between the normal-age limits for entering and for completing each of the several grades of the elementary school as these are given in Tables LX and LXI, two differences will be observed: (1) the normal age for entering and the normal age for completing each of the several grades are a half year higher in Table LXI than in Table LX; and (2) the age-grade standards for entering and for completing each of the several grades in Table LXI permit a range in ages of an entire year, whereas the age-grade standards in Table LX permit a range in ages of only

[1] Twenty-two per cent. of the pupils entering the 1A grade of the elementary schools of the City of New York in 1910-11 were seven years of age and older. See Annual Report of the City Superintendent of Schools for 1910-11, page 61.

TABLE LXI

SHOWS THE NORMAL-AGE LIMITS FOR ENTERING AND THE NORMAL-AGE LIMITS FOR COMPLETING EACH OF THE GRADES OF THE ELEMENTARY SCHOOL, WHEN JUST PRIOR TO FIFTEEN IS ACCEPTED AS THE UPPER NORMAL-AGE LIMIT FOR COMPLETING THE ELEMENTARY SCHOOL COURSE OF STUDY

Grades	Normal-Age Limit for Entering	Normal-Age Limit for Completing
1A	6 up to 7	6½ up to 7½
1B	6½ up to 7½	7 up to 8
2A	7 up to 8	7½ up to 8½
2B	7½ up to 8½	8 up to 9
3A	8 up to 9	8½ up to 9½
3B	8½ up to 9½	9 up to 10
4A	9 up to 10	9½ up to 10½
4B	9½ up to 10½	10 up to 11
5A	10 up to 11	10½ up to 11½
5B	10½ up to 11½	11 up to 12
6A	11 up to 12	11½ up to 12½
6B	11½ up to 12½	12 up to 13
7A	12 up to 13	12½ up to 13½
7B	12½ up to 13½	13 up to 14
8A	13 up to 14	13½ up to 14½
8B	13½ up to 14½	14 up to 15

a half year. This difference of a half year in the upper normal-age limit for entering and a half year in the upper normal-age limit for completing each of the grades, together with the difference of a half year in the range of the normal-age limits for entering and for completing each of the grades, materially affect the reported number of pupils normal age and over age.[1] In consequence, to determine whether or not pupils are under age, normal age, or over age, in view of the age-grade standards given in Table LXI, is to report for a school system a maximum number of pupils of normal age and a minimum number of pupils over age.

[1] See Table LXII, pages 229 and 230.

To accept up to fifteen years of age as the upper normal-age limit to complete the elementary school and to use the age-grade standards based thereon, as given in Table LXI, in making age-grade reports, is not only unwise, because of the facts cited (see page 222) in support of making up to fourteen and a half the upper normal-age limit for finishing the elementary school course of study, but unwise because of the following additional reasons:

(1) Because to make up-to-fifteen the normal age for completing the elementary school course and to report this as the normal age fails to impress parents with the fact that unless their children enter school at the legal age of entrance (six), and continue regular in attendance, they will probably drop from school without being able to complete the course.

(2) Because to make up-to-fifteen the normal age for completing the elementary school fails to impress on school officials the necessity of so adapting the standards of the school and the course of study to the abilities and needs of different groups of children, that children entering at six but only able to continue until they are fourteen or shortly thereafter may complete an entire elementary school course of instruction.

Effect on Statistics for New York City of the Age-Grade Standards Used

Reference to the age-grade standards for "being in the grade," proposed and employed by the City Superintendent of Schools (see page 211), will reveal the fact that he is in the second group of writers and school officials; that is, among those who hold that the upper normal-age limit for completing the elementary school is just prior to the attainment of the fifteenth birthday. Had the City Superintendent of Schools made up-to-fifteen, together with the legal age of entrance (six), the basis of determining the normal-age limits for entering and for completing each of the several grades, 1A, 1B, 2A, etc. (see Table LXI), and had he determined under age, normal age, and over age from the point of view of the normal-age limits for entering and for completing each of the several grades, even then he would employ the age-grade standards which yield a larger reported number of pupils of normal age and a smaller reported number of over-age pupils than when the age-grade standards (see Table LX) are employed, based on finishing the elementary school just prior to becoming fourteen and a half. (See Table LXII.)

The City Superintendent of Schools, however, did not use up to fifteen years of age, together with the legal age of entrance (six), to determine the normal-age limits for entering and for completing each of the several grades, the 1A grade, the 1B grade, the 2A grade, etc., but, as we have seen, he used these ages to determine the normal ages for "being in the grades" of the several years, first-year grades, second-year grades, etc.; he does not make his age-grade reports from the point of view of entering or of completing each of the several grades, the 1A grade, the 1B grade, etc., but, as we have seen, from the point of view of "being in the grades" of each of the several years; and finally, since 1905, his age-grade reports are not only for "being in the grades" of each of the several years, but, as we have seen, are made *after promotion.* All of which contribute to one end, viz., a very high reported number of pupils of normal age and a very low reported number of pupils over age in the elementary schools. (See Tables LXII-1, LXII-2, and LXIII.)

3. DIFFERENCES IN REPORTED PER CENT. OF OVER-AGE PUPILS WHEN DIFFERENT AGE-GRADE STANDARDS ARE USED

Age-grade Table LXII-1 conforms in every respect to the age-grade reports as made by the City Superintendent of Schools, with two exceptions: the age-grade standards

TABLE LXII

SHOWS THE NUMBER AND THE PER CENT. OF PUPILS UNDER AGE, NORMAL AGE, AND OVER AGE, WHEN AN AGE-GRADE REPORT IS BASED ON THE AGE-GRADE STANDARDS FOR ENTERING AND FOR COMPLETING EACH OF THE GRADES

(1) WHEN THE AGE-GRADE STANDARDS ARE DETERMINED IN VIEW OF UP-TO-FIFTEEN AS THE UPPER NORMAL-AGE LIMIT FOR COMPLETING THE ELEMENTARY SCHOOL

Grades	Register as of June 30 after Promotion	Under Age		Normal Age		Over Age	
		Number Under Age	Per Cent. of Register Under Age	Number Normal Age	Per Cent. of Register Normal Age	Number Over Age	Per Cent. of Register Over Age
1A	131	4	3.05	82	62.60	45	34.35
1B	394	129	32.74	203	51.52	62	15.74
2A	486	144	29.63	234	48.15	108	22.22
2B	418	73	17.47	216	51.67	129	30.86
3A	486	106	21.81	234	48.15	146	30.04
3B	452	81	17.92	197	43.58	174	38.50
4A	477	89	18.66	216	45.28	172	36.06
4B	457	73	15.97	168	36.76	216	47.27
5A	473	63	13.32	190	40.17	220	46.51
5B	416	45	10.82	138	33.17	233	56.01
6A	548	84	15.33	184	33.58	280	51.09
6B	462	59	12.77	141	30.52	262	56.71
7A	436	74	16.97	125	28.67	237	54.36
7B	577	80	13.86	189	32.76	308	53.38
8A	515	101	19.61	191	37.09	223	43.30
8B	400	68	17.00	147	36.75	185	46.25
Total	7,128	1,273	17.86	2,855	40.05	3,000	42.09

TABLE LXII (*Continued*)

(2) WHEN THE AGE-GRADE STANDARDS ARE DETERMINED IN VIEW OF UP-TO-FOURTEEN-AND-A-HALF AS THE UPPER NORMAL-AGE LIMIT FOR COMPLETING THE ELEMENTARY SCHOOL

Grades	Register on June 30 after Promotion	Under Age		Normal Age		Over Age	
		Number Under Age	Per Cent. of Register Under Age	Number Normal Age	Per Cent. of Register Normal Age	Number Over Age	Per Cent. of Register Over Age
1A.......	131	4	3.05	50	38.17	77	58.78
1B.......	394	129	32.74	134	34.01	131	33.25
2A.......	486	144	29.63	162	33.33	180	37.04
2B.......	418	73	17.47	128	30.62	217	51.91
3A.......	486	106	21.81	126	25.93	254	52.26
3B.......	452	81	17.92	115	25.44	256	56.64
4A.......	477	89	18.66	105	22.01	283	59.33
4B.......	457	73	15.97	100	21.88	284	62.15
5A.......	473	63	13.32	99	20.93	311	65.75
5B.......	416	45	10.82	78	18.75	293	70.43
6A.......	548	84	15.33	91	16.61	373	68.06
6B.......	462	59	12.77	71	15.37	332	71.86
7A.......	436	74	16.97	45	10.32	317	72.71
7B.......	577	80	13.86	96	16.64	401	69.50
8A.......	515	101	19.61	78	15.15	336	65.24
8B.......	400	68	17.00	77	19.25	255	63.75
Total.....	7,128	1,273	17.86	1,555	21.81	4,300	60.33

are for entering and for completing, and are for each of the several grades when up-to-fifteen is accepted as the upper normal-age limit for completing the elementary school. Age-grade Table LXII-2 conforms in every respect to the age-grade reports of the City Superintendent of Schools, with three exceptions: the age-grade standards are for entering and for completing, and are for each of

TABLE LXIII

SHOWS THE NUMBER AND THE PER CENT. OF PUPILS UNDER AGE, NORMAL AGE, AND OVER AGE, WHEN AN AGE-GRADE REPORT IS BASED ON THE AGE-GRADE STANDARDS FOR BEING IN THE GRADE, OF THE SEVERAL YEARS, WHEN THESE AGE-GRADE STANDARDS ARE DETERMINED IN VIEW OF UP-TO-FIFTEEN AS THE UPPER NORMAL-AGE LIMIT FOR COMPLETING THE ELEMENTARY SCHOOL, AND WHEN THE AGE-GRADE REPORT IS MADE AFTER PROMOTION (AS AGE-GRADE REPORTS HAVE BEEN MADE BY THE CITY SUPERINTENDENT OF SCHOOLS SINCE 1905)

Grades	Register June 30 after Promotion	Under Age		Normal Age		Over Age	
		Number Under Age	Per Cent. of Register Under Age	Number Normal Age	Per Cent. of Register Normal Age	Number Over Age	Per Cent of Register Over Age
1st Year.....	525	17	3.24	476	90.67	32	6.09
2nd Year.....	904	147	16.26	663	73.34	94	10.40
3rd Year.....	938	122	13.01	662	70.57	154	16.42
4th Year.....	934	106	11.35	603	64.56	225	24.09
5th Year.....	889	73	8.21	549	61.76	267	30.03
6th Year.....	1,010	102	10.10	561	55.54	347	34.36
7th Year.....	1,013	108	10.66	578	57.06	327	32.28
8th Year.....	915	131	14.32	575	62.84	209	22.84
Total........	7,128	806	11.31	4,667	65.47	1,655	23.22

the several grades, when these are determined in view of up-to-fourteen-and-a-half as the upper normal-age limit for completing the elementary school. Age-grade Table LXIII conforms in every respect to the age-grade reports as made by the City Superintendent of Schools since 1905[1]; the pupils are those on register June 30th; the ages are as of June 30th; the age-grade standards are those for being in the grades of the several years when determined in view of up-to-fifteen as the upper normal-age limit for completing the elementary schools; and whether pupils are under age,

[1] See Annual Report of the City Superintendent of Schools for 1905, pages 58 ff.; and for 1911, pages 53 ff.

normal age, or over age is determined after promotion. In consequence, age-grade Table LXII-1 shows for the five schools in question the per cent. of pupils under age, normal age, and over age, as it should be reported when an age-grade report is based on the register as of June 30th, and when up-to-fifteen is accepted as the upper normal-age

	Per Cent.		
	Under Age	Normal Age	Over Age
Table LXII-1—Shows for the pupils and schools in question when under age, normal age, and over age are correctly determined, and when-up-to fifteen is taken as the normal age to complete the elementary school......................	17.86	40.05	42.09
Table LXII-2—Shows for the same pupils and the same schools, when under age, normal age, and over age are correctly determined and when up-to-fourteen-and-a-half is taken as the normal age to complete the elementary school......	17.86	21.81	60.33
Table LXIII—Shows for these same pupils and these same schools as would be reported by the City Superintendent of Schools, who takes up-to-fifteen as the normal age to complete the elementary school..............................	11.31	65.47	23.22

limit for completing the elementary school. Table LXII-2 shows for these same pupils and the same schools the per cent. of pupils under age, normal age, and over age, as should be reported, when up-to-fourteen-and-a-half is accepted as the upper normal-age limit for completing the elementary school. Age-grade Table LXIII shows for the same pupils and for the same schools the per cent. under age, normal age, and over age as would be reported by the

City Superintendent of Schools. (Up-to-fifteen is accepted by the City Superintendent of Schools as the upper normal-age limit for completing the elementary school.)

The City Superintendent of Schools, by using the age-grade standards for "being in the grades" of the several years, and by making his age-grade reports as he does, records, therefore, in view of Table LXII-1, 6.55 per cent. fewer pupils under age, 25.42 per cent. more pupils of normal age, and 18.87 per cent. fewer pupils over age than there probably are in the elementary schools of the City of New York, and in view of Table LXII-2, he reports 6.55 per cent. too few pupils under age, 43.66 per cent. too many pupils of normal age, and 37.11 per cent. too few pupils over age. These differences, varying according to whether up-to-fifteen or up-to-fourteen-and-a-half is accepted as the upper normal-age limit for completing the elementary school, are to be found in all the age-grade reports made by the City Superintendent of Schools for 1905 to 1911 inclusive.

CHAPTER XVI

WHEN AND HOW TO MAKE AGE-GRADE REPORTS

WHETHER or not a pupil is under age, normal age, or over age can be accurately determined, as we have seen, only from the point of view either of the normal-age limits for entering or of the normal-age limits for completing each of the several grades. Accordingly, age-grade reports to be reliable and accurate must be made either at the end or at the beginning of a school term or school year.

AGE-GRADE REPORTS MADE AT THE END OF A SCHOOL TERM OR YEAR

The laws of most of the states, including the State of New York, require superintendents of schools to make an annual report for the official school year to the State Department of Education. With the recognition of their significance, over-age tables showing the ages and grades of pupils—the basis of age-grade reports—have been included in the annual report required of superintendents of schools by the educational departments of several states. Owing, at least partly, to the state requirement of an annual report for the official school year on the ages and grades of pupils, superintendents of schools make age-grade reports, as a rule, at the end of the year only.

When age-grade reports are made at the end of the year, to be included in the annual report for the official school year, such age-grade reports are based, almost always, on the age and grade, at the end of the year, of each and every pupil who has been on the register during the course of the official year, of any one of the several schools of the system.[1] Such an age-grade report gives, therefore, for all the different pupils who have been on the register during the official year, the number, at the end of the year, under age, normal age, or over age.

Indeed, the primary object of state authorities in requiring such age-grade reports and the primary object of superintendents of schools in making such reports is to gain definite information with respect to the number of pupils, at the end of the year, of the total or net register for the official year, under age, normal age, and over age, to the end that definite data may be at hand on which to base such administrative policies and action that the number of overage pupils may be reduced during the succeeding official school year.

Requirements of an Exact Age-Grade Report Where Promotions Are Annual

A reliable and accurate age-grade report for the official school year for a system of schools having annual promotion involves:

(1) That the age-grade report be made for each of the several grades.

(2) That the age-grade report for each grade be based on the total or net register of the grade for the official school year, that is, be based on the age of each and every pupil on the register of the grade at the end of the year and on the age of each and every pupil—exclusive of pupils transferred or promoted—who has been on the register of the grade during the course of the year, but who has dropped from school either temporarily or permanently, and consequently is not on the register of the grade at the end of the year.

[1] Annual Report of the Schools of Cincinnati for 1911, page 81.

(3) That the age-grade report be made after promotion and non-promotion, but before the grades and classes are reorganized for the new year; that is, both promoted and non-promoted pupils should be reported as of the register of the grade in which they have been during the whole or part of the official year, and in which they are registered at the end of the year before the reorganization of the grades and the classes for the new year.

(4) That whether promoted pupils are under age, normal age, or over age be determined in view of the normal-age limit for completing the grade in which they have been registered a part or the whole of the year ending and hence in view of the normal-age limits for completing the grade from which they are to be advanced.

(5) That whether non-promoted pupils are under age, normal age, or over age be determined from the point of view of the normal-age limits for completing the grade they last finished. Since non-promoted pupils are for all practical purposes just entering the grade from which they have failed to be advanced, whether non-promoted pupils are under age, normal age, or over age may be determined practically as well from the point of view of the normal-age limits for entering the grade in which they have been registered during the whole or a part of the year ending, and from which they have failed to be promoted.[1]

(6) That all pupils—exclusive of those transferred or promoted—who have been on the register of a given grade sometime during the official year, but who have dropped from school either temporarily or permanently, hence are not on the register of the grade at the end of the year, be

[1] The probable error in determining non-promoted pupils from the point of view of the age-grade standards for entering the grade in which they have been registered during the whole or a part of the year, but from which they have just failed to be advanced, is only .028 of one per cent.

regarded as non-promoted pupils. Whether such pupils are under age, normal age, or over age is then determined in the same way as in the case of other non-promoted pupils. The age-grade report for promoted pupils, for non-promoted pupils, and for pupils who have dropped from school either temporarily or permanently should be made separately in order to distinguish between the per cent. of under-age, normal-age, and over-age pupils, among promoted and non-promoted pupils and among pupils who have dropped out. These separate reports should then be combined to show the per cent. of under age, normal age, and over age for the grades as a whole.

Age-Grade Reports Where Promotions Are Semi-Annual

The foregoing considerations have to do, as stated, with the making, at the end of the year, of an age-grade report for the official school year, in a system of schools having annual promotions. In a system of schools having semi-annual promotions, such as in the City of New York, *it is better not to attempt to make an age-grade report for the official year as a whole, but to make a separate age-grade report for each of the official terms.* If this is done, the age-grade report for the official term is made in the same way as such a report for the official year.

If, however, in a system of schools having semi-annual promotions it is deemed desirable to make an age-grade report for the official year as a whole, the age-grade report for each of the grades should be made on the basis of the ages of all pupils on the register of the grade, at the end of the year; and on the basis of the ages of all pupils, exclusive of those transferred or promoted, who have been on the register of the grade during the course of the official year, but who have dropped from school either temporarily or permanently, the report itself is made in the same way as in a system of schools having annual promotions.

AGE-GRADE REPORTS MADE AT THE BEGINNING OF THE SCHOOL TERM OR YEAR

In contrast to age-grade reports made at the end of a term or year for the official year, the primary purpose of an age-grade report made at the beginning of a term or year is to give definite knowledge of the number of pupils actually in each classroom and in each school of the system under age, normal age, and over age, to the end that this information may be used by school officials, principals, and teachers in properly classifying pupils and in properly adapting the materials and methods of instruction to the varying abilities and needs of different groups of children. In a word, age-grade reports made at the end of a term or year shed light on age-grade conditions in the system as a whole and supply the basis of general administrative policies, such as making provision for special classes and providing different courses of instruction for over-age pupils; whereas age-grade reports made at the beginning of the term or year place at the disposal of school officials, principals, and teachers information which enables them so to apply their general administrative policies that the best interests of each child are conserved.

An age-grade report for the beginning of a term or school year, to be most helpful to principals and teachers in classifying and carrying on the instruction of pupils, should be made on the first day that schools open for instruction, or as soon as possible thereafter. Such a report should include all pupils who were in the particular class and grade who failed of promotion and all pupils who were promoted to the particular class and grade when the schools closed for instruction at the end of the preceding term or year. There should also be included in such a report all pupils who enter the particular classes and grades from time to time after the beginning of the term.[1] In a word, an age-grade report

[1] For a suggestive method of tabulating and exhibiting such an age-grade report for a given class see the card prepared by Dr. Leonard Ayres of the Russell Sage Foundation.

for the beginning of a term, to be most helpful, should show correctly the age-grade condition in the particular class. It also follows from the foregoing discussions that such an age-grade report, to be reliable and accurate, must be made from the point of view of the normal-age limits for entering each of the several grades.

Where it is deemed desirable to make an age-grade report at the beginning of the term *for the system as a whole,* sufficient time, after the opening of the schools for instruction, must be permitted to elapse, at least one or two weeks, so that a large part if not all of the pupils who are to be in school are actually in attendance. Otherwise, the report will give but a partial view of the actual existing age-grade conditions.

WHEN AGE-GRADE REPORTS ARE MADE BY THE CITY SUPERINTENDENT OF SCHOOLS

The annual reports of the City Superintendent of Schools are for the official year beginning August 1st and ending July 31st. The age-grade reports made by the City Superintendent of Schools appear in his annual reports. This being true, it would be expected that his age-grade reports would be for the official year, and give, by official terms or for the official year as a whole, the number of pupils of the total or net register under age, normal age, and over age.

While this may have been the intention of the City Superintendent of Schools, an examination of his age-grade reports reveals the fact that they are neither for the official term nor for the official year as a whole. Aside from the method employed in making them, the age-grade reports of the City Superintendent of Schools are based on the register as of June 30th, instead of being based on the total or net register for the official year, as should be done when the report is for the official year. Thus the tens of thousands[1] of pupils who have been on the register during the

[1] See pages 185-189.

course of the official year, but who have dropped from school either temporarily or permanently, are entirely ignored; instead of his age-grade reports being made after pupils are promoted and non-promoted, but before the grades are reorganized for the new year, they are made after the grades and classes are organized for the new year; hence, pupils are not reported from the grade in which they have been during the whole or a part of the year past, but from the grade they will be in at the beginning of the new year.[1] In consequence, the age-grade reports of the City Superintendent of Schools do not have the value for administrative purposes which belongs to age-grade reports made at the end of the year for the official year as a whole.

Notwithstanding the age-grade reports of the City Superintendent of Schools appear in his annual reports and for this reason the inference is that they have to do with the official year for which the annual report is made, his reports have certain of the characteristics of age-grade reports made at the beginning of a school term or year for the system as a whole. His age-grade reports, however, instead of being based on the ages and grades of the children on the register in the new year, as should be done when the report is for the beginning of the new term or year,[2] are based on the ages and grades of the children on register June 30th after promotion, and instead of his age-grade reports being made after the greater part, if not all, of the pupils who will be in school during the new term or year are actually in attendance, they are made at the end of the preceding year when the schools are closed for instruction, hence no account is taken of the ages and grades of the army of pupils who will enter the elementary schools of the City of New York for the first time during the new term or year. In consequence, the age-grade reports of the City

[1] See Annual Report of the City Superintendent of Schools for 1905, pages 58 ff.; and for 1911, pages 53 ff.

[2] See pages 238-239.

Superintendent of Schools are lacking the practical worth which belongs to age-grade reports made at the beginning of a school term or year, for the system as a whole, or of a current age-grade report made at the beginning of a term, for a particular class and grade.

The age-grade reports made annually by the City Superintendent of Schools since 1904 have, therefore, neither the value for administrative purposes belonging to age-grade reports made at the end of the year for the official year, nor the practical worth belonging to such reports made at the beginning of a new term or year, for neither do they supply definite information on the age-grade status in the system as a whole, nor do they supply definite information useful to principals and teachers in the classification and instruction of children.

CHAPTER XVII

WHEN AND HOW TO TAKE THE AGES OF PUPILS

IF the school term or the school year, i. e., the period during which the schools are open for instruction, began and ended on the same date as the official term or the official school year, there would be no question about when the ages of children should be taken in making age-grade reports. But the official school year may begin August 1st, whereas the schools may not be open for instruction until September 1st; the schools may close for instruction June 30th, whereas the end of the official school year may not be until July 31st. This being so, confusion has arisen about the proper time to take the ages of children to be used as the basis of age-grade reports. In consequence, there is no consensus of opinion on when the ages of children should be taken, and there is little uniformity in the time they are taken; the time often varies within the same system of schools and within the same age-grade report.[1]

The time to take the ages of pupils depends on whether the age-grade report is for an official school year and made at the end of the year or is for the beginning of an official school year and made at the beginning of the year.

WHEN THE AGE-GRADE REPORT IS MADE AT THE END OF THE YEAR, AND FOR THE OFFICIAL SCHOOL YEAR

It should be obvious that when an age-grade report is to be made at the end of the school year for the official year

[1] Annual Report of the Superintendent of Public Schools of the City of Philadelphia for 1911, pages 104 ff.

as a whole, the ages of the children cannot be taken as of the date of their first enrollment in the schools in the given official year.[1] Because, should the ages of the pupils taken in this way be used as the basis of such an age-grade report, the ages of all children would be lower from one to eleven months than the actual ages at the time the report was made. It is equally obvious that the ages of children cannot be taken as of the birthday occurring within the official school year for which the age-grade report is made.[2] Because to take the ages of children in this way would be to use as the basis of the age-grade report ages lower by from zero to twelve months than the actual ages of the children. Similarly, and for a like reason, it is incorrect to take the ages of children as of a specific date during the course of the official school year, e. g., December 8th.[3]

When an age-grade report is made at the end of the year for the official year as a whole, there are but two dates for taking the ages of pupils which need to be considered: (a) the date at the end of the year when the schools close for instruction; and (b) the date of the close of the official school year.

The argument for taking the ages of children as of the date of the closing of the schools for instruction is that the real work of the schools is done when they close for instruction, hence this is the proper date on which to take the ages of children in judging of their progress through the schools.

The arguments for taking the ages of children as of the date of the close of the official school year are:

(1) The question of taking the ages of children as of the date of closing of the schools for instruction only arises

[1] See Report of Board of Education of the City of Chicago for 1911, pages 147 ff.

[2] See Directions of the United States Bureau of Education for 1910-11.

[3] Strayer: *Age-Grade Census of Schools and Colleges*, page 10; Annual Report of the City Superintendent of Public Schools of the City of Philadelphia for 1911, pages 104 ff.

when this date does not coincide with the date of the end of the official year. For example, in the City of New York, the schools close for instruction about June 30th, whereas the official school year ends July 31st.

(2) The end of the official year remains the same from year to year, whereas the date of the closing of the schools for instruction fluctuates; hence, to take the ages of the children as of the date of the close of the official year gives uniformity to the time of taking the ages and gives a corresponding uniformity to the age-grade reports made on the basis thereof.

(3) The primary purpose of an age-grade report made at the end of the year is to show the actual age-grade status, at the end of the official school year, of all the different pupils who have been in the schools during the course of the official year; hence, to take the ages of the children as of a date other than of the close of the official year is to give the age-grade status as of that date and not as of the end of the official year, hence is to lose sight of the object of such an age-grade report.

(4) Finally, the normal length of time to complete each of the several grades is fixed and must necessarily be fixed, in school systems having semi-annual promotions on the basis of the calendar half year (six months), and in school systems having annual promotions on the basis of the calendar year (twelve months).[1] The normal length of time to complete a grade (either six calendar months or a calendar year), together with the accepted normal age for completing the elementary school and the legal age of entrance, serve as the basis of determining the normal-age limits for entering and for completing each of the several grades. The age-grade standards, in view of which under age, normal age, and over age are judged, are, therefore, based on calendar units of a half year or a year.

In making age-grade reports, to take the ages of children

[1] See page 223.

as of the date of the closing of the schools for instruction at the end of the mid-year, or as of the date of the closing of the schools for instruction at the end of the year, is equivalent to making the actual length of time the schools are open for instruction during the term, or during the school year, the normal length of time for completing each of the several grades, hence is to introduce a second, and, as a rule, a shorter measure of the normal length of time for completing each of the several grades, shorter by from one to two months, than the calendar unit of time employed in fixing the normal-age limits for entering and for completing each of the several grades. Or, it is to use one unit of measure—a short one—in taking the ages of children, and a second unit of measure—a long one—in judging of whether or not they are under age, normal age, or over age. The result of which is to report too high the number of pupils under age and to report too low the number of pupils of normal age and over age.[1]

For the foregoing reasons, when an age-grade report is made at the end of the year for the official year, the ages of the children should be taken as of the date of the close of the official school year.

WHEN AN AGE-GRADE REPORT IS MADE FOR THE BEGINNING OF THE YEAR

Confusion about when to take the ages of the children, when an age-grade report is made for the beginning of the year, arises (a) from the fact that the date of the beginning of the official school year does not always coincide with the date of opening the schools for instruction, and (b) from the fact that an age-grade report for the beginning of the year, to be reliable and accurate, must be made at the beginning and during the course of the term, or sometime after the schools are opened for instruction. There are four possible dates on which the ages of the children may be taken in making an age-grade report for the

[1] See Table LXIV, page 248.

beginning of the year: (a) the date of the beginning of the official school year; (b) the date of the opening of the schools for instruction; (c) the date on which the child enters school; and (d) the date on which the register is taken for the report, when made for the system as a whole.

An age-grade report for the beginning of the year and for a given class and grade should be made currently as children enter the given class, and when for the system as a whole, it should be made sometime after the opening of the schools for instruction. To take the ages of the children as of the date of their first entrance to school or as of the date the register is taken for the report when for the system as a whole is, as a rule, to record ages from zero to one, two, and three months older than if the ages were for the beginning of the official year. In an age-grade report for the beginning of a school term or year, under age, normal age, and over age are determined in view of the normal-age limits fixed for entering each of the several grades, and these age limits in turn date from the beginning of the official year. Hence, to take the ages of the children as of a date later than the date of the opening of the official school year is to increase the reported number of over-age pupils. Ages as of the date of the entrance of pupils to school cannot therefore be used in a report at the beginning of the year for a given class and grade, nor can the ages as of the date the register is taken be used for such a report when for the system as a whole.

The remaining possible dates for taking the ages in making such an age-grade report at the beginning of the term or year are (a) the date of the beginning of the official school year, and (b) the date of the opening of the schools for instruction. The respective arguments for using each of these dates parallel the respective arguments given above for taking the ages of the children, in making an age-grade report at the end of the year, as of the date of the closing of the schools for instruction, and for taking the ages as of the date of the end of the official school year. Consequently, it is not necessary to repeat the arguments for taking the ages of the children, to be used as the basis of an age-grade report, for the beginning of the year, as of the date of the opening of schools for instruction, or to repeat those for taking the ages as of the date of the beginning of the official school year.

The primary purpose of an age-grade report for the beginning of the school year is, as we have seen,[1] to supply definite knowledge of the number of pupils in each classroom and in each school under age, normal age, and over age. In view of this purpose, there can be but one time for taking the ages of children to be used as the basis of such a report, viz., the date of the beginning of the official school year.

WHEN AGES ARE TAKEN BY THE CITY SUPERINTENDENT OF SCHOOLS

The ages of children used by the City Superintendent of Schools, in making his age-grade report for the elementary schools for 1911, were taken as of June 28th, the date of the closing of the schools for instruction.[2]

In making an age-grade report at the end of the year, to use as the basis thereof, the ages of children as of the date of the closing of the schools for instruction is, as we have seen,[3] to use a short measure of the time to complete a grade—the length of time the schools are open for instruction, approximately ten months—and to use a long measure of the time to complete a grade—twelve months—when judging whether or not pupils are under age, normal age, or over age. The effect is the same as when goods are bought on long measure and sold on short measure. Hence, for the City Superintendent of Schools to take the ages of children as of the date of the closing of the schools for instruction and to use these ages as the basis of his age-

[1] See page 234. [2] Elementary School Circular No. 27, 1911-12.
[3] See page 244.

grade reports is for him to report the number of pupils under age too high and to report the number of pupils of normal age and over age too low.

TABLE LXIV

SHOWS THE NUMBER AND THE PER CENT. OF PUPILS UNDER AGE, NORMAL AGE, AND OVER AGE, WHEN AN AGE-GRADE REPORT IS MADE, AS MADE BY THE CITY SUPERINTENDENT OF SCHOOLS SINCE 1905

(1) WITH THE AGES OF PUPILS AS OF JUNE 30TH

Grades	Register as of June 30 after Promotion	Under Age		Normal Age		Over Age	
		Number Under Age	Per Cent. of Register Under Age	Number Normal Age	Per Cent. of Register Normal Age	Number Over Age	Per Cent. of Register Over Age
1st Year.........	525	17	3.24	476	90.67	32	6.09
2nd Year.........	904	147	16.26	663	73.34	94	10.40
3rd Year.........	938	122	13.01	662	70.57	154	16.42
4th Year.........	934	106	11.35	603	64.56	225	24.09
5th Year.........	889	73	8.21	549	61.76	267	30.03
6th Year.........	1,010	102	10.10	561	55.54	347	34.36
7th Year.........	1,013	108	10.66	578	57.06	327	32.28
8th Year.........	915	131	14.32	575	62.84	209	22.84
Total...........	7,128	806	11.31	4,667	65.47	1,655	23.22

Age-grade Table LXIV-1 conforms in every respect to the age-grade reports as made by the City Superintendent of Schools since 1905. Age-grade Table LXIV-2 conforms in every respect to the age-grade reports as made by the City Superintendent of Schools since 1905, with one exception, the ages of the pupils are as of July 31st, the close of the official year. In consequence, Table LXIV shows the effect on the reported number of pupils under age, normal age, and over age, of taking the ages of pupils as of June 30th, the usual date of the closing of the schools for instruction, instead of, as should be done, when the age-grade report is made at the end of the year, as of July 31st, the end of the official school year.

Table LXIV-1 shows for the five schools in question that of the pupils on register after promotion 11.31 per cent.

TABLE LXIV (*Continued*)

(2) WITH THE EXCEPTION THAT THE AGES OF PUPILS ARE AS OF JULY 31ST

Grades	Register as of June 30 after Promotion	Under Age		Normal Age		Over Age	
		Number Under Age	Per Cent. of Register Under Age	Number Normal Age	Per Cent. of Register Normal Age	Number Over Age	Per Cent. of Register Over Age
1st Year.........	525	13	2.48	473	90.09	39	7.43
2nd Year.........	904	97	10.73	699	77.32	108	11.95
3rd Year.........	938	87	9.28	677	72.17	174	18.55
4th Year.........	934	82	8.78	612	65.52	240	25.70
5th Year.........	889	54	6.07	554	62.32	281	31.61
6th Year.........	1,010	84	8.32	547	54.16	379	37.52
7th Year.........	1,013	85	8.39	573	56.57	355	35.04
8th Year.........	915	105	11.47	583	63.72	227	24.81
Total............	7,128	607	8.52	4,718	66.19	1,803	25.29

were under age, 65.47 per cent. were of normal age, and 23.22 per cent. were over age. Table LXIV-2 shows for the same schools and for the same pupils that 8.52 per cent. were under age, 66.19 per cent. were of normal age, and that 25.29 per cent. were over age. In a word, the City Superintendent of Schools, by taking the ages of pupils as of June 28th or June 30th, as the case may be, is able to report, in view of Table LXIV, 2.79 per cent. more pupils under age, .72 of 1 per cent. fewer pupils of normal age, and

2.07 per cent. fewer pupils over age, than he would probably be able to report were the ages of the children taken as they should be, when age-grade reports are made at the end of the year, viz., as of the date of the close of the official school year.

HOW TO TAKE THE AGES OF PUPILS

But little less confusion exists with respect to how to take the ages of pupils than exists with respect to when to take their ages.

The basis of determining the ages of children, as of a given date, is the date of birth: year, month, and day. In getting the date of birth—year, month, and day—great care should be exercised. Under no condition should the teacher ask the pupils in her classroom the dates of their births and record these dates in her register to be used later in determining the ages of pupils. The date of birth—year, month, and day—recorded in the teacher's register should in all cases be taken from the pupil's record card.

In getting the date of birth—year, month, and day—for the pupil's record card, the parent should be made to go on record, and in all cases of doubt documentary evidence should be demanded, such, for example, as birth certificates. To repeat, too much care cannot be exercised in getting the exact date of birth, and this should be acquired once for all when the pupil enters school for the first time.

With the date of birth—year, month, and day—as the basis, the age of a child as of the beginning or the end of the official school term or school year can be readily determined. For reasons which will appear later, the ages of children should always be computed in terms of years, months, and days, thirty days being counted as a month.[1]

The normal-age limits for entering and for completing each of the several grades are fixed, it will be remembered,[2]

[1] In case pupils are born in the month of February, 28 days should be counted as a month.

[2] See pages 222-225.

in terms of years, months, and days. For example, when up to fifteen is accepted as the upper normal-age limit for completing the elementary school, the normal-age limits for completing the 1A grade are from 6 years, 6 months, and no days through 7 years, 5 months, and 29 days inclusive; for the 1B, from 7 years, no months, and no days, through 7 years, 11 months, and 29 days inclusive, and so on. Accordingly, if pupils are to be grouped with accuracy on the basis of age, it is necessary to have their ages in years, months, and days. When their ages are so taken, it is possible to group them with absolute accuracy according to the age limits fixed for entering or for completing each of the several grades.

CHAPTER XVIII

THE CHILDREN TO INCLUDE IN AGE-GRADE REPORTS

THE BASIS OF THE QUESTION

A DECADE ago the elementary school was a simple institution, having as a rule one organization, one course of study, and one general classification of pupils. The present-day elementary school is a complex institution comprising a number of different schools, each having its own organization, its own course of study, and caring for a distinct class of pupils. Within the present-day elementary school are included: (1) regular classes, to which normal children are assigned; (2) rapid-advancement classes, in which over-age pupils may do three terms of work in two terms; (3) E classes—classes for over-age and retarded pupils; (4) C classes—classes for non-English-speaking pupils; (5) D classes—classes for over-age and retarded pupils seeking employment certificates; (6) defective-speech classes—classes for children having speech defects; (7) classes for anæmic children; (8) classes for tubercular children; (9) truant, probationary, and parental schools; (10) classes for the blind; (11) classes for the deaf; (12) classes for crippled children; (13) ungraded classes—classes for mentally defective children; (14) trade-schools for boys; (15) trade-schools for girls; and, at times, still other classes for children having special needs and interests.

In view of the diversified activities and the complex organization of the present-day elementary school, the question arises: What pupils should be included in an age-grade report having as its purpose to give, at the end or at the beginning of the official school term or year, the number of under-age, normal-age, and over-age children in the elementary schools?

THE CHILDREN TO INCLUDE

In making an age-grade report, in addition to having fixed normal-age limits for entering and for completing each of the grades and having the ages of the children as of the date of the close or the beginning of the official school term or year, it is also necessary to have the children classified either as to completion or as to entrance to one or the other of the grades. Otherwise it is impossible to determine whether or not pupils are under age, normal age, or over age. Only those pupils, therefore, can be included in an age-grade report for the elementary schools who can be classified as having completed or as entering one or the other of the grades.

In classes for the blind, for the deaf, for crippled children, for mentally defective, for anæmic and tubercular children, and in trade-schools for boys and for girls, the grades of the elementary school are, as a rule, ignored. It is, therefore, impossible to classify with any degree of accuracy children in such classes as having completed or as entering one or the other of the grades, and, in consequence, it is impossible to include the children of such classes in the body of an age-report.[1]

In rapid-advancement classes, in E classes, C classes, D classes, in defective-speech classes, in truant, parental, and probationary schools, the instruction follows more or less

[1] But the number of such children in each kind of special class and the ages of such children should be reported and incorporated in an age-grade report as a separate item. In case such pupils can be classified with reasonable accuracy on the basis of entrance or completion of one or the other of the several regular grades, they should, of course, be included in the body of the age-grade report under the heading of the respective kind of special class to which they belong.

along the lines of the regular elementary school course of study. In consequence, it is possible to classify the children in such classes with more or less accuracy according as they have completed or are entering one or the other of the grades. Hence, the children in such classes can be included.

While all pupils, except those in ungraded classes for physically and mentally defective children, and probably those in trade-schools for boys and for girls,[1] should be included in an age-grade report for the elementary schools, it adds both to the clarity and to the value of such a report if a separate report is made for each sex and for each distinct class of pupils; for example, a separate age-grade report for pupils in regular classes, for those in rapid-advancement classes, for those in E classes, and so on. These several and separate age-grade reports are then combined to show the total number of under-age, normal-age, and over-age pupils in the elementary schools, exclusive of those in ungraded classes[1] for physically and mentally defective children and those in trade schools.[2]

Finally, in view of the purpose of an age-grade report made at the end of the year for the official year, such an age-grade report should include not only all pupils, exclusive of those transferred or promoted, in the foregoing classes, on register at the close of the official year, but all pupils who have been on the register of these classes for a whole or a part of the official year, but who have dropped from school either temporarily or permanently; that is, age-grade reports made at the end of the year for the official year should be based on the total or net register. (See pages 234-237.)

Whereas, when an age-grade report is made at the beginning of the year for a given class and grade, there should be included all pupils in the foregoing classes, exclusive of

[1] See note, page 253.

[2] For a good example of such separate age reports, see Annual Report of the Superintendent of Public Schools of the City of Philadelphia for 1911, pages 104 ff.

those transferred, who were in the given class during the whole or a part of the previous term or year, and who were not promoted, and all pupils promoted to the given class at the end of the previous year; there should also be included all pupils who have entered the given class for the first time during the given term; when such a report is made for the system as a whole, it should be based on the total or net register for such classes up to and including the day on which the register is taken for the report.

CHILDREN TO BE INCLUDED IN AGE-GRADE REPORTS FOR THE ELEMENTARY SCHOOLS OF THE CITY OF NEW YORK

In view of the foregoing discussion, there should be included in a complete and exact age-grade report for the elementary schools of the City of New York, both when the report is for the official year, and when the report is for the beginning of the term or year, at least the pupils in the following classes:

(1) In the regular classes of each of the several grades
(2) In rapid-advancement classes
(3) In E classes
(4) In C classes
(5) In D classes
(6) In defective-speech classes
(7) In truant, parental, and probationary schools

CHILDREN INCLUDED IN AGE-GRADE REPORTS MADE FOR THE ELEMENTARY SCHOOLS OF THE CITY OF NEW YORK

In making his age-grade reports for 1904 and for 1905, there were included by the City Superintendent of Schools all the different children on register June 30th, but he did not include in these reports all the different children, exclusive of those transferred or promoted, who were on the register during the course of the official school year. While there were, therefore, included in the age-grade reports for 1904 and for 1905, children—a few hundred—who should have been excluded, viz., pupils in classes for mentally defective children,[1] there were omitted from these reports the tens of thousands of children who dropped from schools temporarily or permanently during the course of the official year, and who were not on the register June 30th.

In his Annual Report for 1905 the City Superintendent of Schools announces what pupils are to be excluded thereafter from his age-grade reports, viz., "pupils in special classes (classes to teach English to immigrant children) and ungraded classes (classes for defective or atypical children)." As a matter of fact, the foregoing children—a total of 2,115—were not only excluded from his age-grade report for 1906, but there were also excluded some 17,544 pupils on register in the newly formed Special D and E classes.[2] In a word, the age-grade report of the City Superintendent of Schools for 1906 included only the pupils on the register at the end of the year when the schools closed for instruction, in the regular classes of the several grades,[3] and this is true of all his later age-grade reports.[4] In consequence, the age-grade reports of the City Superintendent of Schools, since 1905, are not age-grade reports for the elementary schools as a whole, but merely age-grade reports for the regular classes of the several grades, and, by reason of taking no account whatever of the tens of thousands of pupils who drop from the regular classes during the course of the official year, they are but partial reports even for the pupils in the regular classes.

[1] Annual Report of the City Superintendent of Schools for 1905, page 63.

[2] Annual Report of the City Superintendent of Schools for 1906, pages 57-58.

[3] Annual Report of the City Superintendent of Schools for 1906, page 57.

[4] See Annual Report of the City Superintendent of Schools for 1907, page 58; and for 1911, page 54.

TABLE LXV

SHOWS THE NUMBER AND PER CENT. OF PUPILS UNDER AGE, NORMAL AGE, AND OVER AGE, WHEN AN AGE-GRADE REPORT IS CORRECTLY MADE, IN A SYSTEM OF SCHOOLS HAVING SEMI-ANNUAL PROMOTIONS, AT THE END OF A TERM FOR THE OFFICIAL TERM

(1) WHEN UP-TO-FIFTEEN IS ACCEPTED AS THE UPPER NORMAL-AGE LIMIT FOR COMPLETING THE ELEMENTARY SCHOOL

Grades	Net or Total Register for 2nd Official Term 1911	Under Age		Normal Age		Over Age	
		Number Under Age	Per Cent. of Register Under Age	Number Normal Age	Per Cent. of Register Normal Age	Number Over Age	Per Cent. of Register Over Age
Regular Classes							
1A....	517	90	17.41	315	60.93	112	21.66
1B....	487	95	19.51	280	57.49	112	23.00
2A....	436	50	11.47	235	53.90	151	34.63
2B....	524	74	14.12	272	51.91	178	33.97
3A....	463	60	12.96	203	43.84	200	43.20
3B....	488	70	14.34	228	46.72	190	38.93
4A....	468	63	13.46	166	35.47	239	51.07
4B....	498	46	9.24	205	41.16	247	49.60
5A....	441	31	7.03	146	33.11	264	59.86
5B....	557	72	12.93	188	33.75	297	53.32
6A....	491	48	9.78	131	26.68	312	63.54
6B....	466	61	13.09	141	30.26	264	56.65
7A....	658	73	11.09	172	26.14	413	62.77
7B....	588	82	13.95	191	32.48	315	53.57
8A....	483	60	12.42	157	32.51	266	55.07
8B....	388	76	19.59	141	36.34	171	44.07
Total...	7,953	1,051	13.22	3,171	39.87	3,731	46.91
C, D, and E Classes							
1A....	6	......	......	......	......	6	100.00
1B....	2	......	......	......	......	2	100.00
2A....	5	......	......	......	......	5	100.00
2B....	16	......	......	......	......	16	100.00
3A....	20	......	......	......	......	20	100.00
3B....	23	......	......	......	......	23	100.00
4A....	40	......	......	1	2.50	39	97.50
4B....	48	1	2.08	2	4.17	45	93.75
5A....	77	1	1.30	......	......	76	98.70
5B....	24	2	8.33	1	4.17	21	87.50
6A....	23	1	4.35	2	8.70	20	86.95
6B....	9	......	......	......	......	9	100.00
7A....	3	......	......	......	......	3	100.00
Total...	296	5	1.69	6	2.03	285	96.28
Grand Total..	8,249	1,056	12.80	3,177	38.51	4,016	48.69

TABLE LXV (*Continued*)

(2) WHEN UP-TO-FOURTEEN-AND-A-HALF IS ACCEPTED AS THE UPPER NORMAL-AGE LIMIT FOR COMPLETING THE ELEMENTARY SCHOOLS

	Grades	Net or Total Register for 2nd Official Term 1911	Under Age		Normal Age		Over Age	
			Number Under Age	Per Cent. of Register Under Age	Number Normal Age	Per Cent. of Register Normal Age	Number Over Age	Per Cent. of Register Over Age
Regular Classes	1A....	517	90	17.41	199	38.49	228	44.10
	1B....	487	95	19.51	194	39.83	198	40.66
	2A....	436	50	11.47	133	30.50	253	58.03
	2B....	524	74	14.12	153	29.20	297	56.68
	3A....	463	60	12.96	120	25.92	283	61.12
	3B....	488	70	14.34	115	23.57	303	62.09
	4A....	468	63	13.46	92	19.66	313	66.88
	4B....	498	46	9.24	104	20.88	348	69.88
	5A....	441	31	7.03	80	18.14	330	74.83
	5B....	557	72	12.93	86	15.44	399	71.63
	6A....	491	48	9.78	67	13.64	376	76.58
	6B....	466	61	13.09	50	10.73	355	76.18
	7A....	658	73	11.09	84	12.77	501	76.14
	7B....	588	82	13.95	83	14.11	423	71.94
	8A....	483	60	12.42	75	15.53	348	72.05
	8B....	388	76	19.59	64	16.49	248	63.92
	Total.	7,953	1,051	13.22	1,699	21.36	5,203	65.42
C, D, and E Classes	1A....	6	......	......	......	......	6	100.00
	1B....	2	......	......	......	......	2	100.00
	2A....	5	......	......	......	......	5	100.00
	2B....	16	......	......	......	......	16	100.00
	3A....	20	......	......	......	......	20	100.00
	3B....	23	......	......	......	......	23	100.00
	4A....	40	......	......	......	......	40	100.00
	4B....	48	1	2.08	1	2.08	46	95.84
	5A....	77	1	1.30	......	......	76	98.70
	5B....	24	2	8.33	1	4.17	21	87.50
	6A....	23	1	4.35	1	4.35	21	91.30
	6B....	9	......	......	......	......	9	100.00
	7A....	3	......	......	......	......	3	100.00
	Total...	296	5	1.69	3	1.01	288	97.30
	Grand Total..	8,249	1,056	12.80	1,702	20.63	5,491	66.57

TABLE LXVI

SHOWS THE NUMBER AND PER CENT. OF PUPILS UNDER AGE, NORMAL AGE, AND OVER AGE, WHEN AN AGE-GRADE REPORT IS MADE AS AGE-GRADE REPORTS ARE MADE BY THE CITY SUPERINTENDENT OF SCHOOLS

Grades	Register as of June 30 after Promotion	Under Age		Normal Age		Over Age	
		Number Under Age	Per Cent. of Register Under Age	Number Normal Age	Per Cent. of Register Normal Age	Number Over Age	Per Cent. of Register Over Age
1st Year.........	525	17	3.24	476	90.67	32	6.09
2nd Year.........	904	147	16.26	663	73.34	94	10.40
3rd Year.........	938	122	13.01	662	70.57	154	16.42
4th Year.........	934	106	11.35	603	64.56	225	24.09
5th Year.........	889	73	8.21	549	61.76	267	30.03
6th Year.........	1,010	102	10.10	561	55.54	347	34.36
7th Year.........	1,013	108	10.66	578	57.06	327	32.28
8th Year.........	915	131	14.32	575	62.84	209	22.84
Total............	7,128	806	11.31	4,667	65.47	1,655	23.22

Age-grade Table LXV-1 is made as an age-grade table should probably be made for the elementary schools of the City of New York, if up-to-fifteen is accepted as the upper normal-age limit for completing the elementary school. Age-grade Table LXV-2 is made as an age-grade report should probably be made for the elementary schools of the City of New York, if up-to-fourteen-and-a-half is accepted as the upper normal-age limit for completing the elementary school. Age-grade Table LXVI conforms in every respect to the age-grade reports as made by the City Superintendent of Schools since 1905. Age-grade Tables LXV and LXVI show, therefore, the effect of the City Superintendent of Schools making his age-grade reports as he does, on the reported number of pupils under age, normal age, and over age.

The City Superintendent of Schools, by limiting his age-grade reports to the regular classes of the several grades, by including in his reports only the pupils on the register in these classes at the end of the term, and by making his age-grade reports as he does, reports, in view of Table LXV-1, for regular classes, 1.91 per cent. fewer pupils under age, 25.60 per cent. more pupils of normal age, and 23.69 per cent. fewer pupils over age, than there probably are in the regular classes of the several grades; while, if his reports are taken as age-grade reports for the elementary schools as a whole, he reports, in view of Table LXV-1, 1.49 per cent. fewer under-age pupils, 29.96 per cent. more pupils of normal age, and 25.47 per cent. fewer pupils over age than there probably are in the elementary schools. Whereas, in view of Table LXV-2, he reports 1.91 per cent. fewer pupils under age, 44.11 per cent. more pupils of normal age, and 42.20 per cent. fewer pupils over age than there probably are in the regular classes of the several grades, and if his reports are taken as age-grade reports for the elementary schools as a whole, he reports in view of Table LXV-2 1.49 per cent. fewer pupils under age, 44.84 per cent. more pupils of normal age, and 43.35 per cent. fewer pupils over age, than there probably are in the elementary schools of the city.

Only by including in his age-grade report the children that he does, and by making his age-grade reports as he does, was the City Superintendent of Schools able in 1911 to report as follows:

"That the decrease in the number of over-age children in the grades has been steady and progressive since 1904, when I first called the attention of the world to this over-age problem, is shown by the following table:

"TABLE XXXII

"SHOWING THE NUMBER OF OVER-AGE CHILDREN IN THE GRADES SINCE 1905

Year	Number of Over-Age Pupils	Per Cent of Whole Number
1905..............	160,549	32.0
1906..............	150,500	30.1
1907..............	158,466	30.4
1908..............	161,373	30.0
1909..............	156,208	28.4
1910..............	146,326	26.1
1911..............	131,858	23.3 "[1]

It is possible for the City Superintendent of Schools, making his age-grade reports as he does, to report a reduction of over-age pupils "in the grades" from 32 per cent.[2] in 1905 to 23.3 per cent. in 1911, a reduction of 8.78 per cent. But the City Superintendent of Schools failed to point out in connection with "Table XXXII" that the per cent. of over-age pupils "in the grades" was only for those pupils on register "in the grades" June 30 when the schools closed for instruction, and that no account whatever had been taken of the thousands of pupils who had been "in the grades" during the course of the official year, but who had dropped from school temporarily or permanently.[3] He failed to point out the fact that the number of pupils taken from the regular classes of the several grades and put into special C, D, and E classes had increased from a few hundred in 1905 to 28,838 in 1911.[4] Naturally, when thou-

[1] Annual Report of the City Superintendent of Schools for 1911, page 59.

[2] It should be noted in this connection that the per cent. of over-age pupils in the regular classes of the grades was not 32 per cent. as given in "Table XXXII," but that 32 per cent. is probably the per cent. of over-age pupils in the elementary schools as a whole, because in this age-grade report pupils in certain special classes were included. See Annual Report of City Superintendent of Schools for 1904, page 43.

[3] 30,995 pupils dropped temporarily or permanently from the elementary schools of the city during the course of the February-June term of 1911. See page 188.

[4] Annual Report of the City Superintendent of Schools for 1911, page 55.

sands of pupils—all presumably over age—are taken from the regular classes in the grades and entirely ignored in an age-grade report, the per cent. of over age in the grades is reduced. By the same mechanical methods the per cent. of over-age pupils in the grades could be reduced to zero.

Until an exact and complete age-grade report is made no one will know what the actual age-grade conditions are in the elementary schools of the city; until such a report is made, it is impossible to judge whether the schools are efficiently or inefficiently administered, to judge whether or not the materials and methods of instruction are adapted to the varying abilities and needs of different groups of children, or to determine the number of pupils for whom special classes should be provided.

CHAPTER XIX

CONCLUSIONS AND RECOMMENDATIONS

CONCLUSIONS

THE discussion of over age and the method of determining it may be summarized briefly:

(1) Over age has social, educational, and financial significance, because:

(a) Over-age children tend to fail to complete the work of the elementary schools, just to the extent that they fall behind their grade for their age.

(b) Over-age children, by tens on tens of thousands, falling behind the grade for their age, enter practical pursuits with only a sixth or seventh grade education.

(c) To provide special classes for the instruction of over-age pupils, as is now done, increases the cost of instructing such pupils, and the presence of a large number of over-age pupils in a system of schools increases the number of classrooms, and, hence, the number of buildings needed to care for a given school population.

(2) Age-grade standards for "being in the grade" are an inexact basis for age-grade reports, because:

(a) A child is not under age, normal age, or over age by reason of being of a certain age and by reason of "being in a certain grade."

A child is under age, normal age, or over age in view of the task in hand, viz., completing the entire elementary school course of study by a given age.

(b) To make age-grade reports on the basis of age-grade standards for "being in the grade" is to *decrease* decidedly the reported number of over-age children.

(3) Whether or not a child is under age, normal age, or over age can be determined exactly only in view of the normal-age limits fixed for entering and for completing each of the several grades of the elementary school.

(4) The age-grade standards for entering and for completing each of the several grades of the elementary school will differ according to whether up to fifteen years of age or up to fourteen and a half years of age is accepted as the upper normal-age limit for completing the elementary school.

(5) Age-grade reports are most reliable and exact when made on the basis of age-grade standards for entering and for completing each of the several grades of the elementary school, and when these age-grade standards are determined in view of up to fourteen years and a half as the upper normal-age limit for completing the elementary school.

(6) Age-grade reports, to be valuable as a means of guidance to the Board of Education and to administrative officers, should be made at the end of the year for the official school year as a whole. Age-grade reports, to be valuable to principals and teachers in the proper classification and instruction of pupils, should be made at the beginning of the school term or year.

(7) When an age-grade report is made at the end of the year for the official year as a whole, the ages of

the children should be taken as of the date of the close of the official school year. When an age-grade report is made at the beginning of the school term or year, the ages of the children should be taken as of the date of the beginning of the official school year.

(8) In making age-grade reports the ages of the children should be based on the date of birth—year, month, and day—and taken in terms of years, months, and days.

(9) There should be included in an age-grade report for the elementary school, all children who can be classified with reasonable accuracy as having completed or as entering one or the other of the several grades of the elementary school. The only pupils in the elementary school who probably cannot be included in such a report are those in ungraded classes for physically and mentally defective pupils and those in trade-schools.

(10) Age-grade reports, whether made at the end of the year, for the official year, or made at the beginning of the year, for a given class of a given grade, or for the system as a whole, should be based on the total or net register.

RECOMMENDATIONS

In view of the foregoing conclusions we recommend:

(1) That the methods employed by the City Superintendent of Schools in making age-grade reports be materially modified.

(2) That an age-grade report be made at the end of the year for the official school year as a whole, to supply the Board of Education and its administrative officers with the basic information needed for their guidance.

(3) That an age-grade report be made at the beginning of the year to supply principals and teach-

ers with the facts upon which they may rely in making classification and in carrying on the instruction of pupils; that these reports be for the several classes of each school and for each school, but not for the system as a whole.

(4) That up to fourteen years and a half be accepted as the upper normal-age limit for completing the elementary school.

(5) That age-grade reports be made according to the provisions of this report.

(6) We would also recommend:

(a) That data be collected at once by the Board of Education on the ages and grades of children; that complete and exact information may be had with respect to the age-grade condition in the elementary schools of the city.

(b) That data be collected at once on the causes of over age in the elementary schools, and

(c) That an immediate investigation be made of to what extent pupils now in special classes are classified and are instructed in view of the causes of their being over age.

Index

INDEX

www.ingramcontent.com/pod-product-compliance
Lightning Source LLC
LaVergne TN
LVHW010548110826
845149LV00003B/595